Palgrave Studies in American Economic History

Series Editor

Barbara Alexander
Babson College
Babson Park, Massachusetts, USA

Since the social upheavals of the 1960s and 1970s and the free-market resurgence of the 1980s, American society has been enmeshed in a continuing process of profound change. Economic change has been oriented around the regulation of business, the information and telecommunication revolutions, and widening roles played by women and minority groups. Authors in the innovation area will assess how America arrived at its current position of technological dominance that is nonetheless under pressure from institutions that arguably are not well-configured for the future. Regulatory and legal historians will evaluate the reasons for concurrent regulatory breakdown and overreach in industries ranging from finance and health care to energy and land use. Finally, researchers working at the intersection of society and economic history will explore continuing struggles around issues of gender, ethnicity, and family structure, and the distribution of income, wealth, and political power. The series will address topics of interest to scholars, undergraduate and graduate students, and general readers drawn to the interplay of economics and cultural issues. Series contributors will be economics and business historians, or economists working with historians.

More information about this series at
http://www.springer.com/series/14650

Donald Stabile

The Political Economy of a Living Wage

Progressives, the New Deal, and Social Justice

palgrave
macmillan

Donald Stabile
St. Mary's College of Maryland,
St. Mary's City, Maryland, USA

Palgrave Studies in American Economic History
ISBN 978-3-319-32472-2 ISBN 978-3-319-32473-9 (eBook)
DOI 10.1007/978-3-319-32473-9

Library of Congress Control Number: 2016945665

Printed on acid-free paper

This Palgrave Macmillan imprint is published by Springer Nature
The registered company is Springer International Publishing AG Switzerland

Acknowledgements

While a scholarly book such as this one is usually the result of individual effort, it also depends on the assistance of a community devoted to scholarship and research. An author does not create the product of his research individually, but relies on others to help in carrying out a project. I would like to acknowledge several types of help that I have received on this book.

First, I want to thank several resources that made the research for this book easier than it otherwise might have been. The staff of the Franklin D. Roosevelt Library in Hyde Park, NY, was very helpful in setting me up as a researcher during a brief research trip. The supervisory archivist of the library, Bob Clark, kindly answered many questions for me by e-mail both before and after that trip. Shane MacDonald of the archival staff at the American Catholic History Research Center and University Archives at The Catholic University of America in Washington, DC, was equally helpful in my research in the John A. Ryan Papers. Julie Day at the Willard Wirtz Library of the US Department of Labor organized my search of union publications very effectively. While this type of archival research was helpful, even more valuable is the vast quantity of scholarly resources now available through the Internet. Although these are all acknowledged by way of being cited in the bibliography, I especially want to thank Gerhard Peters and John T. Woolley of *The American Presidency Project* for creating a website of presidential papers that allowed me to locate references to a living wage in President Roosevelt's speeches and other forms of communication. The Social Security Administration's website on the history of the Social Security Act contributed greatly to my writing of Chapter 5.

Second, several individuals helped me at various stages of the production of this book. Bruce Kaufman supplied me with many useful suggestions regarding areas of coverage that I should add to the book, recommended readings to round out my knowledge of the issues related to the Progressive Era and the New Deal and generally provided encouragement that kept me going on the project. My good friend and colleague, Andy Kozak, read and commented on several of the chapters I had written before he began his fight against the cancer that ended his life, way too soon. Otherwise, this book would have been a collaboration with Andy and he would have appreciated John Ryan's approach with much greater acumen than I have. Another good friend, MaryAnn Liberatore, helped me get a large amount of research done at the Roosevelt Library by tackling the microfilmed archives while I looked through boxes of paper documents.

Finally, I wish to thank the staff at Palgrave Macmillan for their help and encouragement in publishing this book. Their anonymous reviewer made many helpful suggestions that enabled me to see the connection between a living wage and the rise of consumerism in USA, which led me to recognize that the connection was ultimately severed when the Progressives focused heavily on consumerism.

As is always the case, none of the persons mentioned above are responsible for the use I made of their help and any flaws or errors contained in the book are mine alone.

Contents

CHAPTER 1

The Political Economy of a Living Wage

On June 16, 1933, President Franklin Delano Roosevelt issued one of the most important statements of his New Deal Administration. His first three months in office had been busy with legislation that aimed at making the financial system of the USA secure. At the end of the frenetic first 100 days, he announced his program for ending the Great Depression, the National Industrial Recovery Act (NIRA). One part of the NIRA was a short-term public works program to put people back to work. The longer-term strategy of the NIRA was for business, labor, and the government to work together and coordinate production, prices, and wages in an effort to reform the capitalist economy. In his presidential statement on signing the NIRA, Roosevelt announced where the reform element of the NIRA was headed, "Its goal is the assurance of a reasonable profit to industry and living wages for labor with the elimination of the piratical methods and practices which have not only harassed honest business but also contributed to the ills of labor."[1]

Viewed from the perspective of the early twenty-first century, Roosevelt's use of the words "living wages" to describe a goal of the NIRA comes across as a remarkable statement, especially because the NIRA was his first program for ending the Great Depression. After all, most of us would think that it has only been during the last two decades that a social movement with a goal of providing workers with a living wage has been growing in the USA. In this book, I will tell the story behind Roosevelt's stated

D. Stabile, *The Political Economy of a Living Wage*,
DOI 10.1007/978-3-319-32473-9_1

goal of the NIRA and examine the degree to which programs of the New Deal reflected the ideas of a living wage movement that existed in the USA for almost three decades before Roosevelt was elected president. My strategy will be to offer a history of the political economy of the concept of a living wage in the USA from the Progressive Era through the beginning of the New Deal. I will then compare the arguments in favor of a living wage with statements made by politicians, pundits, business and union leaders, and academics who favored the New Deal to see the extent to which their justifications of the New Deal were consistent with the arguments made by advocates for a living wage. The overall finding of the book is that the idea of a living wage was present in the New Deal to a greater extent than has been previously recognized. The New Deal advocates for a living wage used a simple formula derived from a broad political economy perspective: collective bargaining, social insurance, and a minimum wage equaled a living wage.

A Living Wage and the Issues It Raises

Present-day advocates for a living wage on a national level have used a strategy of expanded social security benefits, revitalization of unions, and a livable minimum wage to achieve their goal. This strategy for a living wage, however, would not be possible without the social reforms of the New Deal. More to the point, it has been overlooked that there was an earlier movement for a living wage that tried to influence those New Deal reforms. By placing Roosevelt's comments on the living wage in the context of its history, I have found that he was reflecting a viewpoint that was expressed in a variety of writings during the three decades before he took office. Still, no one has studied Roosevelt's relationship to the ideas expressed by the movement for a living wage. To give some examples, Daniel Fusfeld, in his study of Roosevelt's economic thinking, never mentions the idea of a living wage.[2] The same can be said of William J. Barber and his book on economic policy during the New Deal. Barber stresses the methods used in the New Deal to increase the purchasing power of workers. As a result, when he quotes from Roosevelt's statement on the NIRA,[3] he points out that it had a goal of increased purchasing power.[4] He does not mention that Roosevelt referred to a living wage multiple times in between his statements on purchasing power. Deborah M. Figart, Ellen Mutari, and Marilyn Power discuss the NIRA in their book, *Living Wages, Equal Wages*, but do not mention Roosevelt's inclusion of a living wage as a goal of the NIRA.[5] Allan Carlson does mention the relationship between the living wage and the New Deal in his brief history of the family wage, but he attributes that relationship to the Secretary of Labor, Frances Perkins, and not to Roosevelt.[6]

By focusing on the living wage as a goal of the New Deal, I will also address another issue in its history. As Ira Katznelson points out, historians have typically divided the New Deal into two phases using 1935 as a boundary year. The first phase marked a period of economic reform with the enactment of legislation such as the NIRA and the Agriculture Adjustment Act; the second phase saw social reform through three programs for economic security: labor relations through the National Labor Relations Act (NLRA), social security due to the unemployment insurance and pensions provided by the Social Security Act (SSA), and the minimum wage provided by the Fair Labor Standards Act (FLSA).[7] Cass Sunstein also criticizes historians for dividing up the New Deal in his study of Roosevelt.[8] Economists have gone further than historians, with Barber describing how Roosevelt made "more than one 'U-turn' in his economic strategies."[9]

To be sure, those economic strategies involved different ways to increase purchasing power. In this book, however, I will join with Katznelson and Sunstein to focus on the continuity in Roosevelt's approach with regard to a living wage because it was, as I will describe throughout this book, a common theme in the New Deal's interest in helping workers attain economic security. Roosevelt's overall goal was to see all workers earned a wage that covered the cost of life—a living wage. Even after World War II took care of the purchasing power problem, Roosevelt retained an interest in a living wage when near the end of the war he set forth a second Bill of Rights with an implicit goal of a living wage, as will be discussed later in this chapter. My intention is to reach a better understanding of the Roosevelt New Deal through an analysis of how its programs for economic security were consistent with the agenda of the living wage movement.

There is another point that needs to be made, however. Many New Deal programs were motivated by the theory that the cause of the Great Depression was underconsumption caused by the lack of purchasing power among workers and overproduction by business. The NLRA and the FLSA aimed to increase the purchasing power of workers by getting them higher wages; the SSA would give them unemployment insurance and pensions to spend. From this perspective, it could be argued that Roosevelt's advocacy for a living wage was a Trojan horse for increasing consumption demand through higher wages for workers. The push for greater purchasing power from workers was a central feature of the New Deal and it was the pursuit of how to achieve it that caused the many changes in policy that Barber describes. Bruce Kaufman analyzes the purchasing power side of the argument with great acumen,[10] and Barber makes it the central theme of his book.[11] I agree with them that the purchasing power argument was central to the New Deal's economic policies.

The problem with this argument, however, is that it works the other way just as well, because the underconsumption theory can also serve as a ploy to secure a living wage. Both parts of this argument were made by supporters of the New Deal and they often went hand in hand. To give one example, in his statement on the NIRA, Roosevelt called for a "change from starvation wages and starvation employment to living wages and sustained employment," adding that "decent living, widely spread among our 125,000,000 people, eventually means the opening up to industry of the richest market which the world has known."[12] While I will offer other examples of advocates for a living wage who also employed the purchasing power approach, I focus on the living wage part of the argument for three reasons. First, it has been overlooked for so long. Second, the living wage argument unifies all of the Roosevelt programs for labor as much as the purchasing power approach does. Kaufman, for example, points out that the NLRA and FLSA continued the effort to improve wages that started with the NIRA.[13] From a living wage perspective, the NLRA, the SSA, and the FLSA all continued the living wage goal of the NIRA. Third, as Kozak and I have argued, Herbert Hoover was just as strong an advocate for increasing the purchasing power of labor as Roosevelt and the New Deal.[14] Walter Lippmann believed that Hoover's "historic position as an innovator has been greatly underestimated and that Mr. Roosevelt's pioneering has been greatly exaggerated,"[15] and Rexford Tugwell, a prominent member of the New Deal, acknowledged that the New Deal programs built on the policies of Hoover.[16] Whatever the merits of the views of Lippmann and Tugwell, I would argue that Roosevelt's direct advocacy for a living wage differentiates him from Hoover in terms of their policies.

In taking this focus, I am not claiming that the living wage was a central goal of the New Deal. The New Deal had a variety of goals ranging from reform of the financial sector of the economy to ending the Great Depression, all through different types of public policy. As a number of scholars have argued, no single idea played a central role in shaping the New Deal. Rather, the New Deal jumped from one idea to another in pursuit of its goals of reforming the economy and ending the Depression. A living wage was one of those ideas but it has been left out of the story. In this sense, I see this book as supplementing previous histories of the New Deal by adding in another idea to the list of the ones that motivated its policies.

Wilfred Beckerman has stressed the importance of identifying the value judgments behind public policy.[17] My perspective is that a focus on a living wage will help to identify the values behind the New Deal's public policy, because those values were consistent with the values of a living wage. There was a surprisingly robust literature on the topic of a living wage that existed in the 1920s and early 1930s and bringing that literature to light as a possible influence on the New Deal will provide an exploration into the values that the New Deal held.

In looking for those values, I am mindful that the living wage is a complex concept. It is hard to define and even harder to measure, as will be described throughout this book. Moreover, not everyone used the term, a living wage, when they wrote about the values behind it. Rather, in the course of this book we will find advocates for a just wage, fair wages, a decent wage, the social minimum, a decent standard of living, an American standard of living, economic security, social justice, or against a wage below subsistence. There are even cases where advocates described what they meant without using a term to describe it. For example, as will be described later in this chapter, in 1944 Roosevelt presented a second Bill of Rights that contained all the elements of a living wage but never called it that. Even the simple formula presented earlier—collective bargaining, social insurance, and a minimum wage equals a living wage—is more about means than about the end result. One purpose of this history of a living wage is to describe what its advocates thought the end result should be. The term they often used for the outcome was economic security. I employ a living wage as a key concept because it offers a clear expression of what Progressives and New Dealers meant by economic security. There are a variety of approaches to economic security: higher wages, charitable alms, and public welfare programs. The persons I have surveyed as supporters of a living wage focused on higher wages through a living wage because they linked economic security to dignity and personal freedom without the taint of the dole. That is why they favored collective bargaining, social insurance, and a minimum wage as adding to economic security regardless of their impact on consumption and its role in ending the Depression. They would have favored that form of economic security even in times of prosperity.

There is a final issue around a living wage that I will address. Historians have written of a trend in economic thinking in the twentieth century that created a transition from an emphasis on production in economic policy to a stress on consumption.[18] To an economist, the issue is best framed through consideration of Say's Law of Markets, named for the French economist Jean Baptiste Say (1767–1832). Say's Law is captured by the familiar circular flow model covered in virtually every introductory economics textbook. In this model, all of the costs of production—labor, land, capital, and entrepreneurial skill—become someone's income—wages, rent, interest, and profit. In turn, this income is spent on the items that have been produced and returned to businesses as revenues. The end result is that a full-employment economy always generates the income necessary to purchase everything produced. Overproduction or underconsumption cannot be a persistent problem. If some of the income generated by production is not spent but is saved, financial markets will adjust the price of saving, that is, interest rates, so that someone else will borrow the saved money and spend it. Prices of products may also have to fall to stimulate spending on consumption or investment goods, and since prices do not fall at the same rate, some sectors of the economy will do better than others when there is a recession. Firms that produced too much might become bankrupt during the recession, but firms that had not overexpanded would end up stronger. In the end, a prolonged period of insufficient demand cannot exist in a market economy as long as prices are flexible.

Up to the Great Depression, the consensus view among economists was that there could not be a sustained period of general overproduction of goods and services resulting in a sustained period of high unemployment. Starting in the 1930s, economists, politicians at the federal level, union leaders, and pundits began shifting the focus from supply to demand as the more important of the two, a shift that culminated in the triumph of Keynesian economics. Historians refer to this shift as a transition from "producerism" to "consumerism," a distinction that mirrors the economists' dichotomy of "supply-side economics" versus "demand side economics." To be sure, this distinction can be overdone. It still remains true that there can be no consumption without production and no consumer demand without the income earned in production. The distinction is more about emphasis than about essentialism. However one distinguishes between the two perspectives, it is clear there was a transition in the emphasis from supply to demand in government policy.

This transition poses another set of questions about a living wage. What part did it play in the transition from producerism to consumerism? How did that transition impact the movement for a living wage that existed in the 1920s and 1930s? The starting point will be with the theory of a living wage with definite ties to the production. Its major premise was that workers contributed to production and needed to be rewarded for that contribution in a way that made them valuable members of the community, with a comfortable life of dignity. Starting in the 1920s, however, a theory of underconsumption became popular and it resonated with many economists, politicians, pundits, business leaders, and unionists as an explanation for business cycles. Underconsumption became the most popular explanation for the Great Depression and the way to solve it was to enhance the purchasing power of labor. A living wage would also enhance the purchasing power of workers whose productivity did not merit it, which is why the two approaches were often linked. But hidden in the link was a difficulty. A living wage was based on the costs to sustain a worker and his family; the purchasing power argument meant that wages had to be high enough to purchase all that was produced. A living wage may have been part of the purchasing power argument but we will see by the end of this book that during the transition from producerism to consumerism, the concept of a living wage lost its significance. Keynes' accentuation of fiscal policy as a way to increase consumption detached consumption from the purchasing power of labor and consequently left a living wage out of the equation.

To put all these issues in historical perspective, for the rest of this chapter I will first look at the history of political economy to see how economic thinkers from the Greek philosophers through Adam Smith up to John Bates Clark supported the concept of a subsistence wage as a living wage. Then, I will investigate the writings of one of the most prominent advocates for a living wage in the US—Monsignor John Augustine Ryan—to give an overview of the arguments in favor of a living wage and the programs that the government could use to bring it about; I will also detail Ryan's definition of social justice. I will then give an overview of the elements of Roosevelt's programs for a living wage, a description of his efforts to define social justice, and an analysis of his support for a living wage in the second Bill of Rights he proposed in 1944 near the end of his years in office. I will show that among classical political economists, as well as Ryan and Roosevelt, there was a shared definition of social justice ensuring that the affluent took care of the working poor so that everyone had a share of the economic prosperity.

A Living Wage in the History of Political Economy

Advocates for a living wage typically support it by arguing that it is necessary for economic justice and a fair economy.[19] Jerold L. Waltman has presented *The Case for the Living Wage*, which focuses on the political aspects of the living wage and justifies it on moral grounds rooted in religion.[20] The typical economist today, however, would argue that justice and fairness are not economic concepts. In a free market economy, such an economist would say, wages represent a market estimation of what a worker adds to the production of goods and services that the society wants. Paying workers a living wage greater than their value added would tamper with the incentive structure and upset the efficiency of a value-added economy. Given the importance economists place on efficiency, they would not support a living wage.

This lack of support for a living wage from economists, however, is a recent occurrence. In this section, I present arguments made by well-known thinkers in the history of political economy, who supported a living wage for three reasons: it was needed to sustain the workforce, to make the workforce more efficient, and to avoid imposing costs on the society.[21] For the most part, my emphasis will be on the great names in English political economy. More than any other school of thought, they concentrated on the issues related to labor and work. Consequently, their writings greatly influenced the advocates for a living wage in the USA in the following way: if those advocates looked for lessons about the living wage in the writings of classical English political economy, as many of them did, they found what they needed. My starting point, however, is with the ancient Greek philosophers, Plato and Aristotle.

Plato (428–347 BCE) disliked the competition of the marketplace and the persons who used it to make a living, because the pursuit of wealth was inimical to creating a society based on virtuous behavior.[22] In his *Republic*, for example, Plato proposed that the guardians and rulers of the state live a communal life with only the minimal livelihood they needed. To keep them from being distracted by the pursuit of wealth, they would, in effect, be provided a wage that ensured them the basic necessities of life. Plato defined necessities as follows: "Are not necessary pleasures those of which we cannot get rid, and of which the satisfaction is a benefit to us?"[23] Here we have a very early definition of a living wage, based on the indispensable elements of life.

Aristotle (384–322 BCE) had a more moderate view of the market and defended private property on the basis that humans needed incentives to care for property.[24] To explain how property could be beneficial to human existence, he argued that it involved the acquisition of the resources needed by a household through its own labor, as supplemented by the use of market transactions, to survive when it was not self-sufficient.[25] Trade took place when two persons bartered surplus items, but since such exchanges were needed to supply "what is needed for natural self-sufficiency," that type of trade remained natural.[26] Trade to make a profit to satisfy the unnatural needs for luxury was not natural, however. In this way, Aristotle set forth a longstanding view that the pursuit of wealth for the purpose of consuming items of what Thorstein Veblen, much later, would call conspicuous consumption was unnatural. The idea that spending on luxuries was "unnatural" set a tone in economics that became a common theme in English political economy and among advocates for a living wage. But first, the economy had to develop.

Writing in the thirteenth century, when commerce was becoming important in the medieval world, St. Thomas Aquinas (1225–1274) continued this line of thought by combining the Holy Scripture with the ideas of the Greeks, especially Aristotle, to develop an economic theory of the just price. He started from the proposition that it was morally proper for humans to seek after material possessions to provide for their sustenance. In a money-based society, to be sure that all members of society had access to necessities, Aquinas argued that prices charged for them had to be just. To be sure, as Murray Rothbard has pointed out, Aquinas' argument reflected a long tradition in Church history in favor of the just price.[27] In keeping with that tradition, Aquinas found it acceptable to use the market price as the just price as long as there was not too much market power on either side of the exchange and no one used coercion. The market (just) price also had to cover the costs of producing the product, so that producers would be ensured a livelihood in the sense that if a merchant or craftsman did not cover their costs they would have to go out of business. To assure that transactions were just, Aquinas argued, both buyers and sellers in the marketplace should follow the Gospel in doing unto others as you would have them do unto you. Both the buyer and the seller had to be informed about each other's needs. Although there were few wage workers in this era, it followed that a wage rate that pushed a worker below a subsistence level eroded his chances for being virtuous and was, therefore, unjust.[28]

As I have argued previously,[29] there is an intellectual chain of thought from Aquinas' just price through Martin Luther and Frances Hutcheson (Smith's teacher) to the subsistence wage of Adam Smith (1723–1790). One difference between Aquinas and the Protestants, however, is that the latter placed greater emphasis on workers and their need to labor to earn a livelihood. We can see this subtle shift in Smith, who held that one of the main purposes of political economy was to find policies "to provide a plentiful revenue or subsistence for the people, or more properly to enable them to provide such a revenue or subsistence for themselves."[30] Consequently, the central part of Smith's case for the market system was that the market let individuals act on clear monetary incentives to follow their self-interest and produce items that would do the most good for society. In the marketplace, competition would bring prices to their "natural rate," at which point business owners would earn a natural profit that was moderate and workers would be earning a natural wage. Smith defined the natural wage as the subsistence wage. He wrote, "A man must always live by his work, and his wages must at least be sufficient to maintain him. They must even upon most occasions be somewhat more, otherwise it would be impossible for him to bring up a family, and the race of such workmen would not last beyond the first generation."[31] If workers did not earn a subsistence wage, the workforce would be overused and the economy would cease to function.

Smith defined the subsistence wage in terms of what it would allow workers to purchase to maintain themselves, which meant that he had to outline the commodities that made up subsistence. He wrote, "By necessaries I understand not only the commodities which are indispensably necessary for the support of life, but whatever the custom of the country renders it indecent for creditable people, even of the lowest order, to be without."[32] As opposed to Plato, Smith argued that the subsistence wage had a decency component to it. This decency component, however, varied from place to place. In England of Smith's days, it included linen shirts and leather shoes, while in Scotland it was proper for women to be barefoot, and in France coarse material was sufficient for shirts.

Smith's definition of a subsistence wage has parallels with the modern concept of the living wage as well as the problems. In both cases, the basic wage must depend on a basket of commodities that enable workers not only to live but also to have a decent life. The problem is that the cost of those necessities as well as the decency items in the basket will vary from place to place as well as over time. In defining the subsistence wage this way, Smith was also making a statement about social justice. He wrote, "No society can surely be flourishing and happy, of which the far greater part of the members are poor and miserable. It is but equity, besides, that they who feed, cloath and lodge the whole body of the people, should have a share of the produce of their own labor as to be themselves tolerably well fed, cloathed and lodged."[33]The real question, one that Smith addressed, was what it would take for the market wage to at least equal his version of a subsistence wage and make social justice a reality.

For Smith, the level of wages had a variety of influences, such as the disagreeableness of the job, the skill required in the job and the cost of attaining that skill, the amount of trust required on the job, and the risk that one might not succeed in the job. Supply and demand conditions could affect wages in the short term, as an expanding industry would have an increased demand for labor that brought about higher wages until more workers entered the industry and brought wages back to their natural level. In the long run, the economy would grow and there would be a general increase in the demand for labor that would lead to rising wages.[34] Here we have Smith's optimistic account of market outcomes. Through trade fueled by self-interest, the division of labor expands, the economy grows, and wages increase. Workers would see a rising subsistence and market forces would have the positive consequence of at least a subsistence wage for all.

While Smith did see that workers in his days earned a wage at or above subsistence, he also saw that there were cases where they might not. In labor market negotiations over wages, he believed that masters (employers) had advantages that gave them the upper hand. This was no accident, for Smith noted, "Whenever the legislature attempts to regulate the differences between masters and their workmen, its counsellors are always the masters." Given these advantages, "masters are always and every where in a sort of tacit, but constant and uniform combination, not to raise the wages of labour."[35] At the time, Smith wrote England's economic system was influenced by a policy of mercantilism, which regulated the economy in an effort to help merchants prosper and enhance the revenues of the crown. Smith was against this mercantilist policy and countered it with his case for the free market.

As Rothbard observes, English mercantilism included laws that put a cap on wages and limited the mobility of labor.[36] If employers were able to use government regulations to keep wages low, a free market system might give workers a better chance for higher wages. To Smith, government intervention was wrong when it granted favors to the wealthy and powerful. In one of his broadsides against mercantilist policy in the woolen trade, he said of the mercantilists thus:

> They endeavour to buy the work of the poor spinners as cheap as possible. They are as intent to keep down the wages of their own weavers as the earnings of the poor spinners, and it is by no means for the benefit of the workman that they endeavour either to raise the price of the complete work or to lower that of the rude materials. It is the industry which is carried on for the benefit of the rich and the powerful that is principally encouraged by our mercantile system. That which is carried on for the benefit of the poor and the indigent is too often either neglected or oppressed.[37]

To Smith, mercantilism was a tight-knit relationship between business and the government—what we now call crony capitalism—and he argued in favor of free markets as a method to end the ways the government in England helped a select group of businesses. He was less concerned when government programs helped the poor. For example, he proposed that the government provide free education for the children of workers, because he did not think workers could afford that schooling on their own. In considering what items to tax to pay for public education, he proposed taxes on the wealthy, including taxes on luxuries. He opposed taxes on wages.[38] To a large extent Smith's writings on labor in *The Wealth of Nations* aimed at a voluntary approach to having employers make life better for workers with the wages and working conditions that made for a decent life.

From our review of Smith so far, we can see he anticipated that the market system had the potential to result in a living wage for workers. He went further, however, to make a case for the social benefits of higher wages for workers. In an early statement of what is now called efficiency wage theory he wrote, "Where wages are high, accordingly, we shall always find workmen more active, diligent, and expeditious than when they are low."[39] A better workforce was more productive which would have the benefit of increasing the wealth of the nation. On the other hand, if wages fell below the subsistence level, workers might not bother to work, instead turn to begging or to crime. These would impose a cost on the society.[40] Smith hoped that businessmen would become more enlightened and voluntarily provide a rising subsistence, that is, a living wage, for workers.

Smith's *Wealth of Nations* remained a source of ideas on political economy for two generations after it was written. John Stuart Mill (1806–1873) became the next synthesizer of economic thinking with his *Principles of Political Economy*. One of his analytical tools was to separate production and distribution into two distinct spheres. In this way, he could argue that while production was governed by unalterable scientific laws, distribution followed social laws that could be changed.[41] The implication of this separation of distribution from production was that it was possible to redistribute income without harming the economy. Regarding labor, it was an obvious scientific fact that if workers did not receive a subsistence wage there would be no production. The issue of whether they did indeed receive a subsistence wage fell into the laws of distribution, however.[42]

To define what he meant by subsistence, Mill made a distinction between productive and unproductive consumption. What workers consumed, he wrote, "in keeping up or improving their health, strength and capacities of work, or in rearing other productive labourers to succeed them is productive consumption." Consumption of luxuries by workers or by idle persons was not productive consumption, since it did not aim at production. Mill's dividing line between productive and unproductive consumption was sustainability. If something were not produced for a year and society survived, it qualified as an item of unproductive consumption.[43] Mill was arguing that the laws of production determined productive consumption, but it was the laws of distribution that gave wealth to idlers seeking unproductive consumption. The laws of distribution could be changed and the standard of living of workers could be improved. Mill wrote, "Society at large is richer by what it expends in maintaining and aiding productive labour."[44]

When he looked at what caused wages to be low, Mill made unproductive consumption a crucial variable. At any time an economy had a stock of capital with which business owners bought machinery and materials and hired workers. The overall stock of capital was derived from the surplus left over after paying workers in the previous time period, and the part of the capital stock spent on hiring workers in the next time period determined the demand for labor and wages. But Mill also saw the capital stock as the fund "from which all are subsisted who are not themselves engaged in production."[45] The point for Mill was that if the capitalists used their profits by spending on unproductive consumption, the demand for labor would be reduced and wages would be low. Moreover, Mill was less optimistic than Smith that there was a minimum level of wages at the subsistence level. Since the subsistence wage had a decency component to it that varied from time to time and place to place, it was possible to "permanently lower the standard of living" of workers and have their "deteriorated condition…become a new minimum."[46] The decency component of the subsistence wage could be reduced. Because wages fell under the laws of distribution and not production, however, Mill also considered methods for increasing them.

In general, Mill did not favor government intervention in economic activities on the ground that the government often intervened on behalf of business; he also wanted to avoid a parental state where the working poor became dependent on the government. From this principle he chastised the living wage advocates of his day for arguing that every employer "*ought to give sufficient wages*; and if he does not willingly, should be compelled to it by general opinion; the test of sufficient wages being their own feelings, or what they suppose to be those of the public."[47] According to Mill, there was no clear standard of what wages should be, no clearly defined living wage that one could use to establish what employers ought to pay.

Instead, Mill argued that workers could help themselves get higher wages through the formation of labor unions, making him one of the first well-known economists to investigate the nature of unions and to wish to see them strengthened as a social institution. Mill objected to the view that government interference in the form of laws against unions was desirable to keep wages low, writing, "If it were possible for the working classes, by combining among themselves, to raise or keep up the general level of wages, it needs hardly be said that this would be a thing not to be punished, but to be welcomed and rejoiced at."[48] Mill also believed that unions would enable workers to gain moral character for pursuing their own interests as well as society's.[49]

The ability of unions to raise the wages of their members without harming others has long been an issue of contention among economists. Mill pointed out that higher wages for union workers could be paid for by employers charging higher prices, which meant that higher wages might cause higher prices to consumers. Mill did not object. His principle was that "the cheapness of goods is desirable only when the cause of it is that their production costs little labour, and not when occasioned by labour's being ill remunerated."[50] Mill believed that it was better to hurt affluent consumers than to mistreat low-paid workers.

Mill also recognized that workers might be underpaid. On Mill's account, market forces of supply and demand did not "thrust a given amount of wages into a labourer's hand." All prices resulted from bargaining in the market, and "poor workers who have to do with rich employers [might] remain long without the amount of wages which the demand for their labour would justify, unless, in vernacular phrase, they stood out for it; and how can they stand out for terms without organized concert?" Because of this need for workers to organize to get the wages the market forces accorded them, Mill concluded that unions, "far from being a hindrance to a free market for labour, are a necessary instrumentality of that free market." Bargaining power imbalances between individual workers and their employers might result in wages below the market rate, and unions were needed to get wages to that rate. Indeed, Mill wondered how an individual worker would even know what the market wage was "except by consultation with his fellows."[51]

It is always difficult to make an imputation of influence in the history of political economy. Mill's *Principles of Political Economy* strongly influenced at least two generations of economists, who followed him in supporting unions. According to Fusfeld, Mill's book was the text young Franklin Roosevelt learned economics from as a student at the Groton School.[52] The important point here is that Mill sanctioned unions as a vehicle for helping workers attain a living wage. The idea to be wary of, Mill warned, is having workers become dependent on advocates of a living wage for pay increases, because that would be paternalistic. The lesson Mill offers is that workers in their own union are a way to have them get a living wage for themselves. This view, however, was criticized by Mill's contemporary, Karl Marx.

Karl Marx (1818–1883) offers us an approach to political economy that focuses on workers and not capitalists as the key element of the economy. This approach is not surprising given his overarching belief in the historical importance of class struggle. To apply his belief in class struggle to the world of capitalists and workers, Marx began his study of capitalism, *Capital*, with the conception that workers were removed from ownership of property, that is, control over access to the means of production. This alienation of workers from the means of production meant that the only thing they had to offer for sale in the marketplace was their general ability to work, what he referred to as their labor power. The exchange value of labor power was the cost to the worker of producing it, the subsistence wage.[53] With his idea that workers were reduced to a common product of labor power with common subsistence needs, Marx might have set forth a theory that wages tended to be limited to the existential needs of workers.

Instead, Marx found that a subsistence level of consumption would differ depending on climate. Moreover, he went on, a worker's subsistence needs and the way they were fulfilled were "themselves products of history, and depend therefore to a great extent on the level of civilization attained by a country." The definition of subsistence for Marx contained "a historical and moral element," that is, the decency component we saw in Smith's writing. It also had to include an element for replacing the workforce in the form of children "in order that this race of peculiar commodity-owners may perpetuate its presence on the market."[54] Here, Marx echoes Smith's idea that subsistence included the sustainability of the workforce.

In volume 2 of *Capital*, Marx expanded on his definition of subsistence by distinguishing between necessities and luxuries. To him, necessities were those items "which enter into the consumption of the working class" and might also be consumed by capitalists. Tobacco, for example, might not be biologically necessary but might be consumed from habit. While this definition was very inclusive, Marx narrowed it by arguing that "articles of luxury enter into the consumption of the capitalist class only."[55] The standard of living that workers enjoyed defined subsistence. This hardly seems a useful definition of a subsistence wage, and in the notebooks he kept to clarify his thinking, Marx added that "needs are produced just as are products and different kinds of work skills." He continued, "The greater the extent to which historic needs…are posited as *necessary*, the higher the level to which real wealth has become developed."[56]

Having raised the issues inherent to defining a subsistence wage, Marx extended his analysis by looking more closely at what workers had to do to earn it. Marx's explanation for wages is one with which we are already familiar, unequal bargaining power. In opposition to Smith and Mill, however, Marx argued that unequal bargaining power was a systemic feature of capitalism and related to class struggle. The advantages employers had regarding workers had to do with their having property and workers having to sell their labor power in order to survive. Once their bargain was made and a wage established, workers lost control over how their labor power was used. They could be made to work longer than was necessary to produce the equivalent of their means of subsistence.[57] The subsistence wage also factored in the number of hours of unpaid labor that had to be worked to earn it.

Moreover, the growth of capital had another impact on the subsistence wage that Marx found in his analysis of machinery. Machines had a great advantage of reducing the strength and skill required of workers. While this could make life easier for workers, instead it increased the potential workforce by including "every member of the worker's family, without distinction of age or sex."[58] The addition of women and children to the workforce redefined the subsistence wage as the amount the whole family earned. The necessary and decency components of the subsistence stayed the same, but more than one family member had to work to earn it. This raises another issue in defining a living wage: should it be based on an individual worker or on a household? If it is based on an individual's income but all members of the household earn it, they may gain a level of affluence above what a living wage should provide. When all members of the household must combine to earn a living wage, the household will be in serious trouble if something happens to one of its members.

We saw earlier that Mill looked toward unions as a way to help workers get a higher wages. For Marx, unions could not be successful in helping workers unless they were organized as national associations to lead workers in the class struggle with capitalists. When unions did not take on this economy-wide role, he forecast their failure, arguing that unions were good at opposing the ills of the capitalist system but did not have the outlook needed to change that system.[59] Unions focused on the immediate needs of their members and did not take a social outlook needed to give all workers a higher wage. Only a transformation of capitalism into socialism could ensure that workers got higher wages.

Mill and Marx signal the end of an era in economic thinking dominated by the ideas of Smith. We can conclude that all three exhibited a great deal of support for workers having a better existence. This support correlated with all of them adhering in some degree to a labor theory of value. It is often argued that their use of the labor theory of value was part of a search for an objective measure of the intrinsic value of commodities as embodied in the mainly labor costs involved in production. In addition, however, the labor theory of value facilitated the focus the early English political economists had on the status of labor, as evidenced in the culmination of Marxian economics. It based prices on the cost of production of a commodity, which meant that wages had to cover the cost of production of workers.

After Mill and Marx, economists began a new approach that stressed the subjective value of the utility of commodities as an organizing theme of economics. In addition, the newer economists adopted an approach that became known as marginalism because it emphasized the increments of value added by factors at the "margin" of production or consumption, that is, the value added by the last unit of consumption or the last input in production. The synthesizer of marginalism was Alfred Marshall (1842–1924). His book, *Principles of Economics*, first published in 1890, replaced Mill's *Principles of Political Economy* as the primary text in economics—a status it held through eight editions during a 30-year period. Still, Marshal used the new approach to continue the labor views of his predecessors.

Marshall was a very moral person who worried about the existence the poor would have from the wages they earned in the labor market; he wanted them to have "the material conditions of a complete life."[60] In writing about the level of wages needed for a complete life, Marshall linked it to those items needed for keeping workers at efficient levels of effort. He wrote, "The income of any class in the ranks of industry is below its necessary level when any increase in their income would in the course of time produce a more than proportionate increase in their efficiency."[61] In this way Marshall associated wages to what was necessary for the efficiency of the workforce.

As to whether workers would earn sufficient wages, Marshall believed that firm owners combined to keep wages down, especially in dealing with lower-paid workers who needed income most. Bargaining power between individual workers and employers was unequal, because owners of large firms employing many workers acted as if they were a combination of employers while workers were unorganized.[62] To counter that power of employers, workers needed to take collective action by forming unions. In the long run, market forces determined the level of wages. In the short run, however, collective bargaining could help workers gain higher wages.

In anticipation of the efficiency wage theory, Marshall stressed the importance of high wages, arguing that increases in wages to workers would be paid for through a greater increase in production. He saw a cumulative process where high wages directly improved the capability of the present generation and indirectly enhanced the capability of the next generation. The next generation, being more efficient, would raise its standard of living, do a better job of educating its children, and improve their prospects. The cycle would go on, leading to improvement of workforce efficiency. Marshall allowed that the reverse scenario was possible, with lower wages setting off poorer children.[63] He was also concerned with the impact of overwork, arguing that the wage rate did not take into account the worker's "wear-and-tear, of which indeed he is himself often rather careless."[64] Overwork led to a lower standard of living for workers and for future generations.

Along with the economists surveyed so far, Marshall was sympathetic toward workers and wanted to see them gain better wages. Although they tacitly followed Aquinas in wanting this just wage for workers, they did so with their own versions of a secular economy organized by market exchanges. Richard T. Ely (1854–1943) went against this tradition of secular argument. Ely was well-known in the USA as the founder of the American Economic Association (AEA) and the author of the largest-selling US textbook on political economy, *An Introduction to Political Economy*, published in 1935. For him, "ethical aims" were "an essential part of economic activity" and political economy did "not tell us merely how things are, but also how they ought to be."[65] The study of the economy should not just aim at understanding what takes place in the economy; it should uncover wrongs and figure out what society ought to do about those wrongs. In this way there would be progress as society increasingly met higher standards of "humanity and justice."[66]

For those higher standards to be met, workers needed to have wages and working conditions sufficient to enhance their capability and they had to use their wages in the right way. In looking at wages, Ely offered several explanations for them. First, he set forth an idea that wages were set by the standard of living of workers. He wrote, "Laborers have an habitual standard of life, a certain style of life, and what they receive as wages enables them on average just to keep up this standard, but to do no more." When women and children went to work to improve the standard of living for the family, Ely found that household income fell to where all members of the family needed to work to attain the standard of living the male had previously earned. He defined this standard as follows: "It should include provision for all real needs and provision for accidents; future emergencies, disability on account of old age, and the like should be included. A deposit in the savings bank and insurance policies ought to be part of the habitual standard of life."[67] The standard was not always met, however, and at times workers suffered from a reduced standard—there could be an absolute decline in the standard or a relative decline when the standard did not keep pace with the growth of wealth in society as a whole.[68] Ely has here raised the two crucial issues of a living wage, whether or not workers earned it in the market and what "real needs" a living wage should meet.

Regarding whether or not workers earned a living wage in the market, Ely found that wages were determined by bargaining power that tilted toward employers.[69] This superior strength came from staying power. Employers could outwait workers who needed wages to survive. To combat this superior bargaining power, workers formed unions. If unions succeeded in raising the living standard for workers, workers must use their improved standards properly. Ely believed that increased standards of living should give the worker "opportunity for the completest development of all his faculties."[70] In this way, he continued Mill's notion of productive consumption, which required him to distinguish between desirable and undesirable wants: "Wants satisfied by those things which serve as a basis for the full and harmonious development of our faculties are desirable wants; wants satisfied by other material things which are not positively helpful or are positively injurious are undesirable wants." The consumption of luxuries fell into the category of undesirable wants because they catered to the individual's vanity and smugness and thereby hindered "the development of a better manhood in us and in all those whom we could influence."[71]

Ely did not fall into the marginalist camp of economists. One US economist who did, John Bates Clark (1847–1938), is noted for his development of the marginal product theory of wages. His development of this theory made him an international figure in economics—the first economist in the USA to attain a high stature. Simply stated, this theory says that in a competitive economy wages will equal the marginal product of labor, that is, the amount that the individual worker adds to total production. This theory implies that low-wage workers are low-productivity workers. If a living wage means increasing workers' pay above their productivity, businesses will not hire them.

Clark, however, was a moral person who believed in fair treatment for workers and developed his marginal product theory with the hope that it might lead to increased wages. Clark lived in the tumultuous times of the second industrial revolution, which in the USA included the growth of large corporations and the emergence of national unions. Because he worried that society was falling apart, he employed a standard for economic analysis that emphasized social cohesion and asked one overriding question: did labor markets provide a wage for workers that allowed them and society to be sustained?

Clark's approach to wages was to look at the bargaining power of workers versus capitalists and he argued that the advantage went to the capitalists. The problem in setting things right was in finding a standard for where wages should be placed. Clark did not see a living wage as a standard.[72] To establish his own standard for wages, Clark used a two-stage method. The first stage was to determine how free competition would determine wages through supply and demand. The second stage would then see how wages deviated from that competitive standard in the real world of large corporations and unions.[73] Once that standard was established, Clark felt that wages could be determined by government-led arbitration.[74] With a standard for wages in place, it might be possible to avoid Smith's warning that government always sided with business in legislating wages.

Clark developed the marginal product theory as a way to establish a standard for wages. His statement of marginal productivity theory, *The Distribution of Wealth*, gave his intention clearly in its opening words: "It is the purpose of this work to show that the distribution of the income of society is controlled by a natural law, and that this law, *if it worked without friction*, would give to every agent of production the amount of wealth which that agent creates."[75] Clark clarified the emphasized statement, noting that his theory operated as "if the changes that are going on in the shape of the industrial world and in the character of its activities were to cease."[76] In short, the idea that workers' wages would equal the value they added to production was a theoretical construct; it only held in an economic model based on perfect competition. To determine how competition established a wage equal to the marginal product of labor, Clark relied on abstract technical thinking that need not concern us here.[77]

What does concern us is that Clark consistently maintained that establishing a standard based on the ideal of competition was only a first approximation and was an incomplete explanation for wages without adding in the elements of the real world.[78] Clark presented those elements in his book, *Essentials of Economic Theory*. In it he saw that an important trend of industry was that economic development through technical innovation tended to pull wages upward. It thus became a crucial question, Clark indicated, to know "when the standard of wages rises as it naturally should."[79] He based his discussion of labor and technical change on the supposition that industry cut costs by reducing the labor component of production. This process was not entirely advantageous to workers, because "new machines are labor displacers."[80] As a result, he argued, "a supply of unemployed labor is always at hand" due to "temporary displacements of laborers" by technical change. This army of the unemployed, to use Clark's term, kept wages low.[81] Unemployed workers set the low end of the wage scale on which all other wages were based and workers might not earn wages equal to their value added.

To attain fairness in a dynamic economy, Clark called for collective bargaining. In defining the extent of bargaining power organized workers could obtain, Clark differentiated between unions as monopolies and as engaged in collective bargaining. Unions secured a monopoly when they had the strength to keep non-members from working in a trade or industry. The competitive alternative to the monopoly power of unions was collective bargaining. By this term, Clark meant that all workers who were willing to take a job in an industry be allowed to join a union, at a fair level of dues, in return for the union bargaining a wage for them.[82] He concluded, "When free from the taint of monopoly, trade unions, as has been shown, help rather than hinder the natural forces of distribution."[83]

When unions went beyond collective bargaining to the use of monopoly practices, Clark recommended arbitration. When the time came to give advice to arbitrators as to where wages should be set, Clark altered his statement of marginal productivity theory as a competitive standard to the following: "The law of final productivity works most effectively when it works automatically, as it does when competing employers make the best bargain with locally organized laborers. The results, then, approach the theoretical standard, though they do not entirely coincide with it."[84] It was wages set by collective bargaining that set the standard that arbitration should employ.

Although he pioneered the idea that under conditions of perfect competition labor market wages would be set as equal to the productivity of workers, Clark was enough of a realist to recognize that labor markets were more complicated than his basic model indicated. His dynamic approach to markets with bargaining power hinted at the notion that labor markets are social organizations and that the wage had to be at a level that led to social cohesion. In this broader conception of the labor markets, labor is not just another commodity with known qualities to be purchased off the shelf. Instead, neither employers nor workers know precisely what they are getting from the wage bargain in terms of the nature of the work and whether the skill and effort required for the job can be met by the workers. Both sides to the wage bargain must have experience with each other to determine the relationship between wages and productivity. Since productivity cannot be known in advance, nor even with hindsight, supply and demand mean that market wages fall into a zone, which Clark identified as a productivity wage gap with a lag between rising productivity and rising wages. If the gap was too small, businesses might not earn enough profits to continue to invest. Too large a gap would reduce workers' morale and effort. Either extreme could reduce economic development.[85]

In general terms, the wage bargain would indicate where in the zone wages will be. A number of social factors such as bargaining power, ideas of fairness, the desire for a reputation as a good employer, the need to enhance the stock market value of the firm, the existence of internal labor markets, and anticipation of future technological innovation will influence the level of wages within the zone. Government-mandated minimum wages, arbitration, or unemployment insurance would be other social elements that determine wage levels within the market zone. The boundaries of the zone, moreover, are not easily identified, which makes the correct market wage even harder to determine. As a result, market wages are much more flexible in relationship to supply and demand than is the case with a commodity.

Clark's lesson regarding a living wage is twofold. First, low wages may indicate the low productivity of the workers earning those wages. That low productivity may reflect those workers' lack of skills, but it may also indicate that they are working with very little capital. Efforts to increase their wages without altering those conditions will prove fruitless. Second and more important, low wages may also be below the productivity of workers earning them, because of their weak bargaining power. Unions are a way for workers to redress that weak bargaining power, but only if they remain free of the taint of monopoly. When unions gained a monopoly, the remedy was government arbitration. Clark never made it clear how often unions gained a monopoly but he seemed to oppose most unions that existed in his day. This meant he would have been in favor of government intervention to set wages at the value-added level his theory anticipated. Clark never made it clear whether that wage rate was a living wage.

I end this brief history of political economy regarding wages with Clark because his marginal product theory became the accepted view among economists about how wages were set, but they only used his first step based on competition. The notion of a subsistence wage, that is, a living wage was lost in the transition to marginalist economics. That loss also entailed the loss of two millennia of arguments in favor of a just price, including a just price for labor. To be sure, proponents of a just price considered the market price to be the best estimate. But they worried, as Smith and Mill especially did, that unequal bargaining power in labor markets might keep wages at a rate below what the market should have paid workers. They also held the view, dating back to Plato, that there was something unseemly about conspicuous consumption, especially when workers were being deprived of a living wage. Although he agreed with the unequal bargaining power argument and disdained conspicuous consumption,[86] Clark shifted the just wage to be equal to what workers added to production. As a result, marginalism discarded what went with the argument for a living wage—the need to sustain the workforce, the unequal bargaining power of labor and the use of unions to redress it, and the idea of productive consumption. It would initially fall on writers concerned with the ethics of wage determination to revive those concepts in their case for a living wage. Once that case was made, economists—as we will see in later chapters—did return to the political economy of a living wage and found ways to counter the marginal product theory. Before getting to their ideas, however, I now turn to a premier advocate of the case for a living wage, John Augustine Ryan.

The Progressive Era: John A. Ryan and the Right to a Living Wage

For over a century the USA has seen a movement to provide poorly paid workers with a living wage. During that time labor activists and unions, Progressive politicians, religious groups, intellectuals, and heterodox economists have led this movement to attain social justice for workers. To give one example, in 1906 a group of Progressive economists including Richard T. Ely, John R. Commons, and Henry R. Seager formed the American Association for Labor Legislation (AALL) to push for laws to protect labor such as workers' compensation insurance and a minimum wage.[87] The AALL had its own journal and began paying more attention to the plight of the working poor. In his book on the AALL, David A. Moss indicates that its leaders were influenced by their background of studying in Germany.[88] Rothbard adds that they returned from Germany with a high regard for an organic theory of large government.[89]

Their penchant for thinking about using an activist government may well have come from Progressive academics and intellectuals in the USA studying in Europe. In Europe, they learned socialist ideas that were more common on that continent due to the influence of thinkers such as Saint-Simon, Fourier, and Marx. In Germany, they saw firsthand the activist government of Bismarck and especially the social welfare programs

Germany developed to take care of the poor. Ely and Clark, for example, studied with the German Historical School of Economics, whose members included Lujo Brentano (1844–1931), an advocate of social insurance as an antidote to socialism in order to preserve capitalism.[90] If they went to England, they would have encountered the Fabian Socialism of Beatrice Webb (1858–1943) and Sidney Webb (1859–1947), who developed the idea of promoting efficiency and fairness for workers through collective bargaining and social insurance.[91] In England, they might also have encountered a living wage movement whose activities produced an article in a top publication, *The Economic Journal*, and several books during the years just before and after the turn of the twentieth century.[92]

Given this readiness to attribute a European influence on US intellectuals, it is often overlooked that in the USA there was a home-grown version of worker protection that promoted its programs in a framework that fit within US cultural norms. As Lawrence B. Glickman has pointed out, workers and union leaders began rallying around the idea of a living wage in the last quarter of the nineteenth century and continued well into the twentieth century.[93] In November 1913, for instance, Samuel Gompers (1850–1924) told the convention of the American Federation of Labor (AFL), of which he was the president, "A fair standard of wages—a living wage, for all employed in an industry, should be the first consideration in production." He added, in a statement that Franklin Roosevelt would make a theme of his administration, "An industry which denies to all its workers and particularly denies to its women and minors who are toilers a living wage is unfit and should not be permitted to exist."[94] It is doubtful, however, that Gompers would have wanted to see government legislating a living wage. He would have felt the same about it as he did about enacting a minimum wage law. In 1912 he wrote, "We want a minimum wage established, but we want it established by the solidarity of the working men themselves through the economic forces of their trade unions, rather than by any legal enactment."[95] This statement remained the policy of the AFL at least until the passage of the FLSA in 1938.

It was not the policy of Progressive reformers, however. As Glickman points out, they took over the concept of a living wage as their own idea.[96] In the process, the Progressives shifted the living wage movement from a grass roots struggle by workers to a top-down policy for the government. They joined the fight for a living wage through government action when John A. Ryan published an influential book, *A Living Wage: Its Ethical and Economic Aspects*.[97] Ryan was a priest, social reformer, college professor, and an author most noted for his advocacy of a living wage. Raised on a farm in Minnesota, he studied for the priesthood and after being ordained earned a PhD with a dissertation that was eventually published as his well-known book on the living wage. Francis L. Broderick, titled his biography of Ryan, *Right Reverend New Dealer: John A. Ryan*,[98] in homage to Ryan's long career as a Progressive thinker and its culmination in his work with the New Deal.

A Living Wage is a lengthy study of the ethics and economics of wages and Ryan considered it to be the first book in English to advocate for a living wage. As Robert Prasch has indicated, many individual thinkers influenced Ryan's work.[99] In his book, Ryan acknowledged the influence of several of them. Foremost was Richard T. Ely (see above) who helped get the book published and wrote an introduction to it. Ryan indicated additional influence from the Webbs, who wrote significantly about the problems faced by workers,[100] and from the encyclical of Pope Leo XIII (1810–1903) on the condition of labor.[101] Pope Leo's encyclical, issued in 1891, included the idea "that the remuneration must be enough to support the wage earner in *reasonable and frugal comfort*."[102] In later books, Ryan used the writings of Mill and Marshall in support of his definition of a living wage[103] and indicated he was further influenced by an Italian priest, Matteo Liberatore (1810–1892), and by the English heterodox economist John A. Hobson (1858–1946), who wrote an early book on the distribution of income.[104]

Ryan's work can be downplayed as simply an ethical justification for a living wage but his intellectual background was an eclectic combination of classical and heterodox political economy with a fusion of economics and ethics as Ely had proposed. Two heterodox political economists from the Wisconsin Institutional School of Economics considered Ryan to be a member of that school, at least in spirit. On November 26, 1935, Ely, a founder of that school of economic thought, wrote to Ryan to express his approval of Ryan's recent book, *A Better Economic Order* (see Chapter 3), and to indicate that he and Ryan agreed on the fundamentals of economics.[105] Several years later, on March 10, 1938, Edwin Witte, another member of the Wisconsin School and an architect of the SSA (see Chapter 5), wrote to Ryan to compliment him on a speech he had just given on underconsumption as a cause of the Great Depression. It is likely that Ryan and Witte had met when both were connected with the Committee on Economic Security that drafted the SSA. Witte wrote, "I think you do not regard yourself as a professional economist, but I believe that you are as sound an economist as anyone who discusses economic problems at the present time."[106] If not exactly a member of the heterodox institutional school, Ryan was certainly an admirer of their work just as they admired his.

Regardless of how we categorize Ryan, it is likely that Liberatore was the most important of these influences. In his book, *Principles of Political Economy*, he defined economics as "The science of public wealth, with regard to its rightful ordering as a means of common well being."[107] Consistent with this definition, Liberatore defended inequality and the rights of property but insisted that those rights included a "duty of beneficence" on the part of property owners in helping others through the use of the superfluous income from their property.[108] The idea of a duty of beneficence dated back to the idea in early Christianity that the accumulation of wealth was acceptable if the wealthy used their wealth to support the poor. This idea carried over into labor market activities. Regarding labor, Liberatore argued that equality of exchange in a labor market meant that a worker loaned his ability to a business owner in return for "that which is necessary for the maintenance of himself and his family."[109] This was a natural price for labor and included enough to support a man, his wife, and two to three children. Because excessive competition often compelled business owners to pay the lowest wage possible, Liberatore believed that the government had to step in to help workers and he supported unions and strikes as another tool in securing the natural price of labor.[110] In short, Liberatore was a follower of the unequal bargaining power argument used by classical political economy, especially Smith and Mill.

With this intellectual background, Ryan found himself at odds with the way business worked in the market economy. Consequently, he devoted his first chapter to criticizing the theory of the market economy for setting forth economic laws that were not as universal as the natural law that he saw as underpinning the living wage. Those economists, following Smith, had set forth individual freedom as the basis of a just economics, but "instead of a regime of justice" their ideas brought about "a period of horror" with low pay, long hours, and unhealthy working conditions.[111] To be sure, as described above, Smith recognized that unequal bargaining power in labor markets might result in low pay and poor working conditions. He was hopeful, however, that employers would voluntarily give up their bargaining advantages.

To counter an economic theory based on freedom of bargaining, Ryan offered an alternative perspective that "the laborer's claim to a Living

Wage is of the nature of a *right*."[112] He then justified this view with a long argument derived from the premise that all men were equal due to their rational nature. God had given all humans a free will and the ability to use reason to develop their personalities to the fullest and they had a right to do so. Since they had this right, they were entitled to a share of the produce of the earth, another lesson he drew from Liberatore.[113] He wrote, "The primary right from which the right to a Living Wage is deduced, is the right to subsist upon the bounty of the earth."[114] He then defined a living wage as a decent livelihood that included meeting the needs of an existence marked by "the dignity of a human being."[115] A living wage also included enough to raise a family. In more concrete terms, a living wage meant enough to provide a worker with food, clothing, and shelter for him and his family until his offspring were able to work, to allow him to save enough to guard against illness, accidents, and the infirmity of age, and to give his family a modest amount of education, entertainment, and the ability to perform religious obligations.[116] For a worker, a living wage was essential for he had no other source of income to compensate for low wages. It also was important to insure that workers would be able to have the capabilities to have meaningful lives.

Ryan then presented statistical estimates of how much income constituted a living wage in the USA during the decade before he wrote, that is, using data from around 1900. From a variety of sources he came up with a living wage of $600 a year, but indicated that in some parts of the country it would have to be more.[117] From that figure, he then used census data and other studies to estimate the number of workers earning below a living wage. Depending on the data, his estimates ranged from 48 percent to 85 percent of adult males and he concluded that "it is altogether probable that sixty per cent of the adult male wage earners" did not earn a living wage.[118]

To address this low-paid workforce, Ryan put the primary obligation on employers. Their position in the economy as employers made them the persons most able to secure a living wage for their workers. As a counter to the marginal product theory of Clark, he dismissed the idea that wages had to be tied to the productivity of workers because it was "utterly impossible to measure the relative productivity of different classes of workers."[119] Nor was it possible to determine how to divide the output due to the combined effort of workers, employers, and capital. The best way to determine wages was to accept a living wage and employers who did not pay one were trampling on the rights of their employees.

To be sure, an employer unable to pay a living wage was "for the time being freed from actual obligation as no one is morally bound to do the impossible."[120] After all, an employer was entitled to a living wage as well. It mattered, however, why the employer was unable to pay a living wage. As had Mill, Ryan argued that if the inability was due to a need for large profits to live a life in excessive luxury, then the employer needed to sacrifice that life to pay a living wage. He must also forgo paying dividends to his stockholders or interest on his own capital or on borrowed capital, as all of these expenditures were "subordinate to the laborer's right to a Living Wage."[121] Consumers were obligated to pass by low prices that were the result of low wages and patronize firms that paid a living wage; low prices should not be based on low wages,[122] another instance where Ryan agreed with Mill. Workers too had an obligation to improve their capabilities and to refrain from strong drink; they should also avail themselves of the group strength of combining into unions.[123]

For over a century, free market economists and businessmen had based their appraisal of success on the profitability of a firm. In a radical departure from this type of assessment, Ryan turned the tables on them by insisting that it was the ability to pay living wages that measured success. A firm that did not pay a living wage might be given time to reach that standard just as a startup firm may take time to earn a profit. But if, after the passage of time, the firm did not pay a living wage it should go out of business. Whether or not Ryan's approach is reasonable is not the issue. The issue, as we will see in subsequent chapters, is that the members of the Progressive movement thought it was reasonable—including Franklin Roosevelt. Their argument, although they never used the term, was that pay below a living wage was a market failure. As Beckerman observes, market failure exists when markets do not provide for maximum social welfare.[124] Economists often think of social welfare from the perspective of consumers getting the most happiness from their purchases. By turning attention to the welfare of low-wage workers, proponents of a living wage, especially Ryan, made market failure apply to labor markets as well as to the market for goods and services.

Ryan was aware that the voluntary sacrificing of high profits by business and low prices by consumers was not likely to succeed, and the formation of unions was a doubtful enterprise. As a result, he put a lot of stock in the government as a way to ensure a living wage. He wrote, "The State has both the right and the duty to compel all employers to pay a living wage."[125] Because of the productive power of industry, a living wage for all was feasible. Government enforcement of a living wage in the USA, however, presented severe obstacles, both social and constitutional. During the time it took to make the changes necessary for removing those obstacles, the federal government in the USA could use indirect methods such as legislating a minimum wage, maximum hours of work, and prohibition of child labor. It could also provide workers with pensions, as "a part of the Living Wage that is due him for his life work."[126] To pay for those pensions, Ryan favored high inheritance taxes on the wealthy and a progressive income tax.[127]

We will see in later chapters that Ryan's obligations for the government would become the strategy of Roosevelt's New Deal in its quest for a living wage through collective bargaining, social insurance, and a minimum wage. Before that happened, Ryan spent a quarter of a century writing and agitating for a living wage in a way that made him a kindred soul to the Progressive reformers. In the process, he expanded on his original writing. For example, in 1909, he set forth a comprehensive list of labor legislation that included a minimum wage, the eight-hour day, protection for peaceful picketing, unemployment insurance and government employment offices, and funds to help workers when they became ill, injured, or elderly.[128]

Ryan's inclusion of a minimum wage law in his program for a living wage raises an issue of the difference between a living wage and the minimum wage. As Prasch has discovered through a review of academic journals during the years 1912–1923, in that period a sizable majority of economists in the USA favored minimum wage laws to protect women and children.[129] Even Clark, whom we saw earlier in this chapter as the innovator of the marginal product theory of wages, was a proponent of the minimum wage, although in a conservative form.[130] The approach that these economists took toward the minimum wage was that it should only cover the basic essentials of a worker's life and should also take into account how much a given industry could afford to pay. Ryan probably agreed that this view of a minimum wage was an important starting point in the path toward a living wage, although he would have pushed for a higher level for that minimum than most of his contemporaries. In addition, he advocated social insurance as a supplement to the minimum wage as part of a living wage program. His overall fight, however, was for a wage that gave workers the chance for a decent life of modest comfort based solely on their pay. The combination of a minimum wage and social insurance was an intermediate step to the living wage. Once this combination was socially accepted, employers would recognize labor's right to a living wage at a rate to provide savings and private insurance to such an extent that the combination of a minimum wage and social insurance would become unnecessary. Most economists who supported the minimum wage legislation were unwilling to go that far. Ryan also departed from them in having less concern over whether businesses could afford to pay a living wage.

A living wage became a part of the program of reform being set forth by the Progressives during the first three decades of the twentieth century. Two stalwarts of the Progressive movement, Herbert Croly and Walter Lippmann, wrote in favor of a living wage.[131] Writing in 1917, Lippmann, for example, called for an Industrial Democracy "where every adult is sufficiently insured for the primary needs of life so that he is capable of making some kind of free contract with other men."[132] That quintessential Progressive, Theodore Roosevelt, included a living wage as part of his mandate for social justice. In a speech at the 1912 convention of the Progressive (Bull Moose) Party, he explained,

> We stand for a living wage. Wages are subnormal if they fail to provide a living for those who devote their time and energy to industrial occupations. The monetary equivalent of a living wage varies according to local conditions, but must include enough to secure the elements of a normal standard of living—a standard high enough to make morality possible, to provide for education and recreation, to care for immature members of the family, to maintain the family during periods of sickness, and to permit of reasonable saving for old age.[133]

In a similar expression of this support for a living wage, the Progressive President, Woodrow Wilson, made it part of his speech accepting the nomination of the Democrat Party in 1916, declaiming,

> We must hearten and quicken the spirit and efficiency of labor throughout our whole industrial system by everywhere and in all occupations doing justice to the laborer, not only by paying a living wage but also by making all the conditions that surround labor what they ought to be. And we must do more than justice. We must safeguard life and promote health and safety in every occupation in which they are threatened or imperilled. That is more than justice, and better, because it is humanity and economy.[134]

Roosevelt's definition of a living wage and Wilson's notion that it was justice became rallying points for the Progressives during World War I and they continued to write about it up to the beginning of the New Deal in 1933, as Chapter 2 will describe. Theodore Roosevelt and Woodrow Wilson also served as role models for Franklin Roosevelt.

When the Great Depression took place, Ryan was highly critical of President Herbert Hoover's efforts to resolve it. His background as a social reformer and his opposition to Hoover should have made him a staunch supporter of Roosevelt, but he was put off by some of Roosevelt's campaign speeches criticizing Hoover for being a spendthrift. He had some minor contact with Raymond Moley and Rexford Tugwell, members of Roosevelt's "brains trust." None of this added to his enthusiasm for Roosevelt when he first became president.[135]

As the New Deal proceeded, Ryan began to like what it was accomplishing with regard to labor under the NIRA. At the invitation of the Secretary of Labor, Frances Perkins, in 1933 he became a member of the advisory council of the US Employment Service and delivered the invocation at the dedication of the new Department of Labor Building.[136] Then in 1934, Hugh Johnson, administrator of the National Recovery Administration (NRA), appointed him to the NRA Industrial Appeals Board, set up to address the problems small businesses were having with the NRA Codes (See Chapter 3). Many of the appeals came from small businesses that were not able to pay the labor costs imposed on them by the NRA Codes, but the appeals board routinely denied their appeal.[137] Ryan indicated that if small business could not meet the wages and hours set by the codes, than "let the small businessman perish."[138]

Ryan and Social Justice

Implicit in Ryan's view that businesses that could not pay a living wage should perish was his definition of social justice. The recipients of the wealth that came from the profits of business were obligated to share that wealth with the working poor by seeing that they were paid a living wage. The living wage took precedence over profits and a luxurious lifestyle, and the obligation to help the poor was a part of social justice until every person had the benefit of at least a living wage. Businesses that could not earn a profit and pay a living wage were not able to meet the obligation of social justice and should be allowed to go bankrupt. Since he was skeptical that businesses would meet this obligation of paying a living wage voluntarily, it was up to government to impose it on them.

One of the goals of this book is to uncover the definition of social justice that advocates for a living wage had in mind—social justice to them meant that the affluent must share their wealth until every person had a living wage. To put Ryan's approach to social justice in perspective let us compare it to the most developed version of social justice elaborated in the twentieth century, John Rawls' *Theory of Justice*. In that book, Rawls made it a goal of social justice that a well-ordered society promoted the good of all and was regulated by a commonly held sense of justice.[139] A well-ordered society would promote equality by arranging it that social and economic inequalities be to the advantage of everyone. Indeed, Rawls' second standard of justice held that social and economic inequalities had to be of advantage to all and open to all; equality was the primary objective unless inequality helped everyone.[140] The standard of treating everyone equally was that the most attention must be placed on the worst-off members of society. They should be helped through the provision of primary goods, "what persons need in their status as free and equal citizens and as normal and fully cooperating members of society over a complete life."[141]

Rawls' standard of the provision of primary goods to the worst-off members of society resembles Ryan's plan of giving a living wage to the lowest-paid workers. Where they differ was in their conceptualization of the society providing a living wage. For Rawls it was a well-ordered society held together by a social contract where all members agreed to engage in cooperative behavior that was mutually beneficial. In this society, the members agreed to this social contract by starting from a position where none of them knew of their ultimate place in the economic structure. By making many behavioral assumptions about the way those persons make decisions—rationality was a big one—Rawls showed how every person would want himself and all other members of society to act on the principles of justice as fairness and agree to a more equal distribution of income once economic activity took place.[142]

Rawls' theory of justice was based on political philosophy but his conditions for its attainment were so restrictive on human behavior it is hard to see how they could ever be accomplished—so much time and effort on the part of the members of society would go into deciding upon a system of justice and a social contract with a result that not much else would get done. To be sure, Rawls employed an ideal society as a way to establish a theory of justice, much as economists make use of the ideal of perfect competition in order to point out the virtue of self-interest. In both cases, there is a great deal of abstraction from reality. With Rawls, for example, Beckerman has pointed out that he assumes that individuals in the original position are risk-averse.[143] As a result, they will opt for a social contract that offers them security with little risk. It has been a general finding of behavioral economics, however, that most individuals are overconfident of their abilities and the economic outcome they will experience.

In contrast to Rawls, Ryan accepted a society where much has already been done, especially in the economy. Great wealth had already been produced; the challenge was to motivate the affluent to share their wealth with the poorest-paid workers through a living wage. In place of Rawls' social contract, Ryan employed a natural rights argument, following the ideas of Liberatore. When motivated properly to act as God wanted them to act, the members of society would choose to act in line with Ryan's theory of social justice as a right to live on the earth. As a priest who had heard many confessions, however, Ryan was doubtful that humans would act as God wanted them to act, at least not until they were properly motivated. That motivation, moreover, would come from the government starting down the road to social justice by enacting laws that would encourage the members of society to act with social justice in mind. This approach to social justice would form a backdrop to Roosevelt's New Deal.

Ryan's New Deal Connections

Broderick has indicated that Ryan's connection with the New Deal was not as direct as many individuals had thought, at least not to an extent of him meeting regularly with Roosevelt and advising him on exactly what to do. Still, his connections with the New Deal were impressive. We can start with the president. In doing so, I have reviewed a lengthy correspondence between Roosevelt and Ryan that took place between 1928 and 1945 and filled three folders in the Ryan correspondence file, as well as letters to and from other members of the New Deal administration.

The first letter between Roosevelt and Ryan in Ryan's correspondence file predates the New Deal. On December 2, 1928, Roosevelt wrote to Ryan asking him to look into the financial difficulties one of Roosevelt's college classmates was having.[144] Ryan did as he was asked and reported back to Roosevelt on January 11, 1929, using the letter to wish Roosevelt that he would be successful in his administration as governor of New York. Ryan also told Roosevelt that he had admired him for his work in 1910 as a member of the New York State Legislature in stopping the candidacy of

William F. Sheehan for the US Senate when senators were chosen by state legislatures.[145] We should not be surprised that Ryan knew of Roosevelt. Perhaps Roosevelt knew about Ryan from contacts in the Progressive movement.

The correspondence between the two men continued and on September 1, 1932, presidential candidate Roosevelt wrote to Ryan requesting that he consider being part of a group that Roosevelt was requesting to be prepared to consult with him once the election was successfully won. Roosevelt gave Raymond Moley, a member of his "brain trust," as the contact person for the group.[146] There is no evidence in the Ryan correspondence file that this group met, but Ryan did serve on advisory committees during the New Deal. The contact person for most of them was the Secretary of Labor, Frances Perkins.

On March 29, 1933, Perkins sent Ryan a general invitation to a conference at the Department of Labor on issues facing labor.[147] She sent him an invitation to be on an advisory committee to the US Employment Service on August 5, 1933.[148] Finally, Perkins, on October 29, 1934, asked Ryan to attend a conference on economic security.[149] Ryan's attendance at the conference very likely led to his serving on one of the advisory committees to the Committee on Economic Security as it went about its business of producing a draft of the SSA (see Chapter 5). In 1936, Roosevelt appointed Ryan as a member of a committee to investigate the problems of farm tenancy.[150] During that year, Roosevelt had met with Ryan at the White House "to discuss several politico-economic matters."[151] Ryan's ties with Roosevelt became even stronger through a radio speech Ryan gave on October 8, 1936, "Roosevelt Safeguards America." The speech was intended to defend the president from criticisms made by Father Charles C. Coughlin, the radio priest.[152] Ryan also gave the benediction at Roosevelt's inauguration in 1937 and in 1945. Again, the two men were not meeting on a regular basis but they did have a mutual admiration for each other that will be discussed later in this chapter and in Chapter 7. Part of that mutual admiration was their shared belief in the benefits of a living wage.

The Roosevelt Program of Economic Security

The economy of the USA had experienced many business cycles of recession and recovery before 1929. Few of those economic cycles have warranted the designation of catastrophic. The Great Depression does warrant that designation, because the decade of the 1930s was a lost decade for the US economy. The downturn began in the August 1929 and lasted 43 months before hitting bottom in March 1933. After the trough of the downturn was reached in March 1933, real GDP grew at an eight percent average annual rate but did not come close to its pre-Depression level until 1937, when another downturn took place. The economy did not reach its full potential during the entire decade of the 1930s and unemployment never fell below double-digit levels.

Roosevelt took office in early 1933 just as the economy was starting to improve. During his first 100 days as president, he provided a New Deal through a flurry of reforms to restore confidence. Banks took a holiday until they were deemed solvent and those that were not solvent were closed. The USA went off the gold standard for domestic transactions. The Securities Act of 1933 began closer regulation of financial markets. Bank deposits became insured through the Federal Deposit Insurance Corporation.[153] Public relief was expanded, as were public works projects, and the Reconstruction Finance Corporation, established by the Hoover administration, continued its operations of making loans to business. The Agricultural Adjustment Act aimed to control farm production and give farmers higher income. Under the NIRA, administrators at the NRA were put in to work with business and labor to establish codes of fair competition that would coordinate production, prices, and wages. Public relief and public works projects were expanded under a theory of "pump priming" where government spending would increase consumer purchasing power and get the economy going.

When the US Supreme Court declared the NIRA to be unconstitutional in May 1935,[154] the Roosevelt Administration continued its goals through the use of the federal government's powers of regulation and taxation. The Congress passed the NLRA in 1935 to enhance the ability of workers to form unions, the SSA in 1935 to provide unemployment insurance and pensions, and the FLSA in 1938 to guarantee workers a minimum wage. To be sure, all of them aimed at increasing the purchasing power of workers as a way to end the Depression, but they also aimed at a living wage. When the economy experienced the recession of 1937–1938, the federal government increased its spending in an effort to manage the economy by increasing purchasing power.

To pay for government spending, Roosevelt took an approach to taxation that was consistent with his interest in a living wage. On June 19, 1935, he sent a Message to Congress on Tax Revision. The Congress had been studying the question of new taxes and the results of those studies enabled the president to make some recommendations based on "the broad principle that if a government is to be prudent its taxes must produce ample revenues without discouraging enterprise, and if it is to be just it must distribute the burden equitably." Roosevelt did not think that the current tax system met this broad principle because it worked toward "the unfair advantage of the few." A progressive income tax with higher tax rates for higher incomes met the principles of fairness and caused little harm to enterprise.[155]

Roosevelt gave his reason for being certain of the benefits of progressive taxation in a statement which will remain a clear argument for the tax policies of the quest for economic security through the redistribution of income. He wrote

> Wealth in the modern world does not come merely from individual effort; it results from a combination of individual effort and of the manifold uses to which the community puts that effort. The individual does not create the product of his industry with his own hands; he utilizes the many processes and forces of mass production to meet the demands of a national and international market.
>
> Therefore, in spite of the great importance in our national life of the efforts and ingenuity of unusual individuals, the people in the mass have inevitably helped to make large fortunes possible. Without mass cooperation great accumulations of wealth would be impossible save by unhealthy speculation. As Andrew Carnegie put it, "Where wealth accrues honorably, the people are always silent partners." Whether it be wealth achieved through the cooperation of the entire community or riches gained by speculation—in either case the ownership of such wealth or riches represents a great public interest and a great ability to pay.[156]

Society helped to produce the wealth that any individual accumulated through the mutual assistance given to him by the community. By levying higher income and inheritance taxes, the government could reclaim some of that wealth for society.

Roosevelt's community approach was consistent with the ideas underlying the living wage. Liberatore, whose writings were a great influence on Ryan (see above), defended inequality and the rights of property but insisted that those rights included a "duty of beneficence" on the part of property owners to help others through the use of the superfluous income from their property.[157] He favored progressive taxation, as did Mill, and Ryan followed them. This outlook was also popular with the middle class, according to economist Paul Studenski (1887–1961), a longtime professor at the New York University. It fit in well with a concept of the government as "a cooperative commonwealth in which all men are born equal and are bound, rich and poor alike, in a fraternal relationship of mutual self-help." Higher tax rates on the wealthy would merely deny them "the superfluities of life."[158]

In his statement on his tax philosophy, Roosevelt made a distinction between inactive and active wealth and wanted to tax only the inactive wealth.[159] The idea that the higher taxes would hit inactive income was Roosevelt's way of saying it was superfluous income. In doing so he was agreeing with Ryan's approach that it was not profits that indicate the success of a business but the ability to pay living wages even if it was done by way of the tax code. They also followed Mill in believing that it was possible to redistribute income without harming the economy's overall production. Both Ryan and Roosevelt shared an implicit definition of social justice as the affluent being obligated to help the working poor up to the point where every individual earned at least a living wage.

Roosevelt and Social Justice

I call this definition implicit because Roosevelt did not indicate directly what he meant by social justice. To be sure, he believed in "the philosophy of social justice through social action."[160] By searching for the keywords "social justice" in the online database of his presidential papers I find that from 1933 to 1940 Roosevelt used the term "social justice" 22 times. He typically talked of its being linked with economic security but did not define it. To give one example, on March 3, 1934, he referred to "our program of national planning for social justice."[161] Here he was referring to the NIRA as a program that included a living wage as a goal. Roosevelt came a bit closer to defining social justice in a press conference on June 7, 1935. He was asked what the social objective of his administration was. He answered

> The social objective, I should say, remains just what it was, which is to do what any honest Government of any country would do: to try to increase the security and the happiness of a larger number of people in all occupations of life and in all parts of the country; to give them more of the good things of life, to give them a greater distribution not only of wealth in the narrow terms, but of wealth in the wider terms; to give them places to go in

> the summertime—recreation; to give them assurance that they are not going to starve in their old age; to give honest business a chance to go ahead and make a reasonable profit, and to give everyone a chance to earn a living.[162]

From this passage, we can see Roosevelt was arguing that social justice meant that the prosperity from economic development and growth had to be shared more equally than it had been in the past.

It also meant that the poor took priority in that more equal sharing. In a campaign speech in Dubuque, IA, on October 9, 1936, Roosevelt added to his definition of social justice when he paid tribute to the late Senator Louis Murphy (1875–1936), Democrat from Iowa, by quoting from the eulogy at Murphy's funeral, "To him social justice meant primarily that the common good must, particularly in such times as these, take precedence over personal gain. He was determined that no one should starve in this land of plenty."[163] Finally, Roosevelt did offer a definition of social justice to a group of ministers visiting the White House on January 31, 1938. He told them, "We call what we have been doing 'human security' and 'social justice.' In the last analysis all of those terms can be described by one word; and that is 'Christianity'."[164] In sum, Roosevelt defined social justice in religious terms of helping one's neighbor through use of the golden rule with an aim of insuring that the wealthy acted in a way that put the common good ahead of their personal gain of profits or luxury; that was the aim of the New Deal reforms with the goal of social justice through a living wage—to give everyone a chance at the good things in life.

It also entailed a changed view of the rights of property. For many centuries, the natural law argument meant that a right was a claim to use one's property as one wanted. To be sure, Liberatore's duty of beneficence aimed at having individuals voluntarily use their surplus property to help the poor, as sort of a personal obligation with benefit of clergy. The right to a living wage, however, went a step further because it entailed a claim on someone else's property. By taking a community perspective, Ryan and Roosevelt and their followers made a living wage a right to a claim of a share of the wealth that the community helped to produce instead of a claim on the private property of autonomous individuals. This perspective is similar to Harvey Rosen's description of an organic theory of society, where society can be conceived as an organism. Every person is a component of the social organism, while the government is what controls it. From this perspective, each person is only important as a member of society and only to the extent that his or her actions are coordinated by the government for the benefit of the society as a whole. The organic view of society is as old as Plato and was adhered to by Aquinas. It was countered by the Smith perspective of free market economics, which Rosen describes as an individualistic conception of society.[165]

This organic view was apparently not universally held in the USA during the 1930s, however, at least not in the Congress. Instead, the reform program of the New Deal with regard to a living wage was modified by the Congress in enacting legislation such as the SSA and the FLSA, as we will see in Chapters 5 and 6; it effectively ended in 1938 with the enactment of the FLSA. After that time, a resurgence of Republicans in the Congress formed a coalition with the Southern Democrats to stop any additional reforms. Then World War II came and reform was taken off the table.

As the war neared its end, however, Roosevelt tried to put reform back on the agenda. In his State of the Union address on January 11, 1944, six years after the New Deal period was over, he outlined his overall program as leading to a second Bill of Rights to provide greater economic security and a living wage. The items in the second Bill of Rights had first been presented in a report of the National Resources Planning Board of January 14, 1941. Samuel Rosenman (1896–1972), Roosevelt's friend, advisor, and speechwriter, attributed the idea of putting them together in a second Bill of Rights as part of the State of the Union address to Chester Bowles (1901–1986), an advertising executive who served in the Roosevelt Administration during the war and later had a political career as a Democrat Party member. Rosenman added, however, that the language those rights took in the speech was Roosevelt's.[166]

The first Bill of Rights had provided political freedoms, but as the industrial economy of the USA developed, those political rights "proved inadequate to assure us equality in the pursuit of happiness." A second Bill of Rights that guaranteed economic rights was needed. Roosevelt set forth a list of economic rights as follows:

> The right to a useful and remunerative job in the industries or shops or farms or mines of the nation;
>
> The right to earn enough to provide adequate food and clothing and recreation;
>
> The right of every farmer to raise and sell his products at a return which will give him and his family a decent living;

> The right of every businessman, large and small, to trade in an atmosphere of freedom from unfair competition and domination by monopolies at home or abroad;
>
> The right of every family to a decent home;
>
> The right to adequate medical care and the opportunity to achieve and enjoy good health;
>
> The right to adequate protection from the economic fears of old age, sickness, accident, and unemployment;
>
> The right to a good education.[167]

Aside from the ones aimed at farmers and small businesses, which were taken care of by the Agricultural Adjustment Act and the Robinson Patman Act, these rights formed the basis of a living wage for labor that Roosevelt had hoped to bring about through the New Deal. Taken as a whole, they are similar in intent to the definition of social justice he gave at his press conference on June 7, 1935. They were also set forth when the war had taken care of the problem of a purchasing power deficiency, although there was still concern that it might come back after the war had ended. These are all indicators that Roosevelt had an abiding interest in a living wage separate from its correlation with the purchasing power argument.

It is risky, however, to attribute a clear vision to Roosevelt. Conventional wisdom holds that he was often inconsistent and many of his policies were devised on an ad hoc basis. One example of this perspective was given by Lippmann, who indicated that aside from his unswerving compassion for the underprivileged, Roosevelt did not have a clearly thought out theory of social justice.[168] Without such a theory, according to this view, Roosevelt was susceptible to many poorly formed ideas and often blundered into policies that did not work out very well. Alan Brinkley adds to this view by considering the second Bill of Rights as something that sounded good.[169]

In contrast, Cass Sunstein considers Roosevelt's 1944 State of the Union address to have been a speech that was outstanding for its vision of the possible future of the US economy.[170] In the speech, the president indicated the need, after the war was over, to bring about "an American standard of living higher than ever before known." A higher standard of living was not enough, however, "if some fraction of our people…is ill-fed, ill-housed, and insecure." The provision of economic security was essential to democracy because "true economic freedom cannot exist without economic security and independence."[171] This last phrase was certainly comparable to Lippmann's definition of Industrial Democracy cited previously in this chapter, "where every adult is sufficiently insured for the primary needs of life so that he is capable of making some kind of free contract with other men."[172] The speech was also consistent with the writings of Ryan. In his autobiography that was written after the New Deal reforms had been enacted, Ryan praised the Roosevelt program, "When I began to advocate the establishment by law of a family living wage, I did not dare hope that so near an approach to it would be made by the federal government less than three and one half decades later."[173]

Roosevelt wrote to Ryan on May 30, 1944, to congratulate him on his 75th birthday, indicating that he was heartened that Ryan was "still fighting for social justice," especially noteworthy because in that fight "you were a pioneer." The president believed that Ryan should be satisfied for "all you have done to enforce recognition of the fundamental right of all to a useful and remunerative job; a decent home; a good education; [and] adequate protection from economic fears in old age." The result of Ryan's fight was that workers could attain "a happy life in keeping with the dignity of human nature."[174] Roosevelt made two important points with this letter. First, he was congratulating Ryan for his advocacy of four specific rights in his second Bill of Rights, which indicated that he believed Ryan was in tune with him on what he wanted to accomplish. Second, the idea that their joint effort on behalf of the working poor would result in their having "a happy life in keeping with the dignity of human nature" was consistent with the capabilities approach that Ryan placed as the basis for his advocacy for social justice and a living wage.

The Rest of This Book

The second Bill of Rights was not presented in the 1930s when the New Deal was in full force, but it was certainly implicit in the reforms that were enacted during that decade. In the rest of this book, I will investigate what politicians, business leaders, economists, union members, and pundits wrote about Roosevelt's efforts to create a living wage. First, in Chapter 2, I will give a background to the New Deal by considering what was written and done about a living wage in the 15 years before Roosevelt's election; in the current chapter I have given the impression of a direct link from Ryan to Roosevelt but a key finding of Chapter 2 is that there was a wider interest in a living wage, inspired by the federal government's promotion of it in World War I. In Chapter 3, I will look more closely at the

NIRA and what its administrators and supporters thought of its goal of a living wage. Then I will concentrate on three components of the second Bill of Rights that Roosevelt offered. Chapter 4 will look at the NLRA and its promise of "a useful and remunerative job." The chapter will describe instances in which collective bargaining was regarded as a right for labor and uncover an argument that it was one way to help workers gain a living wage. Chapter 5 will consider the SSA as a way to provide "the right to adequate protection from the economic fears of old age, sickness, accident, and unemployment." That chapter will highlight views of the Act that were consistent with the living wage and will give examples of critics of the Act who said it fell short of a living wage. Chapter 6 will take up the FLSA as having a goal of giving workers "the right to earn enough to provide adequate food and clothing and recreation." I will give several examples of individuals who argued that the minimum wage should be a living wage. Finally, Chapter 7 will summarize my findings and present contemporary perspectives on the New Deal programs of economic security. In these chapters, I will be looking at the regulatory and taxation programs of the New Deal most directly concerned with a living wage.

I will also be considering the most important question of all: What went wrong? Members of the New Deal and its supporters were optimistic that their programs would bring about their ideal of a living wage. The programs were based on a simple formula, collective bargaining plus social insurance plus a minimum wage equaled a living wage. Over 75 years later there are still many workers in the USA who do not earn a living wage. Were the New Dealers misguided by a flaw intrinsic to their formula? Or were there factors in play that the formula did not include?

In answering these questions as well as in making a case for the New Deal as having a goal of a living wage, I will be reviewing interpretations by supporters of the New Deal programs consistent with a living wage. I do not profess to have exhaustively selected every person who wrote in favor of the New Deal, but have tried to offer a sample that ranges from well-known politicians and business leaders to obscure economists and union officials. Where possible, I have tried to give biographical details of each person. The reader should take note that this book presents a history of the political economy of a living wage rather than a broad-based economic or a political history of New Deal policies. That focus will also appear to be one-sided in favor of the living wage arguments. That apparent bias represents the way the debate took place. Not surprisingly, in the world of ideas the proponents of a living wage favored the New Deal, even though many of them thought it did not go far enough toward their ideal. Opponents of the New Deal, however, rarely attacked it on the grounds that it supported a living wage.

Notes

1. Roosevelt, 1933g.
2. Fusfeld, 1956.
3. Roosevelt, 1933f.
4. Barber, 1996, p. 29.
5. Figart, Mutari, and Power, 2002, pp. 97–98.
6. Carlson, 1988, p. 26.
7. Katznelson, 2013, pp. 4659–4692.
8. Sunstein, 2004, pp. 730–35.
9. Barber, 1996, p. 1.
10. Kaufman, 2012.
11. Barber, 1996.
12. Roosevelt, 1933f.
13. Kaufman, 2012, p. 520.
14. Stabile and Kozak, 2012, pp. 100–106.
15. Lippmann,1935, p. 13.
16. Tugwell, 1977, p. xiv.
17. Beckerman, 2011, p. 24.
18. Brinkley, 1996; Glickman, 1997; Donohue, 2003.
19. Pollin and Luce, 2000, title page and 1.
20. Waltman, 2004, pp. 29–53.
21. Stabile, 2008, pp. 4–8.
22. Plato, 1888, pp. 50–54 and 109–10.
23. Plato, 1888, p. 266.
24. Aristotle, 1986, p. 40.
25. Aristotle, 1986, pp. 19–28.
26. Aristotle, 1986, p. 28.
27. Rothbard, 2006, pp. 832–1228.
28. Aquinas, 1968, pp. 124–5 and Aquinas, 1953, p. 145.
29. Stabile, 1997b, pp. 296–8.
30. Smith, 1976 [1776], vol. I, p. 449.
31. Smith, 1976 [1776], vol. I, p. 76.
32. Smith, 1976 [1776], vol. II, p. 399–400.
33. Smith, 1976 [1776], vol. I, p. 88.
34. Smith, 1976 [1776], vol. I., pp. 74–76 and 112–119; vol. II, p. 400.
35. Smith, 1976 [1776], vol. I., pp. 91–92.

36. Rothbard, 2006, pp. 4588, 4595, 4601, 5739, and 6120–30.
37. Smith, 1976 [1776], vol. II, p. 161.
38. Smith, 1976 [1776], vol. II, p. 246.
39. Smith, 1976 [1776], vol. I., p. 91.
40. Smith, 1976 [1776], vol. I., p. 82.
41. Mill, 1960, p. 175.
42. Mill, 1969 [1909], p. 31.
43. Mill, 1969 [1909], pp. 46-52.
44. Mill, 1969 [1909], p. 73.
45. Mill, 1969 [1909], pp. 54 and 163–4.
46. Mill, 1969 [1909], p. 347.
47. Mill, 1969 [1909], p. 361–2, italics in the original.
48. Mill, 1969 [1909], pp. 933–4.
49. Mill, 1969 [1909], p. 938
50. Mill, 1969 [1909], p. 935.
51. Mill, 1969 [1909], p. 937.
52. Fusfeld 1956, pp. 17–20.
53. Marx, 1977, p. 274.
54. Marx, 1977, p. 275.
55. Marx, 1967, p. 403.
56. Marx, 1973, p. 527.
57. Marx, 1977, p. 769.
58. Marx, 1977, p. 517.
59. Elliot 1981, p. 291.
60. Marshall, 1895, pp. 2–3.
61. Marshall, 1895, pp. 137–9.
62. Marshall, 1895, pp. 646–9.
63. Marshall, 1895, pp. 596–7 and p. 641.
64. Marshall, 1895, p. 781.
65. Ely, 1893, p. 101.
66. Ely, 1893, p. 38.
67. Ely, 1893, p. 222.
68. Ely, 1893, p. 69.
69. Ely, 1893, p. 77.
70. Ely, 1893, p. 85.
71. Ely, 1893, pp. 153.
72. Clark, 1886, pp. 51–54.
73. Clark, 1886, p. 110.
74. Clark, 1886, p.137.
75. Clark, 1965 [1899], p. v, emphasis added,
76. Clark, 1965 [1899], p. vi.
77. For details see Stabile, 2000, pp. 593–96.

78. Clark, 1965 [1899], pp. 73–74.
79. Clark, 1968 [1907], p. viii.
80. Clark, 1968 [1907], pp. 256–8.
81. Clark, 1968 [1907], pp. 451–2.
82. Clark, 1968 [1907], pp. 487–8.
83. Clark, 1968 [1907], p. 503.
84. Clark, 1968 [1907], p. 475.
85. Stabile, 2000, pp. 597–99.
86. Stabile, 1997a, pp. 817–21.
87. Moss, 1996, pp. 1–4.
88. Moss, 1996, p. 15
89. Rothbard, 2006, pp. 22402–4.
90. Kaku, 2001, pp. 81–82.
91. Kaufman and Barry, 2014, p. 1206; Figart, Mutari and Power, 2002, pp. 39–40.
92. Stabile, 2008, pp. 2–3 and 112–13.
93. Glickman, 1997, pp. 3, 62, and 131.
94. Gompers, 2015.
95. Gompers, 2015.
96. Glickman, 1997, p. 131.
97. Ryan, 1906.
98. Broderick, 1963.
99. Prasch, 2010, pp. 41–45.
100. Kaufman, 2000.
101. Prasch 2010, p. 46.
102. Ryan, 1906, p. 33, italics in the original.
103. Ryan, 1920, pp. 95–96.
104. Ryan, 1941, pp. 46 and 64–67.
105. Ely, 1935.
106. Witte, 1938.
107. Liberatore 1891, p. xvii.
108. Liberatore 1891, pp. 151–54.
109. Liberatore 1891, p. 181.
110. Liberatore 1891, pp. 161, 183 and 195.
111. Ryan, 1906, p. 17.
112. Ryan, 1906, p. 43.
113. Liberatore 1891, p. 154.
114. Ryan, 1906, p. 68.
115. Ryan, 1906, p. 72.
116. Ryan, 1906, pp. 132–36.
117. Ryan, 1906, pp. 138–59.
118. Ryan, 1906, p. 176.

119. Ryan, 1906, p. 244.
120. Ryan, 1906, p. 249.
121. Ryan, 1906, p. 261.
122. Ryan, 1906, p. 267.
123. Ryan, 1906, p. 280–95.
124. Beckerman, 2011, p. 15.
125. Ryan, 1906, p. 301.
126. Ryan, 1906, pp. 318–21.
127. Ryan, 1906, pp. 322–23.
128. Broderick 1963, p. 57.
129. Prasch, 1999, p. 222.
130. Prasch 2000, pp. 257–8.
131. Glickman 1997, pp. 3 and 151.
132. Goodwin 2014, p. 205.
133. Roosevelt, 1912.
134. Wilson, 1916.
135. Broderick, 1963, pp. 209–211.
136. Ryan, 1941, p. 270.
137. Broderick, 1963, pp. 213–218.
138. Broderick 1963, p. 218.
139. Rawls, 1999, p. 6.
140. Rawls, 1999, pp. 53–54.
141. Rawls, 1999, p. xiii.
142. Rawls, 1999, pp. 454–62.
143. Beckerman, 2011, p. 127.
144. Roosevelt, 1928.
145. Ryan, 1929.
146. Roosevelt, 1932a.
147. Perkins, 1933a.
148. Perkins, 1933c.
149. Perkins, 1934b.
150. Roosevelt, 1936f.
151. Ryan, 1939.
152. Ryan, 1936.
153. Eichengreen, 2015, pp. 4710–5310.
154. Schechter, 1935.
155. Roosevelt, 1935d.
156. Roosevelt, 1935e.
157. Liberatore 1891, pp. 151–54.
158. Studenski, 1936, p. 30.
159. Roosevelt, 1935d.
160. Roosevelt, 1932c.

161. Roosevelt, 1934a.
162. Roosevelt, 1935d.
163. Roosevelt, 1936d.
164. Roosevelt, 1938a.
165. Rosen, 2005, pp. 4–5.
166. Rosenman, 1952, pp. 425–26.
167. Roosevelt, 1944a, pp. 40–2.
168. Goodwin, 2014, p. 248.
169. Brinkley, 1996, pp. 3095–99.
170. Sunstein, 2004, p. 101.
171. Sunstein, 2004, pp. 3875–3885.
172. Goodwin, 2014, p. 205.
173. Ryan, 1941, p. 259–260.
174. Roosevelt, 1944b.

CHAPTER 2

A Living Wage from World War I Through the Onset of the Great Depression

The period from the beginning of the US entry into World War I in 1917 through the early years of the Great Depression was one of the most eventful times in the USA in terms of large-scale, new experiences. The war marked the first time the USA had participated in a global conflict and it ended the war as an important, if not the most important, member of the world economy. The decade that followed, the 1920s, was a time of innovation in business methods and in new products, with a result that the US economy had the best prosperity it had ever seen. That prosperity, however, ended with an economic downturn in 1929, which became the worst recession in US history before the economy hit bottom in March 1933; it was surely appropriate to label it the Great Depression.

These epochal events coming one after another obviously changed the USA in far-reaching ways. Less obvious was a quieter change that took off during this period, a quest for a living wage. As described in the previous chapter, a movement for a living wage had been going on in labor circles since the last quarter of the nineteenth century. Joseph Dorfman credits E.R.A. Seligman as the first prominent economist to raise the issue of a living wage with an article in the *Gunton Institute Bulletin* of March 1898. In that article, Seligman argued that it would not be easy for government to mandate a living wage in every occupation, but it could at least insist that contractors doing government work pay a living wage.[1] We will see in this chapter that advocates for a living wage believed they had attained

D. Stabile, *The Political Economy of a Living Wage*,
DOI 10.1007/978-3-319-32473-9_2

Seligman's beginning at the national level during World War I through the activities of the War Industries Board (WIB).

Seligman's early article notwithstanding, it is likely that John Ryan's book on a living wage had brought the concept to the attention of Progressive reformers. Whomever we credit for inaugurating the concept of a living wage, that concept gained greater importance during the 1920s through US participation in World War I. To coordinate production the federal government established the WIB. That story is well known. As Thomas C. Leonard has observed, a standard interpretation has it that the WIB was very successful in planning the production needed to fight the war and gave the Progressives confidence that government could plan the economy.[2] In her study of the transition among the Progressives from a focus on production to a stress on consumerism, Kathleen Donohue makes the point that the effectiveness of the WIB in increasing the efficiency of industry influenced political thinkers throughout the 1920s and 1930s.[3] A lesser-known story is that the WIB included strategies for helping workers in war industries earn a living wage. Those strategies enabled supporters of a living wage to achieve a broader acceptance of their goal. That broader acceptance continued to grow during the 1920s.

In this chapter I will first look at how the federal government in the USA planned the economy to fight World War I and uncover that a living wage was part of the plan. Then I will describe how reformers continued to promote a living wage during the period of reconstruction immediately after the war. We will follow this promotion through the 1920s and investigate its culmination into proposals for the federal government to end the Depression by managing the economy, much as it had during the war. These proposals also included a living wage.

Ryan Revises His Ideas

Before looking at the war and a living wage, let us check in on Ryan. For the decade after publishing his first book, he had been very busy. *A Living Wage* had been reprinted three times and he had written a second book, *Distributive Justice: The Right and Wrong of Our Present Distribution of Wealth*, which was published in 1916. The second book is much broader than the first by its consideration of income distribution among all social classes. In doing so, Ryan added important background information to his focus on a living wage. He also clarified and revised some of the ideas he had presented in the first book and these will be our main concern.

One of the first clarifications he added was his position on socialism. He opposed it as antihuman and impractical.[4] He was especially skeptical of the socialist belief that humans could be motivated to work effectively through "altruistic sentiments" without the motivation of money; the Church had been trying to incite altruism for centuries and with little success.[5] Humans may be "equal as moral entities," but they were unequal in terms of their abilities, and the complete equality of income prized by socialists was not feasible.[6]

The main problem with capitalism was that it had developed a potential to excessive profits. When profits were earned in a competitive market, they were acceptable if the business had acted fairly and honestly and treated its workers well. A business that made large profits through technological innovation was also entitled to keep what it had earned. Large companies operating as monopolies and making high profits from high prices were unacceptable and the fortunes they produced should be taken away with high, progressive taxes.[7] One area of concern for Ryan was the issue of "a minimum living profit." Did businessmen have a right to a living income where their profits enabled them to live in decent comfort? Ryan insisted that there were no absolute industrial rights, not to a living profit, not even to a living wage.[8] In both cases it was market conditions that determined the outcome. A businessman who earned less than a living profit was probably inefficient compared to his competitors and had to be weeded out; it was time for him to put his capital into something else and not rely on sweatshop conditions and low wages to earn a living profit. Or he could go to work for someone else and make a claim for a living wage. Consumers would not pay high prices to an inefficient business just to provide its owner with living profits.[9] Profits were thus acceptable if they were earned fairly and honestly in a competitive marketplace and if the employees were paid a living wage. Excessive profits were unjust and should be dedicated to charity or else face progressive taxation.

When he turned his attention to labor and wages, Ryan gave the same perspective as in his earlier book, as he freely admitted. His arguments became more sophisticated, however, as he had added to his knowledge about economics. For example, he considered the credibility of economists' theories about fair wages and found them all lacking. He dismissed the idea that wages were fair because they were the result of a free contract with a reminder that a person who faced a choice of work or starvation was not really confronted with an opportunity cost but with a dire choice. The market price could not be considered fair because it did not take into account the needs of the worker nor the effort he put forth in his work. The rigorous view that wages equaled the marginal product of labor fell apart, as Ryan noted, because of the difficulty of calculating it in circumstances where production was cooperative.[10]

In the ten years between his two books, moreover, he had learned that capitalism was embedded in a dynamic economy and accommodating change was important for securing a living wage. He recognized that markets changed from alterations in the technology of production, from new products, and from different consumer tastes. As a result, he qualified his ethical statements by admitting that workers did not have a right to a living wage in a particular job. If competitive conditions in the marketplace reduced the price a business received for its product, then wages would have to be reduced as well, at least for a short time. Workers in that condition might have to find another job that paid a living wage.[11] In this way the rigidities caused by inflexible prices could be avoided.

Another problem Ryan discovered was the difficulty in using a money measure of a living wage. When he estimated the level of a living wage in his first book, 11 years earlier, Ryan had fixed it at $600 a year. Since then prices had risen by 25 to 45 percent. That meant that his measure of a living wage had to be increased to $750 a year. Adherents of a living wage should not be fooled into thinking that increases in wages meant their goal was being reached. Once the higher wages were adjusted for inflation the fact still remained that a large majority of workers did not earn a living wage.[12]

When it came to policies to get workers a living wage, Ryan returned to his suggestions of a minimum wage imposed by the government and collective bargaining by unions. He now had a better understanding of each policy, however. With the minimum wage, he recognized that there were a number of responses that might result from imposing it. The traditional view of economists was that higher wages would lead to unemployment. In contrast, Ryan set forth the idea that higher wages might encourage workers to become more efficient on their own or because their employers adopted new technology to enhance their efficiency. It was also possible that profits would be reduced by the payment of higher wages. Ryan had no objection if it were excessive profits that were being reduced; a living wage came before the payment of interest and dividends to the wealthy. If profits fell to such an extent that a firm went bankrupt, Ryan found this to be acceptable. Previously he had argued that a business that could not afford to pay a living wage be given time to improve. Now he argued that such firms should not be allowed to exist. Any unemployment that resulted from a minimum wage policy would be small compared to the welfare gains from living wages.[13]

Ryan also found unions and collective bargaining to be more problematic than he had first thought. He now had data to show that union members were a small proportion of the workforce and their numbers did not appear to be growing. In addition, unions were not responding to the changes in the economy from technological innovation. The rise of mass production had created a large number of unskilled workers and unions were doing nothing to organize them. Instead, they were sticking with getting higher wages for skilled craft workers.[14] Earlier in the book, Ryan had worried about the ethical issue of some workers earning above a living wage while others did not earn a living wage.[15] Unions were not addressing this issue. As Ryan had to know, workers and union leaders had been rallying around the idea of a living wage since the last quarter of the nineteenth century.[16] He apparently believed that their quest for a living wage was limited to helping a small number of union members in craft unions. They did not have the social justice perspective consistent with a living wage for all workers, a view Ryan shared with Marx (see Chapter 1).

In arguing for policies to advance the cause of a living wage, Ryan recognized that there were limits on what the government could do. He had argued that the community had an obligation to pay workers a living wage but since it was private business and not the government that paid wages, the obligation rested on them. Private businesses received the output of labor and thus had to compensate labor for the output it produced. Ryan then used a hypothetical statement to make his point, without realizing that it was a prediction of things soon to come. He wrote, "If the State were in receipt of the production of industry…it would naturally be charged with the obligation [of paying a living wage] that now rests immediately upon the employer."[17] His point was that if government was buying a large amount of the products of labor everyone would accept that it had to pay a high enough price to secure a living wage for the workers who produced goods for the government; the same logic should apply to employers and consumers. Little did he realize that within a year, the federal government would be buying a large amount of the products of labor and it would find ways to live up to its obligations that workers be paid a living wage.

World War I, National Planning, and a Living Wage

When World War I began, the Progressives believed that it would give them an opportunity to continue their movement for reform in the USA. The war stirred up patriotism and made the public more loyal to the government; this community spirit surely could be transferred to public approval of other government programs. Moreover, to fight the war the government had to use national planning. In the integrated, technological economy that the USA had become, that planning would be essential. As a part of national planning, workers would be granted a living wage.

The war came, and the federal government, through the WIB, took over the railroads and a good deal more, including shipping and the distribution of food and fuel. Labor unions were brought into the fold with the promise of collective bargaining in the war industries. The Progressives joined the war effort in action as well as in the spirit they thought it brought to economic affairs. They framed their efforts with the term "Industrial Democracy" and argued that true democracy must be economic as well as political. This required that the country "establish democracy in the commercial government which is the real government of the state."[18]

The Progressives noted the way government was taking charge of industry during the war and took it as a sign that the Progressive pundits had been right in labeling business as inefficient. Taking over business to plan for the war was necessary, and the Progressives felt certain that the experience of the war would clearly show the inefficiency of current business practices and the efficacy of national planning. The experiences would also show the feasibility of attaining a living wage for all workers. As Bruce Kaufman describes, there was also a business approach to Industrial Democracy. Businesses in the USA, as they grew larger in size and scope, had to grapple with "the labor problem" of ensuring that workers were managed in a way that was conducive to their cooperation with management. To solve the labor problem, businesses used scientific management, welfare capitalism, industrial relations, employee representation plans, and collective bargaining to gain the goodwill of workers.[19]

Both political Progressives and forward-looking business leaders hoped for the fruition of their ideas with their anticipation that they could win support from labor. The Progressives, for example, realized that they were a middle-class movement and that to win elections they needed to gain support from other social classes. The war effort had helped labor and its unions and taught them that they could be part of Industrial Democracy. For example, Hugh Frayne (1869–1934), chairman of the WIB's Labor Division, had been a longtime union leader and was general organizer for the AFL. Right after the war, Frayne recounted some of the difficulties the WIB had with resolving labor issues. The difficulties came mainly from the employer "who has been unfair." These employers insisted on keeping wages low during the war, even though prices had increased. Frayne's judgment was that the employer "who is unwilling to pay a living wage can no longer masquerade under the guise of patriotism and expect to be maintained in that position by the government of the United States."[20]

Because the WIB had been unable to make headway in improving relations between business and labor, President Woodrow Wilson issued a proclamation establishing the National War Labor Board (NWLB) in 1918. In the November 1919 issue of the *Harvard Law Review*, Richard B. Gregg (1885–1974) provided an account of the Board's work. Gregg was a Harvard-educated attorney with a background of working in the area of industrial relations; the consulting firm he helped to form in 1916 was one of the first to advise business on human resource management.[21] In his account of the work of the Board, he outlined the principles of its operations as proclaimed by Wilson. Among them were principles held dear by labor unions, such as the right to organize and bargain collectively and protection to workers from being dismissed for union activities.[22] Of special pertinence to the topic of this book, Gregg quoted Wilson's proclamation on creating the NWLB. Here is what the president had to say about a living wage

1. The right of all workers, including common laborers, to a living wage is hereby declared.
2. In fixing wages, minimum rates of pay shall be established which will insure the subsistence of the worker and his family in health and reasonable comfort.[23]

As noted in Chapter 1, Ryan had quoted Pope Leo's encyclical on the condition of labor "that the remuneration must be enough to support the wage earner in *reasonable and frugal comfort*."[24] Wilson came teasingly close to the same quotation in his proclamation on the NWLB.

As Gregg pointed out, the Board had no legal status and thus did not have the ability to enforce its decisions. Instead, it relied on the war powers of the president directly or as delegated to other departments.[25] He cited two cases where the Board used these powers to enforce a decision granting workers a living wage. In one case, the Board determined that the employees of the Frick Co. should have "a minimum wage established not in reference to the economic power of the workers to compel it, but in reference to a determinable standard of living." The wages the Board awarded the workers were consistent with "what should actually constitute the living wage in accordance with [the Board's] principles."[26] In a second case involving street railway workers, the Board instituted wage increases without consideration of "whether or not the companies could afford the increases. The payment of a living wage was made a first charge on the business."[27]

These two cases were indicative of US government support for a living wage. In the first case, the Board used its own calculations as to what was a living wage. In the second, it went as far as Ryan had proposed. He had argued that a living wage came before the payment of profits or interest.[28] By making payment of a living wage "a first charge on the business," the NWLB accomplished what Ryan had proposed.

There is one other way the war advanced the cause of a living wage, or at least its adherents thought so. In September 1918, assistant secretary of the treasury Thomas B. Love (1870–1948) reported on the importance of war risk insurance. Starting in 1914, the war risk insurance program of the federal government insured US ships at sea from damages resulting from the war. The program was expanded in October 1917 to include the employment contract between the US government and its citizens serving in the military. Because the federal government was now a large employer it should base its employment contracts on what Love called a "generally agreed" standard of "a living wage." Moreover, a living wage should provide the worker with a subsistence income for himself and his family as well as protection from disability, illness, and old age and protection for his family in the event of his death. These were high standards for a living wage and Love argued that the government was meeting them with regard to members of the military and their families. Soldiers and sailors were provided with food, clothing, and medical care in addition to their basic pay. Their families were given an allotment as part of that basic pay. When those in the military were disabled by the war they were given disability pay for as long as they needed it; in the event of their death their families were taken care of.[29]

Love drew two conclusions from this new labor contract between the government and those serving in the military. First, he noted, the pay scheme for the military was "certainly the most liberal provision made by any government in the history of the world."[30] The US government was setting a precedent by paying its soldiers and sailors a living wage. Second, he added that this provision of a living wage to those in the military "will have an added value in that it will point the way...for a rational and sound system of employment which will be mutually beneficial to society and to the worker for peace times as well as for war."[31]

As indicated by the individuals whose writings are featured in this section, the federal government in the USA was taking a lead in the movement for a living wage, at least during the war. It used its wartime powers to implement a living wage in several cases before the NWLB and it paid its military what could be considered a living wage. Would this support for a living wage be carried over into peacetime?

The Period of Reconstruction

The period immediately following World War I was often referred to at the time as one of reconstruction. As the US economy made a transition from war to peace, many thinkers thought it would offer an opportunity to make the economy over, that is, to reconstruct it on a basis that would offer workers a better chance for a decent life. President Wilson made a living wage a key ingredient in the reconstruction program. He outlined the program in his annual message to the Congress on December 2, 1919, and included his policy for labor

> To analyze the particulars in the demands of labor is to admit the justice of their complaint in many matters that lie at their basis. The workman demands an adequate wage, sufficient to permit him to live in comfort, unhampered by the fear of poverty and want in his old age. He demands the right to live and the right to work amidst sanitary surroundings, both in home and in workshop, surroundings that develop and do not retard his own health and wellbeing; and the right to provide for his children's wants in the matter of health and education. In other words, it is his desire to make the conditions of his life and the lives of those dear to him tolerable and easy to bear.[32]

Although he did not use the term "living wage," Wilson did speak in a way that was consistent with the definition of the term, even as he suggested that a need to provide profits might constrain wage payments. His policy included improving labor's right to collective bargaining and stated one of its goals as, "Labor not only is entitled to an adequate wage, but capital should receive a reasonable return upon its investment..."[33]

We can see this approach to reconstruction mirrored in an article by noted journalist Robert W. Bruère (1876–1964), "Can We Eliminate Labor Unrest?" For Bruère, a living wage would go a long way toward giving a positive answer to that question. He noted that the federal government had set forth a "minimum comfort wage for an average American family" of $1400. He added, "A national minimum wage of $1,400 would be a good beginning toward the elimination of labor unrest." In providing that minimum wage, it was important that the worker has the respect that came from being "free from the taint of pseudo-charity." It was also important that a living wage be set as a family wage. Too many employers thought of the family wage as what members of a family could earn through all of them working. To Bruère, the family wage should be "the wage paid to the head of the family alone."[34] No head of a family should be forced to allow other members of the family to be exploited to bring total household income up to a living wage. To provide workers with the dignity of independence from the largess of employers as well as to attain for them a family wage, Bruère maintained that every worker should be "joining and energetically supporting the union of his industry or trade."[35]

A similar approach to labor issues was advanced by industrialist Henry P. Kendall (1878–1959) in an article, "Post-War Standards for Industrial Relations." To him, the labor problem was the most pressing issue facing the USA. He proposed several solutions but thought that the best approach was a system of wage boards modeled after the NWLB. Like that Board, Kendall's proposed wage boards would operate under general principles that included "the right of workers to organize in joint action" and "the right of all workers, including common laborers, to a living wage."[36] He urged business leaders to join with him in advocating for his plan and in working with organized labor.

This pattern of using the experiences of the war as a model for the post-war period can also be found in an article by Henry R. Seager (1870–1930), "Effect of Present Methods on Future Wage Adjustments." Seager was professor of political economy at Columbia University and served three terms as the president of AALL and a term as the president of the AEA in 1922. He spent the war as the secretary of the Shipbuilding Labor Adjustment Board. He used his experience as well as his training in economics to analyze how well the wage-setting methods of the different boards of the war could be used in the future. Regarding the NWLB, he noted that its efforts to implement a living wage among the workers in the industries central to the war effort had met with resentment by the businessmen in charge of those industries because "no department of the government was responsible for reimbursing the employers for the higher wages they had to pay."[37] If the Board were allowed to continue its function, this resentment would grow. To Seager, the only way a peacetime wage board could function effectively was "as part of the machinery voluntarily created through collective bargaining."[38]

With collective bargaining and a government wage board, it would be possible to retain the principle of a living wage that existed during the war. Seager was insistent on the principle and found it key to the new approach he was recommending. He wrote, "That underlying all wage adjustments there should be acceptance of the principle that a wage sufficient to maintain the wage earner and his family in full economic efficiency will be denied by no one." To be sure, there would be differences in opinion about what a living wage would be, with the result that "the living wage is thus an indeterminate but highly important basic standard."[39] But there were government agencies at work collecting the data that would enable a close approximation to what a living wage should be. Wage adjustment boards could use that data and, when combined with collective bargaining, would offer a "constructive plan for substituting co-operation for conflict and bringing us nearer the new day of which we all dream, when the aims of industrial justice and the aims of industrial efficiency will at last be reconciled in a true industrial democracy."[40]

Another perspective on the work of the NWLB was presented by Basil M. Manly (1886–1954), the joint chairman of the Board, in an article, "Moral Influences in the Adjustment of Industrial Disputes." According to Manly, the Board had a moral influence in its "code of principles." Those principles, he added, included "collective bargaining and the living wage, and are so well-known that they need not be quoted."[41] To be sure, the Board was not always able to live up to its principles. In one case, for example, the Board fixed the wage at more than the workers had asked, believing that the extra wages were need to ensure a living wage. In making this award, the Board hoped to set a standard for all wage settlements under its jurisdiction, but it found that its members could not agree on that standard. A plan was put into place for reaching an agreement, but the war ended before the plan could be finished. After the war, the Board's ability to be effective declined because the ultimate source of its power and prestige, President Wilson, had gone to Europe to work on the Peace Treaty. Without his moral influence, the Board could not function effectively.[42] Still, Manly felt that there was a role to be played by the federal government in maintaining a moral influence in industrial relations.

A labor perspective on the NWLB was provided by William Jett Lauck (1879–1949), a prolific writer on labor issues with a keen interest in the issues surrounding a living wage. In 1922, he displayed this interest in a book, *The Industrial Code: A Survey of the Postwar Industrial Situation*. His goal was to show the changes that were taking place in industry after the innovations brought about during the war became accepted. One of the important innovations during the war was the leadership of President Wilson in making a living wage a goal of the NWLB.[43]

This leadership continued after the war when Wilson called for several industrial conferences where business, labor, and the government could discuss issues of concern. In the second of those conferences, Lauck reported, a consensus was reached that "considered from the standpoint of public interest, it is fundamental that the basic wages of all employees should be adequate to maintain the employee and his family in reasonable comfort." Low wages, he added, were dangerous because they brought with them "disease, degeneration and dangerous discontent."[44]

Lauck favored using studies of workers' budgets, such as were being conducted by the Bureau of Labor Statistics as a way to determine a living wage. He also supported other efforts by the federal government to bring about a living wage and called the NWLB "one of the most beneficial governmental organizations of the war" because of its main principles of a living wage for all workers and the right of workers to organize unions. He urged the Congress to continue those principles through peacetime legislation.[45] As had Ryan, Lauck considered that a living wage "should be made a first charge against industry before dividends are considered."[46] In pushing for a living wage, moreover, Lauck included a consumerist perspective by adding, "High wages are desirable" to provide "greater purchasing power" to stimulate business and the economy.[47]

Lauck, moreover, did more that talk about a living wage. He tried to measure its feasibility in an undated report "The Practicality of a Living Wage" (the data he used date the report as the early 1920s). Whenever he talked about a living wage, Lauck found that a question kept being brought up: "Is the productivity of the country sufficient to assure a standard of living of at least modest comfort to each of the millions in the country?"[48] To answer the question Lauck made his own calculation by comparing an annual standard budget prepared by the Bureau of Labor Statistics in 1919 and applying that budget to actual production in the USA in 1914, the last year for which he had data. Lauck argued that potential output would be a better data sample to use, because he believed that national production was hampered by ineffectual methods of industrial organization and a living wage would have an immediate payoff of improving the health of workers and adding to their efficiency. As his data set did not have information on housing, Lauck focused on the output of food and clothing and found that it was "sufficient to maintain the population of the country at a minimum level of health and comfort."[49]

His results, as flawed as his data was, were a big step in addressing whether a living wage was practical. He was also in advance of other supporters of a living wage in looking at the dynamic changes a living wage made in the overall economy. Later in this chapter, we will encounter several persons who did not think the USA could afford a living wage in terms of its total national income. Those individuals used national income per worker as their standard, however. Lauck indicated that a living wage would enhance labor's efficiency and its purchasing power, both of which should cause national income to increase. In thinking this way, he took an approach that was consistent with what unions believed.

Unions Favor the Living Wage Policy of the NWLB

As noted in Chapter 1, unions had long been supporters of a living wage.[50] To some degree that interest in a living wage attracted the attention of the Progressive reformers who took up the same cause and wanted to use government to bring about a living wage for all workers. For unions, the Progressive takeover of their program for a living wage could be seen as a threat. After all, Samuel Gompers had argued that any pursuit of a living wage was best handled by collective bargain under union leadership. That attitude did not change as a result of the efforts of the NWLB to secure a living wage during the war. Gompers and others in the union movement understood that what a government dominated by business interests gave them, it could also take away from them. That is what they thought was happening in the immediate post-war era, as unionized workers saw their wage increases during the war eroded by inflation and by the recession of 1920–1921.

We can see this union attitude in several articles in the *American Federationist*, the chief publication of the AFL. The AFL took a keen interest in the NWLB and its advocacy for a living wage. In May 1918, it published an article on the activities of the NWLB, indicating that its "underlying principle is the dignity and value of human life in the declaration that every worker has a right to a living wage."[51] It was also important that the NWLB supported the right of workers to organize into unions. An even stronger statement of the AFL's approval of the work of the NWLB took the form of an article by Frank P. Walsh (1864–1939), the labor co-chair of the NWLB. Walsh indicated that in the written standards of the NWLB "most of the basic trade union principles were announced as axioms." He saw the NWLB as bringing about a revolution in labor relations. An important part of that revolution was the arbitration cases the Board resolved in its pursuit of a living wage. Business opponents in those cases had argued that the increased pay would reduce their profits and force them into bankruptcy. In response, Walsh indicated, the Board took the approach that property had no preference over labor, because a living wage was "a first lien on all industrial property." With respect to bankruptcy, he added, "The industry which can not pay a living wage has no right to exist. ... If private enterprise can not pay a living wage, then public enterprise will."[52] He also used Wilson's support for a living wage as part of his argument.

In writing this way, Walsh made statements that were in line with what Ryan had written. Ryan also found that a living wage took preference over profits, and businesses that could not pay a living wage after being given a chance should be allowed to go out of business. It is hard to know, however, the direction in which the influence flowed, because unions had held these positions for a long time. And they continued to hold them. In February 1919, the *American Federationist* ran an editorial by Matthew Woll (1880–1956), president of the International Photo-Engravers Union of North America, headed, "Insist on a Living Wage." Woll indicated that in the USA the worker was free, but to exercise that freedom, workers needed the "means of livelihood." World War I had provided better opportunities for higher wages, but in the post-war period wages were being cut back. "This demand for a living wage," he went on, "is in fact a rebellion against the maladministration" of industry. Moreover, the AFL had accepted the principle of a living wage and its "next step is to maintain this living wage where it is established and to establish it for workers where it does not obtain." The living wage was a basic right and "to realize it is the sure and true destiny of organized labor."[53]

Woll, too, wrote in terms similar to Ryan's view that collective bargaining was essential for securing a living wage and that unions could be a vehicle for making a living wage a right of all workers. In the same issue of the *American Federationist*, however, there was another article that added a new wrinkle to a living wage. The article presented the "American Federation of Labor Reconstruction Program" that called for Industrial Democracy to end the autocracy at the workplace through union action. It then shifted gears to offer a union philosophy related to a living wage:

> Unemployment is caused by underconsumption. Underconsumption is caused by low or insufficient wages. Just wages will prevent industrial stagnation and lessen periodical unemployment. Give workers a just wage and their consuming capacity is correspondingly increased...Just wages will create a market at home which will surpass any market that may exist elsewhere.[54]

Unions could be relied upon to attain those just wages. In arguing this way, the AFL was making a first step in the transition from producerism to consumerism noted in Chapter 1. The idea of increasing the purchasing power of labor to solve underconsumption would be a common theme in the New Deal.

A similar support for a living wage can be found in the publication of one of the AFL's largest members, the United Mine Workers. The approach of the NWLB regarding a living wage received favorable coverage in the *United Mine Workers Journal* during 1918. On April 4, an article, "Terms Agreed Upon by War Labor Board," cited the rights of employees of the NWLB goals and highlighted the right of a living wage.[55] Two months later, on June 13, there appeared an article with the headline, "Living Wage Upheld by Frank Walsh."[56] And on July 25 the *United Mine Workers Journal* applauded the NWLB decision in one of its cases, the Waynesboro Case, to give workers a living wage.[57]

With the end of the war, the mine works retained their interest in a living wage. An editorial in the October 15, 1921, issue of the *United Mine Workers Journal* made it clear that a worker was entitled "to a living wage, or rates of pay sufficient to maintain himself and his family according to an American standard of living, on a basis of health, decency and reasonable comfort." Without that standard of living, "there could not be intelligent and sound citizenship and the future was without hope."[58] The issue of how to establish that standard of living was addressed in an article a year later titled, "The Living Wage." In asking what a living wage was, the article answered that it should not be an arbitrary standard. Nor should it be set as "a limit to what a man may do and the amount he may earn." No one wanted to be told that they would be paid "according to a standard we shall set for you." That was why unions and not government boards should be involved in the establishment of wage rates.[59]

In terms of establishing where a living wage should be set, the Mine Workers Union's approach, as set forth by its president, John L. Lewis (1880–1969) on May 15, 1922, was that "the demand of the coal mine workers for a living wage is not an impractical, visionary idea." Rather, it was based on the capability of the economy to produce enough goods and services to provide every worker a living wage.[60] A month later an "Official Circular" in the *United Mine Workers Journal* took up the struggle for a living wage for all workers by stating, "In fighting for such principles [as a living wage], the organized mine worker is not merely fighting for himself and his dependents, but is waging a fight for the benefit of the wage earners of the country."[61] The need for the fight, an article by Charles Lowe added on September 14, 1922, had to do with the unequal distribution of wealth. Using an argument Ryan would have liked, Lowe noted, "God gave the coal to man, and He did not intend that a few men should gain control of the output."[62] Indeed, had he read these articles, as well he might have, Ryan would have been impressed. The mine workers were employing a definition of a living wage similar to his views, claimed to be fighting for all workers, and justified it on an argument similar to his that God gave the bounty of the earth to all humans and all had a right to share in it.

The fact that the NWLB had not succeeded in attaining a living wage only meant to union leaders that its efforts had to be redoubled. But a redoubling of efforts to secure a living wage would not be likely under the return to normal life brought about by the election of Republican Warren G. Harding to the presidency.

The Economy of the 1920s

Harding ran for president on the promise of a return to normalcy. If by normalcy he meant a return to economic prosperity, he delivered. The 1920s were a period of economic growth and prosperity never seen before in the USA. The Federal Reserve index of industrial production went from 81 in January 1920 to 114 in July 1929—a 40.6 percent increase; real income grew at an average of 4.6 percent a year from 1920 to 1929,[63] and 1929 was the best year the US economy had experienced up to that time. To be sure, economic recessions were common during the 1920s. The first began in January 1920 and a recovery did not begin until July 1921; other recessions took place from May 1923 to July 1924, October 1926 to November 1927, and the final downturn began in August 1929. These recessions took up 52 months of the ten-year period.

In addition to being a decade of economic growth, the 1920s were also a decade of economic transformation, brought about by the development of new technologies in production and in product development. The automobile came of age in the 1920s, and the radio and films with sound launched new industries. A contemporary estimate by Joseph Schumpeter found that 90 percent of the change in economic activity in the 1920s came from the automobile, chemical, and electrical industries.[64] These trends ushered in a new mass consumption society with a greatly increased range of choices for consumers. As a result, economic conditions in the US were very good. Until the 1929 crash, leaders in the federal government could justifiably claim that their laissez faire policies had worked very well. The 1920s started out by being billed as a return to normalcy, but in terms of economic growth and technological change they were anything but normal. Herbert Hoover ran for president in 1928 on a platform of prosperity and the continuation of the government policies that had brought it; he won a substantial victory. Confidence in the economy remained high throughout the decade.

Not everyone had that confidence. The triumph of market capitalism in the USA in the 1920s did not turn the critics of markets silent. They continued to find places where the economy was weak and prosperity was not shared by every person in the USA. The movement for a living wage among the Progressives grew along with the economy. One surprising advocate for the idea that all was not well in the economy was Hoover.

Herbert Hoover and the New Economy

Herbert Hoover (1874–1964) had a career that reinforces the idea that the USA is a land of opportunity. Born into a modest family background in the small town of West Branch, Iowa, he was orphaned at age nine. He moved to Oregon and worked in his uncle's store. When Stanford University opened its doors in 1891, he enrolled and graduated with a degree in geology. For him, the best use of a geology degree was in mining and he worked for many years as a mining engineer, becoming affluent in the process. Perhaps because of his Quaker background, he then had a career in public and humanitarian service, starting with his organizing a food relief program for Belgium in 1914 during the early days of World War I. When the USA entered the war, Hoover became head of the US Food Administration. From 1921–1929, he was the US Secretary of Commerce. In 1928, he was elected president, serving one term until 1933.

When Harding appointed him as the Secretary of Commerce in 1921, Hoover saw his new post as an opportunity to gain greater prominence for the work of efficiency in industry through cooperation. His chief approach for cooperation was to encourage trade associations, organizations of businesses that made up a particular industry. Hoover was a strong proponent of trade associations and believed that the information they shared would help alleviate the severity of business cycles. His intent was to make it feasible for every industry in the USA to use their trade associations and the information they provided to promote better decision making by industry planning groups. The result, he anticipated, would be industrial efficiency and intelligent competition.

Regarding the business cycle, Hoover had formed a Committee on Business Cycles in 1921 with an aim of finding out what could be done to mitigate the social damage caused by recessions. In a report to the Congress on the Committee's findings, Hoover wrote that the government should time its public works projects to slow down construction spending during a boom by delaying them and to offset recessions by increasing those projects.[65] This was a new approach at the time and we will see that Hoover used it in the early years of the Great Depression. In doing so, he hoped to avoid the two extreme ideas "that all human ills can be cured by government regulation" and "that all regulation is a sin."[66]

For the rest of the 1920s, the federal government would back away from the type of intervention Hoover called for. In addition, the unprecedented prosperity of the 1920s might have obviated the need for a living wage. Still, there were advocates for a living wage that kept the need for it as a part of public discourse.

Economic Analysis of a Living Wage

From Adam Smith down through Alfred Marshall, economists had always taken a keen interest in the well-being of workers. They did not use the term a living wage, but the term they did use, the subsistence wage, had much the same meaning (See Chapter 1). Once Ryan and World War I had made the term a living wage popular, economists began using it and considering its implications.

The first of them is Dorothea Davis Kittredge (1890–1978). She had earned an MA in economics from George Washington University and her research led her to write an article, "A Suggestion for Determining a Living Wage," published in *The American Economic Review* in June 1923. She began the article by pointing out that there was broad disagreement over how to define a living wage. Her suggestion was to get agreement on some large and measurable variable, "some big factor which a living wage must render possible, and which is capable of clear-definition."[67] The variable she selected was health, because it was tangible and could easily be assessed by a medical doctor.

The problem Kittredge was addressing was inflation, changes in the cost of living. Because the war had brought about a period of high inflation, economists recognized "the fallacy of attempting to define a living wage on the basis of a money standard."[68] A living wage, instead, had to be defined in terms of the quantities of things it would purchase, that is, what were the goods and services that were needed for a family to live. The federal government collected data to determine average budgets for families, but these had been criticized for being too hypothetical and resulting in a very high standard for a living wage. A better approach for research on a living wage would be to have it undertaken by "physicians, dieticians, and experts qualified to rate standards of housing, sanitation, and other essential factors." This research could be done under the auspices of the federal government, but whoever undertook it, there was a "great need for scientific research to ascertain what constitutes a living wage."[69]

The issue of the relationship between a living wage and inflation was also addressed by Alvin Johnson (1874–1971). Johnson earned a PhD from Columbia University under the direction of John Bates Clark. He served for many years as professor of economics at the Cornell University, before taking part in the founding of the New School for Social Research. Although much of his work was highly orthodox, he found faults with traditional economics, especially in its treatment of wages and its opposition to a minimum wage.[70] In 1926, he published an article in *The American Economic Review* titled "Real Wages and the Control of Industry." He began the article by explaining two theories of wage determination that existed in economics. The first was that the wage was whatever was fixed by supply and demand. The second he called the "industrial democratic conception." It held that labor had first priority in the division of the fruits of industrial production. This meant that "a decent minimum of wages shall be paid before capital or management should receive any return, and that any industry which is economically incompetent to pay such wages is parasitic and undesirable and ought to go out of business."[71] Ryan had taken a similar position (See above).

In a period of economic growth there were bound to be changes in the real wage, but an approach that made wages a function of industrial progress through innovation could not be adjusted to take into account an increase in the cost of living. Only a living wage could be used to reflect changes in the real wage. The idea of a living wage had gained prominence in Europe and the USA with very favorable results for focusing attention on the real wage. Johnson wrote,

> Calculations of what the laborer could buy with his money brought home at last to the average citizen and tardily to the public authorities a sense of the moral necessity of giving labor a special place in the economic system. Labor could not be left hanging to the whip of supply and demand. A reasonable subsistence became a paramount moral claim on industry.[72]

Popular opinion had accepted the idea that workers earning low real wages ought to be paid more. But it was indifferent about paying more than that. To Johnson this meant that the focus should still be on attaining a living wage. He wrote, "with the exception of a few favored trades, most of American labor has still to achieve a fair standard of real wage." The problem was that "the fixing of wages on a purchasing power basis involves difficulties of definition."[73]

Because we now live in an era where many of us are familiar with the consumer price index and the way it is used to index wages to produce a fixed real wage, we may find the concerns expressed by Kittredge and Johnson to be overdone. But they lived in an era where price indexes were only starting to be developed. And the idea that large numbers of workers did not earn a living wage also seems difficult to accept. What was needed at the time, and is still needed today, was a solid economic argument in favor of a living wage. Such a theory was presented by an economist in the 1920s and we turn to it next.

John Maurice Clark, Overhead Costs, and a Living Wage

John Maurice Clark (1884–1963), the son of John Bates Clark (See Chapter 1), was a longtime professor of economics at Columbia University and a prominent member of the Institutional School of Economics. He served a term as the president of the AEA in 1935. Clark had a wide range of interests in economics and is now best remembered for his concept of the accelerator, where he argued that small changes in the demand for their product could induce businesses to make larger changes in their investment plans, thereby causing upward or downward swings in the economy (Clark 1923b, pp. 50–59). In this section, I am going to focus on a small component of his work that is related to a living wage.

That interest in a living wage can be found in a few pages in his most important book, *Studies in the Economics of Overhead Costs*. In that book, he presented an economic case for a living wage. His argument started with the idea that every society had a set amount of labor available to its economy to be used in production. From a social perspective, the use of this labor was an overhead charge to society that was not accounted for in the overall costs of production. Clark stated the case as follows: "There is a minimum of maintenance of the laborer's health and working capacity which must be borne by someone, whether the laborer works or not" or else "the community suffers a loss through the deterioration of its working power."[74] Workers were responsible for their own sustainability. When their wages were not adequate to maintain them and if the community did not make additional provisions for them, members of the labor force might deteriorate.

Clark did not see a market solution to this problem, due to the prisoners' dilemma paradox. Employers who considered paying workers a premium above the going wage to cover the overhead cost of labor would not do so without assurance of being compensated with higher productivity. If they did, they would risk having higher costs, which would place them at a competitive disadvantage and reduce their profits. Clark wrote, "The overhead cost of labor is a collective burden upon industry in general, but the market does not allocate to each employer the share for which his own enterprise is responsible."[75] Under the institutional framework of capitalism, businesses shifted many of the costs of maintaining the workforce onto society through layoffs and wage reductions, leaving it to the society to sustain the workforce. What was a fixed cost for society was a variable cost for business. The problem related to unequal bargaining power between business and labor. Clark pointed out, "In an economy based on the division of labor, people are not self-sufficing, and if others will not exchange with them, they cannot live at all."[76]

Clark expanded on this idea in a second book, *The Social Control of Business*. In that book he argued that wage bargains were the result of unequal strength between employers and workers. Clark saw this inequality as a national problem requiring government intervention. He justified that intervention on the basis of a public interest in reducing the social overhead costs of labor. He stated the case as follows:

> Whether through ignorance, inertia or sheer necessity, workers will work under conditions that will shorten their work lives or injure their future efficiency, and they are not able to charge any adequate premium for such kinds of work. This might perhaps be treated as nobody's business but the workers', save for the fact that their children and other dependents have an interest in their working-efficiency, also their future employers, or the taxpayers or contributors to charity who must pay for the rescue work which may become necessary, or the business out of whose product the funds for relief must come—in short, there is a "public interest" in the avoidance of such wastes.[77]

Clark believed that low wages for workers imposed costs on others.

As a result, Clark sought government intervention to mandate a "social minimum" in terms of a standard of living, that is, a living wage. Policies to help the working poor, he argued, might "actually pay for themselves in the long run by increasing the working efficiency of the personnel,"[78] giving an early version of what economists now call the efficiency wage theory. But even if they did not, ending the system that permitted uncompensated damages to the workforce was crucial to economic efficiency.

Clark justified his support of minimum wage laws on the following basis:

> An industry which does not pay a living wage is really imposing part of its costs on other industries, since it is out of those industries that the living expenses of the underpaid workers must be made up, if they are to be made up at all. And if not, there is a loss of working-power which falls as a diffused burden, often handicapping succeeding generations.[79]

Firms that did not pay a living wage were creating costs that fell on the society at large. Clark's point was that through the shifting of costs onto society, individual businesses were receiving a subsidy. Subsidies typically result in a particular form of market failure and detract from maximum social welfare.[80] Clark's viewpoint hinted at Ryan's conclusion that businesses that could not pay a living wage should be eliminated from the economy. By holding down the wages that their competitors could pay, they harmed all of the society.

The concept of a social minimum that would shift the costs back to business, however, ran afoul of meager data—in Clark's case, lacking a system of social cost accounting. A proper social cost accounting system "would undertake to set a true social value on all the human values and costs of industry."[81] Clark's proposals for a social minimum and social accounting were intended to provide insights into a basic problem, defining the standard of living in terms of goods and work levels. That definition required answers to two questions: what wants should be supported and "should added wages be granted subject to the condition that recipients made proper use of them?"[82] To provide answers to these questions Clark proposed a system of social planning using national councils. To him the issue of a living wage was a national one and it could not be solved by local activities.

While I am highlighting Clark as a prominent expounder of the idea of the social overhead costs of labor, there was already recognition of this problem in business circles through the development of human resource management programs, more commonly referred to as welfare capitalism. Detractors of capitalism think of welfare capitalism as a means to subvert unions. Proponents of welfare capitalism believed it would reduce the problems of managing labor by treating workers fairly. One of those early proponents, Sumner Slichter, argued that the "good will of the workers" was a "capital asset" that had to be protected.[83] The problem with this approach to treating labor's goodwill as an overhead cost (asset) was that it cost money to implement. Those costs, moreover, were tangible, whereas the direct benefits to the business were intangible. In addition, the approach included indirect social benefits that accrued to society at large, such as the better health of the workforce. It would take a very committed business to undertake programs of welfare to attain the goodwill of its workers, raising its costs, when its competitors did not follow suit. There needed to be an overarching force such as the government to get firms to follow the path to better working conditions and employee benefits, Clark argued, as well as an effective method of social cost accounting that allowed those businesses to allocate the direct and indirect benefits of the programs of welfare capitalism to their income statements.

From his study of overhead costs, Clark also set forth a theory of business cycles. The first part of the theory related to the problem that expenditures for the capital equipment that constituted overhead were concentrated into short time periods. Whenever a business had an increase in demand at a time when it was operating at full capacity, it would build new facilities to increase its productive capacity. But new facilities were a considerable expense, which meant that small changes in consumer demand could lead to larger changes in investment demand. Clark referred to this as the accelerator.[84]

The result of this accelerator process was that booms and recessions had reinforcing effects that amplified their total force. During a boom, a rise in consumer demand increased the demand for capital equipment, and the producers of capital equipment would expand and hire more workers, whose pay would add to consumer demand and lead to more demand for capital equipment, and so on. As consumer demand leveled off, however, the demand for capital equipment would decline, leading to contractions in the production of capital equipment, the unemployment of workers in the capital equipment industries, lower consumer demand and the beginning of a recessionary spiral. Businessmen would like to buy capital during the trough of the recession when prices were low, but they could never be sure when the bottom had been reached.[85] With this perspective, Clark could conclude that the market economy was not a good way to control the business cycle, and he proposed national planning as a way to control it. But there was another way overhead costs contributed to those cycles.

In a separate article in 1923, Clark analyzed how his theory of overhead costs shed light on how to offset a recession. What was needed was a coordinated program to convert wages into a fixed cost for business and Clark suggested that unions should use their bargaining power to win a wage system that gave workers "a substantial minimum retainer plus a moderate charge proportioned to work actually done."[86] If all firms in the economy followed this approach, there would be steadier production and consumption and a recession might be avoided as the result would be a "general stabilization" of wages, prices, and total demand.[87] By keeping workers employed during a recession, business would be able to maintain total demand in the economy by sustaining steady consumption.

Clark is a central figure in this book but not because he continued to develop his views on a living wage. I will describe in the next chapter how he backed away from an interest in a living wage as required by social cost accounting when he determined that the NRA had not been workable as a way to allocate social costs. He is central because, as will be described in subsequent chapters, his idea of the social overhead costs of labor was used by others to support living wage arguments.

Two Business Leaders on a Living Wage

As noted in Chapter 1, economists had always had an interest in some form of a living wage, even if they did not always use that term. More surprising, there were also business leaders who found the concept of a living wage to be important. In this section, we will take a look at what they had to say.

The first business leader we will look at is Sam A. Lewisohn (1894–1951). Lewisohn was the son of a well-known financier, Adolph Lewisohn. After attending Princeton University and the Columbia University Law School, Sam Lewisohn practiced law for several years before joining his father's firm. Always civic minded, he worked in the War Risk Insurance Bureau of the federal government during the war. In 1921, he was a member of the economic advisory committee of the President's Conference on Unemployment and president of the American Management Association. His 1923 article, "The Living Wage and the National Income," was published in the *Political Science Quarterly*.

Before looking at the topic indicated by the title, Lewisohn thought it advisable to set forth his own view of a living wage. It consisted of three beliefs which are worth quoting in full:

> First, that the underlying purpose of industry is not the private adventure or profit of employers but the economic well-being of all.
>
> Second, that the welfare of wage-earners is one of the most important if not the most important question in the conduct of industry.
>
> Third, that the primary responsibility is upon the employing group to endeavor so to perfect the industrial process that each worker may be provided with a wage that will give him at least all the ordinary comforts of life.[88]

Lewisohn clearly favored a living wage and his placing the primary responsibility for attaining it on employers was in line with what Ryan had argued.

There were limits to how far that responsibility could go, however, and Lewisohn found one difficulty from thinking about whether a living wage was consistent with the level of national income. It was well known that wages, in general, and a living wage, in particular, were always related to the level of national income. A prosperous country typically paid higher wages than a poor one. But when it came to determining a living wage this relationship was often forgotten. Instead, a living wage was defined on the basis of a standard of comfortable living. To highlight the problem, Lewisohn took the national income per employed person and compared it to many estimates of the level of income needed for a living wage and found that giving every employed person a living wage would result in a figure higher than the national income.[89]

Lewisohn did not conclude that a living wage was impossible, only that it could not be attained immediately. The economy would have to become more productive before a living wage could be effectively attained and that would take time. Meanwhile, by making exaggerated claims for what was feasible in terms of a living wage its adherents were giving the Conservatives a good talking point and giving false hope to the working poor. Economists needed to do a better job of describing how far away the USA was from a living wage while also making it clear that any immediate goal of securing a living wage must be modest.[90]

Another business leader with an interest in a living wage was Edward Filene (1860–1937). Filene took a small family store started by his father and expanded it into a major department store. In the store, he utilized advanced views of management to improve the wages and working conditions of his employees. He had testified in favor of a minimum wage law for the District of Columbia, arguing, "A decent wage, then, seems to us the basis of intelligent work."[91] His advanced views were very visible in an article, "The Minimum Wage and Efficiency," he published in the September 1923 issue of *The American Economic Review*. In that article, he was worried that the post-war period was seeing a reduction in the wages of workers. To counter this decline, he wanted to see a minimum wage law in place. He justified the law as follows:

> Wages naturally tend to go down toward the standard set by the meanest and most short-sighted employers. It may as well be said that inability to pay a living wage is not always the reason why such a wage is refused. There are greedy employers…men who for the sake of profit want to squeeze the last penny from their help.[92]

It was up to the government to end this race to the bottom of wages with a minimum wage law.

At this point, Filene, like many at the time, looked to state governments for a minimum wage legislation. A common argument made against this approach was that it would force some businesses to leave the states that enacted a minimum wage. Filene responded by insisting that he favored their departure. "Any business that cannot pay a living wage," he went on, "is not good for the state and has no place in it. By not paying its employees an adequate wage, it forces them to be supported, at least in part, by their relatives, friends, or by the public."[93]

Another argument against a minimum wage was that some workers would not be able to produce enough to earn it. They would be laid off and cause higher unemployment. To Filene, however, that unemployment was a signal that more needed to be done. If the result of a minimum wage law was "a large number of people who cannot earn a living wage," the government would have to give them "sufficient training so that they can earn a living."[94] In this way, the minimum wage would be the impetus for greater efficiency and the reduction of waste.

The notion that businessmen such as Lewisohn and Filene would favor a living wage may seem surprising, but, as Bruce Kaufman has pointed out, there was a component of the business community that took a positive view of the idea of treating workers well.[95] These business leaders wanted a voluntary "Industrial Democracy" that would use forward-looking industrial relations to bring about a distribution of income that was more favorable toward labor. In addition to supporting a living wage, Filene and Lewisohn were advocates for welfare capitalism.[96]

Stuart Chase Finds Waste in the Economy

The reduction of waste in industry was a powerful theme among the Progressives in the 1920s. From the actions undertaken by the WIB during the war as well as from reports such as the one produced by engineers under the leadership of Hoover,[97] the wastefulness of industry became generally accepted. One person who led this attack on waste was Stuart Chase (1888–1985). Chase had graduated from Harvard University with a broad interest in economics. During the 1920s, he wrote an influential book, *The Tragedy of Waste*.[98] In it, he took an engineering perspective to the US economy to analyze how wasteful it was.

Chase's concern was with the relationship between waste and real as opposed to mythical prosperity. His definition of waste was what society produced that was beyond basic human wants. "A sound theory of waste," he wrote, meant that "necessities have right of way over luxuries,"[99] an idea we have seen expressed by John Stuart Mill as described in Chapter 1. To make the distinction between necessities and luxuries more clear, he gave lists for both. Under necessities, he listed food, shelter, clothing, education, recreation, government and community control, the safeguarding of health, religion, and art forms—all the elements of a living wage. Regarding wastes in consumption, Chase came up with the military establishment, harmful drugs, commercialized vice and crime, adulterated products, speculation and gambling, quackery in medicine, super luxuries and their cheap imitation, fashions, commercialized recreation (spectator sports), perversions of professional services, and advertising.

Here, Chase presents a perspective on necessities that was very narrow, as narrow as the definition provided by Plato as being what the rulers of society should be given to prevent their being distracted by wealth (see Chapter 1). None of the economists surveyed in Chapter 1 took Plato's definition of subsistence as their own. The definition of subsistence for Marx, for example, contained "a historical and moral element," that was similar to the decency component in Smith's writing. Because the subsistence items of a worker could become greater, the subsistence wage would always be a relative concept in comparison to the consumption of the wealthy. Chase, however, saw it as an absolute concept in which the consumption items of the wealthy should never trickle down to the rest of society, even in a cheaper version.

The wasteful spending of the wealthy was due to the maldistribution of income. To equalize income and solve the problem of waste, Chase gave "an analysis of the war control of industry."[100] During World War I, the US government had done an excellent job in planning the industrial production needed to equip its military.[101] To be sure, the needs of war were easy to identify, which made it easier to set priorities about what to produce. Ludwig von Mises (1881–1973) had challenged the idea of central planning by arguing that government planners could not collect and gather the information needed to make informed decisions over what to produce and how to produce it.[102] The WIB had avoided this problem because it had a limited number of items to purchase for the war. In a similar way, Chase went to such great lengths to identify basic human needs. Once they were identified, that made it easier to make plans about what to produce. He asked, "Suppose that the war control of industry had been maintained to direct a war against poverty and low living standards."[103] Could we not have won that war as well?

To win it, Chase hypothesized a national planning agency taking an inventory of productive capacity and determining how those resources compared to a survey of needs. Instead of those needs being defined in terms of war materiel, they would be organized in terms of housing, food, clothing, schools, roads, and electric power.[104] Once the needs were defined, the national planning agency could survey industry in terms of plant capacity and location, determine raw material and transportation requirements, and then set up a plan to produce what was necessary to meet basic human needs. That process would result in real prosperity, for Chase thought that national economic planning as he envisioned it could "double and triple the standard of living."[105] In short, national planning would lead to a living wage for all members of society by reducing waste in production and consumption.

Chase's arguments about consumption represented an alternative approach to a living wage. Chase found a great deal of waste in consumption, because even the poor practiced conspicuous consumption. Remove the items that were not essential to survival from a worker's budget and a living wage became much more attainable. It also meant that the Progressive intellectuals would be defining a living wage for workers. Because supporters of a living wage made a life of dignity a part of their ideal, the items of what a living wage had to purchase were a moving target, which meant that a living wage had to continually improve. A life with dignity, moreover, included the dignity of deciding for themselves how to spend their pay, no matter how much their taste might offend those who found waste in consumption. Earlier in this chapter, we saw that unions believed that no one wanted to be told that they would be paid "according to a standard we shall set for you."[106] That same belief would apply to their consumption spending.

Chase's argument that there was a great deal of waste from producers and consumers in the market economy and eliminating it to pay for a living wage was certainly a good talking point. As noted earlier, Lewisohn had raised the issue of whether the national income of the USA was large enough to sustain payment of a living wage. But there was another issue that Chase overlooked—was there really enough consumption spending to purchase all that an efficient economy produced. This was the question unions were asking. It gained greater salience among the Progressive reformers through the work of two popular economic writers.

Foster and Catchings Worry About Consumption

Although the 1920s saw a great deal of prosperity, they also were marked by several recessions. Halfway through the decade, William Trufant Foster (1879–1950) and Waddill Catchings (1879–1960) published a series of books[107] that presented the idea that recessions were due to the way savings reduced spending by consumers. Foster was an academic who eventually became the president of Reed College, while Catchings had a long career as an investment banker. They stated their point quite clearly in the preface of their book, *Profits*: "Why must industry as a whole slow down because of 'overproduction, when millions are suffering from 'underconsumption'?'" Their answer was that at some point in "a period of increased productivity" the time came "when the people who want the goods which have already been produced lack the money wherewith to purchase them." That was an obvious answer, but the real question then became, "*What causes this deficiency of purchasing power*?"[108] Their answer was that savings meant a reduction in consumption and was the primary cause of the underconsumption that produced recessions.

Foster and Catchings investigated many of the ways that had been suggested as a solution to their "dilemma of thrift." To the argument of Say's Law that a lack of consumer spending would cause the price of goods to fall, encouraging more spending, they responded that falling prices put businessmen in a fear of falling profits, which discouraged them from producing and led to cutbacks in output and layoffs, reducing consumer spending even more.[109]

Foster and Catchings went on to consider the idea that government should adjust its spending to offset the business cycle by saving in good times and spending when consumer demand fell. Such a policy was sound when it added to consumer spending when that was what was needed and it might delay a recession. The government could not sustain its spending for long enough to solve the problem of underconsumption and the recession it ultimately brought. At best, it could stabilize the economy for a time by making spending more steady over the course of a few years, but such spending "does not in the long run offset the deficiencies in demand."[110] Yes, government spending on public works projects at the right time limited the economy to "moderate declines" where "there might have been a collapse." But because taxes took money away from individuals and "the people collectively spend their money more wastefully than they do individually," the government and its leaders "should devise better methods of dealing with the problem of deficient consumer demand than constant increases in public expenditures."[111]

Another explanation for the problem of underconsumption was the unequal distribution of income. Even with their extravagant spending, the wealthy could not buy all that was produced. A wider distribution of wealth, however, might make a difference. If stock ownership were more widespread, so dividends fell into more hands, more of those dividends would be spent on consumption instead of being saved. This might offset some of the underconsumption but "even if every member of society were a capitalist, this would not offset deficiencies of consumer income which have already been caused by the use of individual and corporate savings to increase production."[112]

One approach that business was developing at the time was the use of consumer credit to allow consumers to purchase goods by borrowing. Consumer credit, however, could not be "extended indefinitely." Foster and Catchings insisted, "What people need is the means of paying for goods, rather than the means of acquiring goods for which they cannot pay."[113] In a later book, they looked at consumer credit in more detail. They found that by letting some people buy more than their current income would have permitted, the problem of underconsumption was offset and the use of consumer credit had kept the economy "from a marked business recession" at the time, that is, 1928.[114] But the gains in sales from consumer credit were not permanent.

There are many problems with the underconsumption argument expressed by Foster and Catchings, especially their approach to Say's Law. To give one example, by using an aggregate approach they considered all prices rising or falling in tandem. But one point of Say's law is that prices do not move uniformly, because that is the whole point of the price system—to use prices as a signal to indicate sectors that are expanding or contracting. My concern in this book, however, is not with analytical issues but with influence and here Foster and Catchings rate high honors. Their arguments had an influence on the economic policies of Hoover and the New Deal to maintain consumption. Eventually, John Maynard Keynes addressed the issue of underconsumption with greater analytical sophistication than Foster and Catchings did (see Chapter 7). Nevertheless, Foster and Catchings pushed business cycle theory away from financial markets and into the broader economy. In doing so, they helped foster an approach to economics that promoted the use of consumerism as a solution for business cycles.

But that approach would take nearly two decades to become generally accepted. Instead, the Progressives tended to hold to a living wage as a solution to economic problems. With their producerist perspective, they remained concerned about whether the economy could afford a living wage. The economist we consider next, Paul H. Douglas, represents this perspective.

Paul H. Douglas and the Family Wage

Paul H. Douglas (1892–1976) is now remembered mainly for having served as Senator (Democrat) from Illinois from 1949 to 1967. Before his entry into political office, he had a long and respectable career in academia as a faculty member at the University of Chicago; he served a term as president of the AEA in 1947. His approach to economics was to combine the standard neoclassical method with Institutionalism, but his views on the need for economic reform were more in tune with the Institutional school.[115] As a part of that reformist stance, he was a consistent supporter of a living wage. As early as 1923, he stated publically at the annual meeting of the AEA that he believed "firmly in the living wage principle."[116] He doubted it was feasible at the time, because the economy could not yet afford to pay every worker a living wage and because the definition of a living wage as a family wage used a standard family size that was uncharacteristic of families in the USA. As Bruce Kaufman and Michael Barry have described, economists in the USA pioneered in establishing an institutional industrial relations theory of economics to treat humans as more than a commodity in order for social welfare and fairness to exist.[117] This industrial relations theory had many elements in common with the living wage perspective of Ryan, and Douglas was one of its proponents.

Douglas investigated the issue of a family living wage with great depth in his book, *Wages and the Family*. In the preface, he indicated that he was writing "to point a way out of the impasse in which the living wage principle finds itself." The principle of a living wage was "deservedly winning acceptance." But Douglas' own research into the size of the national income of the USA convinced him that it would not be possible to pay all workers the living wage "that was commonly advocated." The problem was that the living wage that was being advocated was based on a family of five. Many workers were single and many others had fewer than four dependents. The solution to this problem was not to abandon the living wage as impossible, but to base it on the pay of a single male and provide additional allowances to males with dependents.[118]

In the introductory chapter of the book, Douglas indicated that there had been a great upsurge by labor in its "demand for a living wage." Moreover, this demand had "deservedly received almost universal acceptance." Indeed, he went on, the NWLB had "expressed the opinion of the vast majority" with its emphasis on a living wage.[119] The problem was that a living wage had not been properly defined. A solid definition had to include how many persons were to be supported by a living wage and what was the standard of living it should cover. Most supporters had settled on five as the number of persons to be supported by a living wage and agreed that those five family members should get more than a bare subsistence. Douglas then took the data calculated for a family budget that gave a subsistence level plus a bit more and multiplied it by the number of employed persons in the USA. The result was that paying workers such a living wage would take over 80 percent of national income. When he added in the idea that some workers had to be paid more than a living wage as an incentive to motivate their extra skill and effort, and considered that interest, profits, and rent would have to be paid, it was impossible to pay a living wage "unless there were a remarkable increase in the per capita amount of national product."[120] For the rest of the book, he argued that a family of five was not typical and if the USA adopted his program of basing a living wage on what a single person earned and then giving additional income subsidies based on family size, the USA could afford a living wage and "largely abolish poverty."[121]

In his writings about a living wage, however, Douglas raised more issues than he solved. First, he did not consider the possibility that his approach might give workers an incentive to have more children to gain the subsidy that he proposed. Second, and more important, he attempted to define what a living wage should be for workers rather than considering what they, or at least unions, thought about it; later in this chapter we will see that unions criticized his approach to a family wage. Finally, and most serious, his approach to a living family wage did not coincide with the standard definition of a living wage as offering workers a life of dignity without the taint of welfare. Supporters of a living wage thought it would obviate the need for welfare, where Douglas' system of aid for workers with children relied on welfare.

Douglas' work is noteworthy for two reasons. First, it indicates that a very prominent economist supported a living wage in principle, although with reservations. Second, his looking back toward the experience of the NWLB as a promoter of a living wage was in keeping with a pattern brought to light in this chapter. All the supporters of a living wage who were part of this pattern took the popular acceptance of the results of the Board as approval of a living wage. He was not the only economic thinker who looked back to the NWLB in the late 1920s.

Jett Lauck Supports a Living Wage as a New Industrial Revolution

In 1929, Jett Lauck, whom we saw earlier as a supporter of a living wage and unions, added to his writings on them with a book, *The New Industrial Revolution and Wages.* The thesis of the book was that a revolution had taken place in the theory and practice of labor relations and it had changed the attitude of business, labor economists, and politicians. The start in the revolution and been with World War I and the NWLB with its principle of a living wage.[122]

In the post-war era, a new consensus developed among industrialists, labor unions, and political leaders that recognized that economic prosperity was based on continual improvements in the standard of living of workers, "as labor would consume more if it could produce more and receive higher compensation."[123] Hoover's activities as the Secretary of Commerce led the way to this new consensus. Its general principle was that increased productivity should be shared with labor, with the result that a living wage "met with a favorable reception."[124] As evidence of that favorable reception, Lauck presented a list of prominent figures and organizations and their statements of a favorable view of a living wage. We have already met several names on his list in this book: John A. Ryan, Theodore Roosevelt, Walter Lippmann, and Henry Seager. Others on the list included, Jacob H. Hollander, professor of political economy at Johns Hopkins University; Federal Judge and former US Senator from Iowa, William S. Keynon; William Allen White, the well-known newspaper editor; General Leonard Wood; Professor Irving Fisher of Yale University; several religious organizations, a number of business executives, the AFL, and President Harding.[125] He especially singled out Owen D. Young, the head of General Electric, for stating the need for higher wages as follows: "No worker with an inadequate wage is free." Rather, "the worker must be made to feel … that he is a property owner."[126] General Electric was working on this new approach and Lauck took this as a sign of the radical change in industry that he was writing about.

To be sure, there was opposition to this radical change that centered on the impracticality of a living wage and Lauck presented its arguments. Supporters responded with studies that showed the practicality of a living wage and Lauck included his own work in the area.[127] He believed that the supporters were getting the upper hand, with the result that in the years since the war the living wage movement had been "sanctioned by enlightened public opinion."[128] The living wage argument, moreover, was tied into two new approaches. First, a living wage had to be related to productive efficiency; the gains from productivity would be shared with workers. Second, the living wage principle was augmented by "the theory that high rates of pay make for increased purchasing power, greater consumption of commodities, and the maintenance of widespread prosperity."[129] Indeed, there was a new "trinity of high production, high earnings and high consumption."[130]

This new trinity was ushering in an era of prosperity. Lauck indicated that during a recession in 1927–1928, when unemployment became a problem, there was recognition of the need "to increase domestic demand for industrial products by developing a higher degree of purchasing power through advancing the rates of pay of industrial workers."[131] We will see later on that this approach would become the policy for ending the Great Depression of the Hoover Administration as well as the Roosevelt New Deal. It retained a linkage between producerist and consumerist views by making a living wage a result of greater productive efficiency and a necessary component of increased consumption spending. We will see that Hoover more than justified the faith Lauck had in the new approach when growth came to an end in 1929.

Hoover and the Great Depression

The Great Depression of the 1930s was the worst of times for the USA. In the economy, the recession began in August 1929 and lasted 43 months before hitting bottom in March 1933. By that time, the real GNP had fallen by 30 percent and the unemployment rate reached 25 percent. Real GNP did not reach its pre-Depression level until 1937. Even with the advantage of hindsight, economic historians still debate what caused the Great Depression and perhaps the best explanation is that it was a perfect storm of many events. Among the explanations that economic historians have given for the Great Depression, the following have been given wide scrutiny: a decline in business investment, turmoil in financial markets, a decline that had to follow the credit-created boom of the 1920s, poor policy by the Federal Reserve in contracting the money supply, the passage of the Smoot–Hawley Tariff, stickiness of wages, issues related to the gold standard, the collapse of the global economy, problems in banking that caused several waves of runs on banks, the collapse of the stock market, declines in personal consumption, and weakening of the housing market.[132]

Throughout the 1920s, Hoover had championed the cause of voluntary cooperation among the major stakeholders in business to provide guidance to market activities. In promoting this form of planning, Hoover hoped to avoid what he saw as the instability of markets and to prevent the growth of government controls. His initial step to head off the recession in 1929 was to set up a series of conferences at the White House to bring together the heads of leading industries in the USA and enable them to take voluntary, but organized, action. The conferences took place in November 1929 and the industry leaders who attended agreed to maintain wages and to avoid laying off workers. Businesses stuck to this agreement for as long as possible, but during a period of deflation such as one that took place in the early 1930s, where prices fell by 25 percent from 1930 to 1933, maintaining wage rates meant that real wages rose. Eventually, businesses had to let go of workers and cut the wages of those they kept. Hoover also created the Reconstruction Finance Corporation as a way for the federal government to help keep banks from failing with loans. The Federal Farm Board, formed in mid-1929, was given funds to make loans to farmers at low interest rates and to buy surplus production in agriculture.

Hoover also tried to help the economy with fiscal policy. For most of the 1920s, the federal government had experienced budget surpluses that it had used to retire debt from World War I. The budget remained in surplus in 1929 and Hoover and the Congress used that surplus to pay for some tax cuts and to fund public works projects. By 1932, however, the federal government faced increasing budget deficits; Hoover and the Congress increased income taxes and excise taxes on a variety of goods and services to get the budget back into balance.[133] Hoover and the Congress also levied the Smoot–Hawley Tariff in 1930, raising the taxes on imports in an effort to keep wages and prices at higher levels; instead the tariff increases further diminished an already declining volume of world trade.

The brief survey of Hoover's policy, while not as comprehensive as he deserves, is sufficient to enable us to interpret it as more interventionist than has been widely understood. His advocacy of high wages and steady employment aimed at forestalling a recession by maintaining consumption at a high level. By securing promises from business leaders that they would maintain wages and employment, Hoover believed he had achieved his goal through voluntary cooperation. He also agreed that it was acceptable to spend a budget surplus on public works projects and tax reductions, but that it was immoral for the federal government to borrow and use deficit finance for the same purpose. Once the government had used up its surplus, it had done the best it could. The real problem, however, was that no one anticipated that the recession that began in 1929 would last as long and be as severe as it turned out to be.

Foster and Catchings and the Need for Consumption

Foster and Catchings had created a stir in the 1920s with their theory that prosperity was always being blocked by too much saving in the economy. It should not surprise us that they used the same argument to explain the Great Depression. We can see this in an article they published, "Riotous Saving," in the November 1930 issue of *Atlantic Monthly*. In it they argued that the USA had the highest standard of living in the world, as measured by the amount of consumption its citizens enjoyed, and the US economy kept increasing the amount of goods it produced. But that was the problem. Foster and Catchings wrote, "We cannot keep producing more oranges or hats or anything else unless we can sell more. And we cannot sell more unless consumers buy more."[134] When business produced goods for sale they generated income. In order for that production to be continued, all the goods had to be sold.

Consumers, however, did not spend all of their income for consumption. They also saved. That was the reason for the Depression taking place and for its continuing. During a period of Depression individuals saved for a "rainy day," that is, they became cautious and increased their savings in case an emergency came along such as their losing their jobs. Those savings might be beneficial for the individual who had them but they were bad for the economy as a whole. The tradition of thrift in the USA had termed extravagant spending as riotous living. Foster and Catchings turned the tables by calling the extra thrift of the Depression "riotous saving."[135] The country needed more extravagant spenders. If the affluent wanted "to help their country, the best thing they can do, right now, is to spend more money."[136]

Foster and Catchings also recognized that the federal government could take measures to help the economy and outlined them in a January 1930 article in the *Review of Reviews*. Titled "Mr. Hoover's Road to Prosperity," the article reviewed the policies the president was pursuing to end the decline in the economy. Foster and Catchings observed, "For the first time in our history, a President of the United States is taking aggressive leadership in guiding private business through a crisis."[137] Previously, presidents had considered economic downturns to be inevitable and had done nothing about them. Hoover was doing something, and his policies were sound, because the point of those policies was to keep consumption at high levels. Foster and Catchings recognized what John Maynard Keynes would later make famous, the idea that private sector jobs would be created by government spending.[138] In holding this view they were in accord with the long-held consumerist views of the AFL.

Unions Continue to Favor a Living Wage

When the Great Depression started to unfold, union leaders continued to use their long-standing commitment to underconsumption as the primary explanation for the economic decline. In the March 1930 issue of the *American Federationist*, there were two articles of a page each to make the point that high wages were the remedy for underconsumption. The first, titled "High Wages Increase Prosperity," featured a series of quotations from prominent business leaders, including Foster, to show their "growing realization that high wages and an increasing standard of living are the foundations of American prosperity."[139] The second article, "Steady Work—Steady Business" offered similar quotations to the effect that layoffs were not good for the economy and "regularity of work is the more efficient method."[140]

The AFL's interest in high wages also included continued support for a living wage. In a regular feature in the *American Federationist* called "Economic Statistics," there was a study of "What is a Living Wage?" A great deal was being said about a living wage but there was still the question of how to define it. Of course, it had to include basic food, clothing, and shelter, but it also had to give workers the chance to save for unemployment or poor health. Just as important, it had to provide "the standard worthy of a human being and an American," such as the "many little things" that made the difference between "living and existence." In support of this last addition, the article cited Lauck's definition of a living wage from his 1929 book.[141] It also disputed the method Douglas devised for calculating a family living wage by reducing the appropriate size of the family to below five members and indicating that there were many single workers. The article countered, "But if a wage-earner is to look forward to marrying and bringing up three children, as every wage-earner should be able to do, he must have enough to save an ample sum at the very start."[142] Unionists might use the definition of a living wage of a Progressive intellectual such as Lauck when it suited them, but they were not averse to disputing the definition when it did not jibe with their interests in higher wages.

In the very next article, the *American Federationist* continued its discussion of the importance of a living wage. Titled "A Market for Our Goods," the article argued that workers needed a living wage to boost their consumption spending and restore prosperity. Efforts to boost consumption spending through installment credit purchases might work for a time, but a better way to maintain prosperous times was "by increasing wages in proportion to production."[143] This perspective was a part of the AFL's long-term consumerist strategy, and its "Books for Workers" section offered a review of a book by a well-known business writer on consumption issues with a telling quotation, "Political parties in every nation primarily represent producers and industries rather than consumers."[144] Consumers needed to become more organized to have a say in government policies, and the AFL was organizing workers along those lines.

Economists Discuss the Depression

At its annual meeting for 1931, the AEA held a discussion on "The Business Depression of Nineteen Hundred Thirty." The participants used the discussion to present their particular analysis of the Depression and what might be done to cure it.

For example, Arthur B. Adams found that the Depression resulted from "a relative shortage of consumers' purchasing power."[145] While this argument resembles that presented earlier by Foster and Catchings, Adams attributed reduced consumption not to savings but to consumers' incomes not keeping pace with prices of consumer goods. During the

1920s, many industries had modernized with mass production technology through "the displacement of labor by machinery." Even though wages had increased during the decade, employment had decreased. The result was that the distribution of income had tilted away from wage earners and toward property owners. Consumer demand had been sustained for a period from the rise of consumer credit, a high level of production taking place in capital goods, foreign demand, and spending from gains made in the stock market. By fall of 1929 "these artificial supports of the market for consumers' goods" had declined, causing the downturn.[146]

Another discussant, Willard L. Thorp, argued that the real problem was that economists were thinking about remedies for recessions when they should be concerned with how to prevent them. Thorp raised the issue of "central control and planning" as a solution to the depressed economy but considered that "there seems to be almost a taboo against suggesting that the only way to eliminate the business cycle may be by definite modification of the present freedom of enterprise."[147] Perhaps there was a taboo on the subject among economists. If so, the Great Depression caused it to be broken.

The Swope Plan and a Living Wage

When the Great Depression took place it was first thought of as a typical recession. It eventually became apparent that it was going to be longer and deeper than anyone had imagined, and a variety of programs were set forth to find a way to end it. The idea that the Depression was caused by underconsumption led to the perception that the cure for the Depression was to increase the purchasing power of labor. This perception also accentuated interest in a living wage. One way of combining both underconsumption and a living wage into a consistent policy was to return to the WIB and the NWLB. We can see this combined approach in the Swope Plan, one of many proposals that floated about in the early 1930s.

Gerard Swope (1872–1957) earned his degree in electrical engineering from the Massachusetts Institute of Technology in 1895; he took a job in the electrical industry and wound up serving as president of General Electric from 1922 to 1939 and from 1942 to 1944. During World War I he joined the US Army and went to work in its procurement division, where he became an assistant to General Hugh S. Johnson at the time when Johnson was the army's procurement representative to the WIB. He was another business leader who took up the industrial relations approach to working with labor and looked favorably on the formation of the United Electrical Workers Union and its efforts to organize the workers at General Electric.[148] He was also well known in the Progressive circles for providing a full range of benefits to the workers of General Electric.[149]

In 1931, at a meeting of the National Electrical Manufacturers Association he offered what became known as the Swope Plan, as a way to end the Depression through planning. The germ of the plan was to take voluntary trade associations and make them mandatory under federal government supervision. As a starting point, they would engage in "stabilization of prices ... to promote stabilization of employment."[150] Trade associations were already performing this work but the Swope Plan would allow them to accomplish more. Each trade association would form a "General Board of Administration" with nine members—three from the trade association, three from the ranks of employees, and three appointed by a federal supervisory agency to represent the public.[151]

The General Board would administer the parts of the Swope Plan related to taking care of workers. Swope proposed a number of items that had long been held dear by the Progressives and forward-looking managers: a workers' compensation program, life and disability insurance, pensions, and unemployment insurance. The insurance plans and the pensions would be funded jointly by workers and employers at a set percent of wages, with a ceiling on the amount of wages used as a basis. The pension plan would be portable, allowing workers to move from job to job; the retirement age was fixed at 70 years. Unemployment insurance would start to pay two weeks after the worker was laid off at a rate of 50 percent of the worker's average pay, with a cap to avoid being too generous to high-income workers. Payments would be made for up to ten weeks in any year, and workers forced to take part-time jobs could collect unemployment insurance to make up the difference with their full-time pay.[152] The programs for labor in the Swope Plan all added up to a living wage; they were also something that General Electric had started on for its employees.[153]

In setting forth this approach to labor, Swope never used the term, a living wage. Rather, he was being consistent with his company's adherence to welfare capitalism. Kaufman observes that Swope and General Electric were among the best in the USA in developing programs to gain the goodwill of workers in an effort to establish a more humane form of capitalism.[154] A key ingredient of welfare capitalism was its effort to treat workers with fairness and to let those workers have a say in what fairness meant. If workers believed that they should be accorded a living wage, then proponents of welfare capitalism would provide it for them in the form of higher wages and improved benefits along with collective bargaining as a way to give them the voice to make their beliefs known to top executives. This was also the living wage formula which was implicitly adhered to by business leaders such as Swope and promoted as a part of a living wage by other business leaders such as Filene and Lewisohn (see above), who were also advocates for welfare capitalism.[155] The difficulty with this approach was that it increased the direct costs of production in the short term, while the direct and indirect benefits of the approach might take longer to materialize. It was a daring plan when competitors gained a short-term competitive advantage by not taking up the same approach, as Clark had pointed out (see above). The plan became even more dangerous during a recession, when costs had to be cut to keep even a firm with advanced welfare programs from going broke. The Swope Plan, by having all firms agree to its "living wage" elements, would allow them to use welfare capitalism.

The overall aim of the Swope Plan was to control competition. For example, firms in a voluntary trade association might all agree to provide pensions to their workers, but this might give them a higher cost structure compared to firms not in the association. This was the problem Clark had highlighted in arguing that the forces of market competition made it hard for the moral business to provide its workers with a living wage. Clark, Chase, and Swope, all agreed that national economic planning was needed to implement a living wage in all industries.

Barbara Nachtrieb Armstrong and a Living Wage Policy

Not all advocates for a living wage went as far as Clark, Chase, and Swope, however. The pivotal year of 1932 saw the appearance of a book that made a provocative statement of what needed to be done to help labor get a living wage. Its author, Barbara Nachtrieb Armstrong (1890–1976) had a law degree and a PhD in economics and was a member of the economics department and the law school at the University of California at Berkeley; she also chaired a subcommittee of the Committee on Economic Security that did the initial work of the SSA, as will be described in Chapter 5, and was a key player in working out the legal issues related to the SSA.[156] She gave her book the prescient title, *Insuring the Essentials: Minimum Wage*

Plus Social Insurance—A Living Wage Program.[157] The title is prescient because it outlined the program the Roosevelt Administration would take as part of its living wage agenda. Armstrong's views on social insurance and the minimum wage will be presented in separate chapters on those topics. Here, I will briefly describe her overall perspective.

Armstrong began the book with a statement of her overriding philosophy: "the burden of support of persons who cannot maintain themselves is an unquestioned social obligation." As a result of this obligation, she added, "a living wage which will assure the worker and his family the essentials of life is of social as well as individual concern." To be sure, the components that made up the standard of living intrinsic to a living wage were complex and beyond the scope of her book. But Armstrong offered a rough definition of a living wage as "a wage sufficient to obviate the need for public charity."[158]

There were two components to this living wage that were essential: a minimum wage that was legally binding and set a standard below which wages could not fall and social insurance to keep income at the level of a living wage when workers were unable to earn a living. A living wage needed to include social insurance because, while the standard of normal living could be calculated, the unpredictable expenses of sickness, accidents, unemployment, and retirement had such a wide range "that no amount could be estimated that would meet the needs of all workers."[159] Private insurance was a possible solution, but it had proved to be too expensive for workers to afford. Unions might secure living wages and union relief funds for their members, but in the USA too many workers were not organized into unions. Another option was private charity, but "the psychological experience undergone by the worker who is relieved by charity…has a disastrous effect upon the self-esteem of the recipient."[160] Social insurance was the most effective way to supplement a minimum wage to secure a living wage and Armstrong devoted nearly 700 pages of her book to surveying what had been done in Europe and what had been attempted in the USA to secure the two components of her living wage, including minimum wage legislation, workers' compensation, health insurance, pensions, and unemployment insurance—all as carried out by the government.

It is difficult to ascertain the extent to which Armstrong's book directly influenced Roosevelt and supporters of the New Deal. That she influenced the discussions that surrounded the crafting of the SSA is clear. Her book very likely led to her membership on the staff of the Committee on

Economic Security, where she helped draft the pension provisions of the SSA. According to Domhoff and Webber, Armstrong believed that Swope had liked her book and as a result had arranged for her to work on the SSA.[161] While many individual writers added to the clamor for social security, her book presented a survey of approaches to the issue. To give one example of her influence, Abraham Epstein, who was a well-known expert on social insurance (See Chapter 5), cited Armstrong numerous times with seven entries in his index in his classic book, *Insecurity: A Challenge to America*,[162] first published in 1933. In a review in the *Columbia Law Review*, Harry Laidler called Armstrong's book a "monumental volume" that should be read by everyone "interested in the problem of economic security" and added that its publication was "a good omen for the future."[163] Given the New Deal's achievement of social insurance and a minimum wage law, along with legal collective bargaining in the next six years, Ladler's forecast was on target.

Conclusion

An important finding of this chapter is the extent to which a living wage was discussed by the Progressive thinkers during the era between World War I and the New Deal. In a variety of academic journals and books, economists, business leaders, pundits, and politicians produced a modest literature on a living wage during the 1920s. Unions also pushed for a living wage in their publications. Most of them looked backward to the WIB and the NWLB as a paradigm for how a living wage could be brought about by government action. They did not blindly follow that paradigm, but raised a number of issues of how to define a living wage, how to adjust it for inflation, how to gauge its feasibility in relation to national income, and whether it should be based on an individual or a family wage. These proponents of a living wage were not deterred by the difficulty some of the issues caused for their ideal and remained steadfast in support of a living wage. They differed over how government action might secure a living wage, however.

Clark, Chase, and Swope, for example, believed that national economic planning was essential to bring about a living wage. Because payment of a living wage would alter the equilibrium of the economy, planning was necessary to keep all the sectors of the economy on track, much as the WIB had controlled economic matters during the war. Moreover, they argued, coordination of prices was crucial to keep companies that did not pay a living wage from undercutting those that did. Clark argued that it would take planning to make sure the economy could cover the social overhead costs of labor that were not being paid in the market economy. Chase considered the wastefulness of the market economy to be the target that planning should aim for. To Swope, planning that produced a living wage would also end the Great Depression.

Other individuals featured in this chapter such as Filene, Douglas, and Armstrong believed government regulation would do the job. The regulation they most favored was a minimum wage law that mandated a living wage. Such legislation would mean defining a living wage. There was some agreement that a living wage should be based on the calculation of a family budget that met the biological and social needs of families, but that definition still had problems. To Douglas, it was important to get the right size of the family on which the budget would be based; Kittredge believed that good health had to be part of the budget. There were also problems in maintaining the standard of a living wage in a period of inflation, as Kittredge and Johnson pointed out. Equally important, as Lewisohn and Douglas argued, the amount decided on as a living wage had to be gauged against national income to determine if it was feasible.

These Progressives, however, missed a point that unions and their supporters, such as Lauck, had made. A living wage could increase national income. First, it could boost labors' efficiency as producers. Second, it would increase workers' capability as consumers, which would enable them to purchase what their new efficiency added to national income. A living wage would counter the underconsumption problem that Foster and Catchings had highlighted. We will see that this consumerist viewpoint became more common in the New Deal.

Whatever the differences in their policy recommendations, these advocates for a living wage all accepted that labor markets are social organizations and that the wage had to be at a level that led to societal improvements. They would all have a chance to try out their policies when Roosevelt was elected to give workers a New Deal. First, the New Deal would try the approach of the planners with the NIRA, the topic of the next chapter. When the NIRA did not work out, the New Deal shifted to the regulatory approach of collective bargaining, social security, and a minimum wage as providing the essentials of a living wage. This second approach will be considered in Chapters 4, 5, and 6.

Notes

1. Dorfman, 1949, p. 254.
2. Leonard, 2012, p. 11.
3. Donohue, 2003, p. 155.
4. Ryan, 1916, pp. 145–170.
5. Ryan, 1916, p. 165.
6. Ryan, 1916, p. 243.
7. Ryan, 1916, pp. 253–296.
8. Ryan, 1916, p. 258.
9. Ryan, 1916, p. 259.
10. Ryan, 1916, p. 329–347.
11. Ryan, 1916, p. 364.
12. Ryan, 1916, pp. 278–280.
13. Ryan, 1916, pp. 409–411.
14. Ryan, 1916, pp. 417–418.
15. Ryan, 1916, p. 381.
16. Glickman, 1997, pp. 3, 62, and 131.
17. Ryan, 1916, p. 365.
18. Richberg, 1917, p. 49.
19. Kaufman, 2008.
20. Frayne, 1918, p. 137.
21. Kaufman, 2008, p. 169.
22. Gregg, 1919, p. 42.
23. Gregg, 1919, p. 44.
24. Ryan, 1906, p. 33, italics in the original.
25. Gregg, 1919, p. 45.
26. Gregg, 1919, p. 53.
27. Gregg, 1919, p. 56.
28. Ryan, 1906, p. 261.
29. Love, 1918, pp. 47–49.
30. Love, 1918, p. 49.
31. Love, 1918, p.50.
32. Wilson, 1919.
33. Wilson, 1919.
34. Bruère, 1919, p. 95.
35. Bruère, 1919, p. 96.
36. Kendall, 1919, p. 165.
37. Seager, 1919, p. 111.
38. Seager, 1919, p. 114.
39. Seager, 1919, p. 116.
40. Seager, 1919, p. 118.

41. Manly, 1922, p. 41.
42. Manly, 1922, p. 41.
43. Lauck, 1922, pp. 123–29.
44. Lauck, 1922, p. 130.
45. Lauck, 1922, p. 424.
46. Lauck, 1922, p. 454.
47. Lauck, 1922, p. 455.
48. Lauck, undated, p. 1.
49. Lauck, undated, p. 1.
50. Glickman, 1997.
51. *American Federationist*, 1918, p. 369.
52. Walsh, 1918, pp. 894–97.
53. Woll, 1919, pp. 151–53.
54. *American Federationist*, 1919, p. 130.
55. *United Mine Workers Journal*, 1918a, p. 10.
56. *United Mine Workers Journal*, 1918b, p. 10.
57. *United Mine Workers Journal*, 1918c, p. 11.
58. *United Mine Workers Journal*, 1921, pp. 14–15.
59. *United Mine Workers Journal*, 1922a, p. 6.
60. Lewis, 1922, p. 12.
61. *United Mine Workers Journal*, 1922b, p. 8.
62. Lowe, 1922, p. 15.
63. Parker, 2007, p. 2.
64. Schumpeter, 1964, p. 305.
65. Hoover, 1951, p. 174.
66. Hoover, 1922, p. 49.
67. Kittredge, 1923, p. 225.
68. Kittredge, 1923, p. 226.
69. Kittredge, 1923, p. 229.
70. Dorfman, 1949, pp. 420–26.
71. Johnson, 1926, p. 54.
72. Johnson, 1926, p. 55.
73. Johnson, 1926, p. 57.
74. Clark, 1923a, p. 16.
75. Clark, 1923a, p. 372.
76. Clark, 1923a, pp. 37 and 42.
77. Clark, 1926, p. 130.
78. Clark, 1926, p. 176.
79. Clark, 1926, p. 451–3.
80. Beckerman, 2011, p. 15.
81. Clark, 1926, p. 100.
82. Clark, 1926, p. 213.

83. Kaufman, 2008, p. 216.
84. Clark, 1923a, pp. 389–90.
85. Clark, 1923a, p. 397.
86. Clark, 1923b, p. 58.
87. Clark, 1923b, p. 59.
88. Levisohn, 1923, p. 219.
89. Lewisohn, 1923, pp. 220–21.
90. Lewisohn, 1923, p. 222–23.
91. National Consumers League, 1919, p. 4.
92. Filene, 1923, p. 411.
93. Filene, 1923, p. 412.
94. Filene, 1923, p. 413–414.
95. Kaufman, 2012, p. 509.
96. Kaufman, 2008, p. 255.
97. Stabile and Kozak, 2012, pp. 81–82.
98. Chase, 1925.
99. Chase, 1925, pp. 29–30.
100. Chase, 1925, p. 3.
101. Chase, 1925, p. 10.
102. von Mises, 1920.
103. Chase, 1925, p. 16.
104. Chase, 1925, p. 18.
105. Chase, 1925, p. 277.
106. *United Mine Workers Journal*, 1922a, p. 6.
107. Foster and Catchings, 1924, 1925 and 1928.
108. Foster and Catchings, 1925, p. v, italics in the original.
109. Foster and Catchings, 1925, pp. 305–6.
110. Foster and Catchings, 1925, p. 340.
111. Foster and Catchings, 1925, pp. 347–8.
112. Foster and Catchings, 1925, pp. 355–7.
113. Foster and Catchings, 1925, p. 411.
114. Foster and Catchings, 1928, p. 62.
115. Rutherford 2011, p. 142.
116. Douglas and Lewisohn, 1923, p. 141.
117. Kaufman and Barry, 2014, p. 1206.
118. Douglas, 1927, p. ix.
119. Douglas, 1927, p, 1.
120. Douglas, 1927, pp. 15–16.
121. Douglas, 1927, p. 272.
122. Lauck, 1929, pp. 1–2 and 48–9.
123. Lauck, 1929, p. 4.
124. Lauck, 1929, p. 93.

125. Lauck, 1929, pp. 100–118.
126. Lauck, 1929, p. 123.
127. Lauck, 1929, pp. 131–140.
128. Lauck, 1929, p. 153.
129. Lauck, 1929, p. 153.
130. Lauck, 1929, p. 247.
131. Lauck, 1929, p. 244.
132. Rothbard, 2000; Smiley, 2002, pp. 11–70; Parker, 2007, pp. 1–28.
133. Rothbard, 2000, pp. 4031–4033.
134. Foster and Catchings, 1930a, p. 667.
135. Foster and Catchings, 1930a, p. 668.
136. Foster and Catchings, 1930a, p. 670.
137. Foster and Catchings, 1930b, p. 50.
138. Foster and Catchings, 1930b, p. 52.
139. *American Federationist*, 1930a, p. 344.
140. *American Federationist*, 1930b, p. 345.
141. *American Federationist*, 1930c, pp. 591–3.
142. *American Federationist*, 1930c, p. 594.
143. *American Federationist*, 1930d, pp. 595–7.
144. *American Federationist*, 1930e, p. 604.
145. AEA, 1931, p. 183.
146. AEA, 1931, p. 184.
147. AEA, 1931, p. 197.
148. Radosh, 1972, p. 176.
149. Armstrong, 1932, p. 537; Tugwell and Hill, 1934, p. 323.
150. Swope, 1931.
151. Swope, 1931.
152. Swope, 1931.
153. Armstrong, 1932, p. 537; Tugwell and Hill, 1934, p. 323.
154. Kaufman, 2008, p. 230 and 275.
155. Kaufman, 2008, p. 255.
156. Dauber, 2013, pp. 133–40; Domhoff and Webber, 2011, pp. 3662–3683.
157. Armstrong, 1932.
158. Armstrong, 1932, p. xiii.
159. Armstrong, 1932, p. xvi.
160. Armstrong, 1932, p. xvii.
161. Domhoff and Webber, 2011, pp. 3267–3269.
162. Epstein, 1936a.
163. Laidler, 1932, pp. 1467–68.

CHAPTER 3

Planning a Living Wage: The National Industrial Recovery Act

As indicated in Chapter 2, during the 1920s and early 1930s, the idea of national economic planning had been proposed by the economist John Maurice Clark, the Progressive pundit Stuart Chase, and the businessman Gerard Swope. They based their proposals on the federal government's WIB in World War I. Their proposals also included the concept of a living wage as had the NWLB of the WIB. In the early and devastating days of the Great Depression, proposals for national economic planning had the support of business, too. To give one example, in 1932, the peak association of business, the US Chamber of Commerce, published an article in its journal, *Nation's Business*, "A Panorama of Economic Planning," that surveyed a variety of proposals for national planning from the Swope Plan to Chase's proposals.[1]

The New Deal responded to this call for planning with an eclectic combination of these programs under the name of the NIRA to be administered by NRA. Since several of the proposals I considered in Chapter 2 looked backward to the WIB, it is no surprise that the NIRA had much in common with it. The NRA borrowed its symbol of compliance, the "Blue Eagle," from a similar symbol used by the WIB and Hugh S. Johnson, who had served a time as the army's liaison to the WIB, was head of the NRA. The NIRA had many objectives, such as stabilizing the economy through the development of purchasing power and establishing fair competition among businesses to avoid ruinous competition. But it also had

D. Stabile, *The Political Economy of a Living Wage*,
DOI 10.1007/978-3-319-32473-9_3

a goal of attaining a living wage for workers. Section 7A of the NIRA, which related to collective bargaining, was based on the experiences of the NWLB.[2]

In this chapter, I will focus on the relationship between the NIRA and a living wage. First, I will consider Roosevelt's statements on the NIRA and its goal of a living wage. Then, I will examine what administrators and supporters of the NIRA said about a living wage. When the NIRA ended, there were many *post mortems* on it and I will present analyses of the NIRA by the supporters of a living wage, along with criticisms from skeptics about a living wage. The conclusion to the chapter will offer an assessment of where the NIRA went wrong. I will begin with a brief description of what the NIRA did.

The National Industrial Recovery Act

The NIRA was passed by the Congress with very little debate on June 16, 1933, to devise a set of industry codes for business behavior to eliminate what was thought to be the ruinous effects of excessive price competition. The key to the codes was for businesses to be able to establish an industry standard of fair prices. Indeed, the Act called for a sharing of the authority for the codes among business, labor, consumers, and the government. Here was the Progressive Era vision of Industrial Democracy, with labor being represented by democratic unions and the rest of society being represented by government officials at the NRA. Both government and labor could thus serve as a countervailing power to business. The public was also to be included as consumers. The NRA had a Consumer Advisory Board, a Labor Advisory Board, and an Industry Advisory Board to ensure that all segments of the economy were represented.

In its initial phase, the NIRA in late July, 1933, set up a "blanket code" to have something in place while each industry code was being worked out. The main provision of the blanket code was that businesses that accepted it agreed to pay their workers a minimum wage as described by the code with variations for the type of work and the location of the business. Businesses that signed the blanket code also agreed to boycott businesses that did not sign the blanket code. This provision to pay a minimum wage meant that businesses had to accept what the federal government set as that wage, which gave them an incentive to produce an industry code as quickly as possible. The number of codes worked out greatly expanded in August, 1933, and the NRA had to increase its staff.[3]

In addition to its goal of minimum wages, Section 7A of the NIRA aimed to help workers by strengthening the right of labor to organize unions and Section 7B aimed at eliminating the practice of wage-cutting. One of the hallmarks of President Herbert Hoover's efforts to end the Depression was to get businesses to agree to hold wages steady on a voluntary basis in order to maintain a high level of consumer spending. The New Deal was a bit more forceful in its efforts to keep wages steady. The industry codes for labor established under the NIRA usually contained provisions establishing minimum wages for the industry, maximum hours of work (a 40-hour week was typical), and prohibitions on child labor. The codes, however, varied depending on the industry and its geographic location—industries in the South had a lower minimum wage. Of all the components of the NIRA, Section 7A was the most controversial.[4] Still, the NIRA called for two elements of the living wage strategy outlined in the previous two chapters, collective bargaining and a minimum wage.

Roosevelt, the NIRA, and a Living Wage

Roosevelt and the New Deal had many goals for the NIRA, including the effort to restore the purchasing power of workers as a way to end the Depression. With respect to my interest in a living wage, I concentrate on the NIRA because Roosevelt's chief and clearest pronouncement in support of a living wage is found in his presidential statements on the NIRA on June 16, 1933. Before he set forth those statements, however, he was already on the record as supporting the general idea of a living wage. In a campaign speech before the Cosmopolitan Club of San Francisco on September 23, 1932, he said, "Every man has a right to life; and this means that he has also a right to make a comfortable living."[5] Two months later, John A. Ryan wrote a letter to Roosevelt's campaign aide and brain truster, Raymond Moley (1886–1975), telling him that this speech showed how much Roosevelt understood "that the problem immediately before us is that of reorganizing our distributive system."[6] This praise from the author of a book titled *Distributive Justice* is an example of how Roosevelt and Ryan were on the same page. Moreover, the president made a similar plea on May 3, 1933, when he addressed the US Chamber of Commerce and asked his audience to refrain from wage reductions and instead keep wages in line with price increases because previously wage levels had "imposed on those who labor an unfair burden" and "prevented their just and equitable share in the profits of industry."[7]

A few weeks later, in a Fireside Chat on May 7, 1933, he expounded on this argument. From his perspective, the overall problem that faced all sectors of the US economy, agriculture, labor, and business, was underconsumption. He added, "All of this has been caused in large part by a complete lack of planning" with the result that everyone in the USA had been wrongly persuaded that the economy could keep producing more each year and "some magician would find ways and means for that increased output to be consumed with reasonable profit to the producer."[8] The magician, of course, was the market system. The market system, however, says that if you want to sell more you must lower the price. Instead of the market, Roosevelt's approach was to form a partnership with the producers, not in sharing profits, but "a partnership in planning." As an example, he considered the cotton manufacturing industry. In that industry, 90 percent of businesses would agree to higher wages, reduced hours for labor, and reduced output. The problem was that an "unfair ten percent" would not make the same agreement and the "fair ninety percent" would have to go along. The government, he went on, "ought to have the right," through the partnership between business and government, to enlist the help of the fair 90 percent to persuade the "unfair ten percent" to agree to arrange better competition and eliminate "the kind of unfair competition that results in long hours, starvation wages and overproduction."[9] Here is a case where the elimination of starvation wages through a living wage would take care of low purchasing power and create greater demand to solve the overproduction problem. If the competition of the market system produced starvation wages, it was up to the federal government to ensure a fairer outcome.

Roosevelt made the same point in a message to the Congress on May 17, 1933. He gave his explanation of the problem faced by business in granting fairer wages to workers. In any industry, there were always a small number of firms paying low wages. Firms that wanted to pay fair wages had to compete with these firms in the prices they charged from their customers. To do so, all firms in the industry, the majority of whom were fair-minded, had to pay unfair wages to be able to compete with the unfair minority. He wrote, "The unfair ten per cent would produce goods so cheaply that the fair ninety per cent would be compelled to meet the unfair conditions. This is where the government comes in." He added an example of the shoe industry where prices had fallen so low that "you can't hire men and pay them a living wage."[10] The problem Roosevelt was bringing up was identical to the one Clark raised when he discussed the issue of business not paying the full social overhead costs of labor and the inability of the market to allow them to do so (See Chapter 2).

These themes resonate in Roosevelt's statement on the NIRA on June 16, 1933. In that statement, he indicated that a goal of the Act was to make a change in industry from "starvation wages" to "a living wage." To accomplish that goal, he added, "There would need to be an industrial covenant to which all employers shall subscribe." As part of the covenant, businesses would agree to a reduction of the hours each worker had to work per week while "paying a living wage for the shorter week." To Roosevelt, a living wage meant "wages of decent living" and he insisted that "no business which depends for existence on paying less than living wages to its workers has any right to continue in this country." To be sure, he recognized that in the market economy businesses could not individually raise wages without losing their competitive edge. If all of business would "act together" and raise wages in concert, "none will be hurt" and labor would be amply rewarded.[11]

Taken out of the historical and intellectual context, Roosevelt's statement on the NIRA seems extraordinary in its advocacy of a living wage. From the perspective provided by the last two chapters, however, we can see that the president was echoing the conventional views of advocates for a living wage. Take his most provocative phrase, "no business which depends for existence on paying less than living wages to its workers has any right to continue in this country." It sounded radical, and perhaps it was, but it was similar to the outlook expressed by Samuel Gompers and Ryan, as described in Chapter 1, and Ryan, Edward Filene, and Clark, as described in Chapter 2. We should also recall that Filene had used a very similar expression, "Any business that cannot pay a living wage is not good for the state and has no place in it."[12] What was new and very exciting to the supporters of a living wage was that the outlook they held was being expressed by the president of the USA.

In his a Fireside Chat of July 24, 1933, Roosevelt made his support of a living wage clear when he told his audience that the idea underlying the NIRA went "back to the basic idea of society and of the nation itself that people acting in a group can accomplish things which no individual acting alone could even hope to bring about."[13] What businesses could accomplish by acting together was the key to getting the economy moving again and Roosevelt was confident of success. He said, "the agreements already approved, or about to be passed on, prove that the plan does raise wages, and that it does put people back to work."[14] The economy would be fairer through a living wage and more robust through increased purchasing power, thanks to the NIRA.

There is also more to the June 16, 1933, statement on the NIRA than what I have indicated while quoting it earlier. A mimeographed copy of the statement in the archives at the Roosevelt Presidential Library has an emphasis that is especially notable with regard to the living wage. In that version of the statement, in the phrase, "by living wages I mean more than a bare subsistence level-I mean the wages of decent living," the words living and decent are underlined.[15] This stress on those two words would seem to tell us that Roosevelt placed importance on living wages and producing a decent standard of living. In addition, the June 16, 1933 statement was published in pamphlet form and sent out to all businesses in the USA as NRA *Bulletin 1*, as way of letting business know what the NRA Codes were supposed to accomplish.[16]

Roosevelt also expressed his agreement with two precursors to the NIRA, the WIB and the Swope Plan. In his statement on the NIRA, Roosevelt harkened back to the WIB: "I had part in the great cooperation of 1917 and 1918 and it is my faith that we can count on our industry once more to join in our general purpose to lift this new threat and to do it without taking any advantage of the public trust which has this day been reposed without stint in the good faith and high purpose of American business."[17]

In a press conference on November 3, 1933, Roosevelt was asked what he thought of the Swope Plan. He answered that he thought it was a very interesting program, adding that an editorial in the *Wall Street Journal* indicated that "Mr. Swope evidently accepts this as an inescapable condition of the times" and the president of the US Chamber of Commerce agreed. Arthur Krock, in a speech in Toronto, made the same point, the president went on, by calling for an economic plan as "an instrument of social welfare." Although Krock's goal was to improve business conditions and reduce unemployment, the president quoted Krock approvingly for saying, "its larger objective is to bring comfort and living security to the greatest number of people. Whether or not you believe it is wise, just, or can work, you should judge it on that basis."[18] The NIRA aimed at the same larger objective. The overall objective of the NIRA, according to Roosevelt, was "the assurance of a reasonable profit to industry and living wages for labor."[19] He repeated this objective in more concrete terms in his reemployment agreement under the NIRA by asking business not to "use any subterfuge" to counter the plan "to shorten hours and to raise wages for the shorter week to a living basis."[20]

When he gave retrospective views on the NIRA, Roosevelt still retained his commitment to the living wage. In a February 20, 1935 message to the Congress seeking an extension of the NIRA, he related how two years earlier, in seeking the NIRA, he had asked the Congress to give him the power "to pay a decent wage." During the two years subsequent to passage of the NIRA, "millions of workers have been released from starvation wages,"[21] that is, they had come closer to a living wage. Finally, to give one example that is related to the NIRA in its other feature of providing for spending on stimulus programs, Roosevelt said that for any public works project under Title II of the NIRA, "No employee on any such project shall be paid less than a just and reasonable wage which shall be compensation sufficient to provide for the hours of labor as limited, a standard of living in decency and comfort."[22] As it had during World War I, the federal government would set an example of paying living wages in its programs for providing work for the unemployed.

This additional information further reinforces an interpretation that Roosevelt was vocal in presenting the idea that a living wage was part of what he wanted to accomplish by the NIRA. I might also add that his statement in his first inaugural address on March 4, 1933, reflected his general approach to economics by saying that his aim was to "apply social values more noble than mere monetary profit."[23] This aim was consistent with Ryan's ethics which held that profits, dividends, and interest were "subordinate to the laborer's right to a Living Wage."[24] In later chapters, I will offer additional statements Roosevelt made about how subsequent New Deal programs for economic security had the same goal. I will also provide examples where the supporters of the New Deal used the term living wage directly in commenting on those programs for economic security along with cases where the living wage was implied.

There is one point about Roosevelt's statements on the living wage that needs to be made again, however. Many New Deal programs were motivated by the theory that the cause of the Great Depression was the lack of purchasing power among workers. From this perspective, it could be argued that Roosevelt's advocacy for a living wage was a proxy for increasing consumption demand through higher wages for workers. This argument, however, works the other way just as well; the underconsumption theory could have been used as a tactic to secure a living wage. Moreover, the two approaches are not mutually exclusive and both were consistently used by supporters of the New Deal. The purchasing power side of the argument has been analyzed many times.[25] As indicated in Chapter 1, I focus on the living wage part of the argument for three reasons. First, it has been overlooked for so long. Second, the living wage argument unifies all of the Roosevelt programs for labor. Third, it is Roosevelt's advocacy for a living wage that differentiates him from Hoover, who also held to the underconsumption argument and the need to address it by giving labor more income.

The NRA and a Living Wage

The NIRA was passed by the Congress on June 16, 1933, and was put in place by the NRA. The NIRA and the codes established under the NRA represented a covenant where, by acting in concert, businesses in each industry would establish minimum wages and maximum hours that would provide the living wage Roosevelt mentioned four times in his statement on the NIRA. The problem Clark and others had raised of firms not being able to increase wages due to competition from businesses that kept wages low would be solved. The codes would also recognize unions and collective bargaining which would enable the setting of industry-wide wage standards. Whether a direct influence or not, the ideas of the persons surveyed in Chapter 2 were consistent with the living wage goal of the NIRA.

Roosevelt's statement on the relationship between the NIRA and the living wage was accepted by top administrators in the NRA. Dudley Cates, the vice-president of the insurance company Marsh & McLennan, who served as second-in -command of the NRA, indicated that the NRA was based on a new philosophy that gave "a new priority to the worker up to a living wage, ahead of any right of capital."[26] In this way, the NRA would end the exploitation of labor by business by giving wages precedence over profits, much as Ryan had argued. Cates included, as one of four main objects of the NRA, "a minimum 'living wage' as a social necessity" and considered that the primary wage policy of the NRA was "the establishing of socially acceptable minimum living wages, to be progressively increased as production increased." He added, however, that wages also had to be based on the ability of an industry to pay a living wage, which meant that the NRA had to "maintain a balance between social and economic values."[27]

Another proponent of the living wage in the NRA was its top administrator, General Hugh S. Johnson (1881–1942). A West Point graduate, he rose to the rank of a general and was the army's liaison to the WIB during World War I. On retiring from the army, he became a business associate of the financier, Bernard Baruch, who had headed the WIB. He was appointed as the administrator of the NRA at its start in June 1933, serving until his resignation in September 1934. He was energetic in his work with the NRA and equally energetic in making the case for that work in a book and numerous articles in the press.

One of those publications that is germane to this book is an article in *The Saturday Evening Post* of January 1935, "The Blue Eagle from Egg to Earth." Written after his resignation from the NRA, Johnson was particularly eager to defend his policies. The criticisms of the NRA resulted from its being part of a new philosophy of government and the economy. Indeed, Johnson "regarded NRA as a holy cause." As would any devotee of a new philosophy, he was hurt from being misunderstood, especially in light of all the good he was doing by bringing the order of government to the chaos of the market economy, making it possible for all sectors of the economy "to act in unison." This united effort was a new approach to economic thinking and it caused discontent among the old-style business leaders who were used to having their way.[28]

One example of this discontent over NRA policies dealt with the level of wages and efforts to ensure that workers earned a living wage. From Johnson's perspective, the philosophy of President Roosevelt on this issue was that "no industry which depends for existence on less than living wages has a right to continue to exist." When the NRA took this philosophy as its marching orders and forced sweatshops to pay a living wage, the operators of those sweatshops said "that NRA oppresses them." They became its enemies. Johnson was willing to have his legacy stand on his rooting out these low-wage industries, even though consumers might benefit from them, because in addition to living wages being in his marching order from the president, "they were also my convictions."[29]

Roosevelt confirmed Johnson's convictions. On September 25, 1934, he wrote to Johnson to accept his resignation as the administrator of the NRA. He praised Johnson because under his leadership the NRA had "accomplished long overdue reforms" including "recognition of the principles of a fair wage."[30] Since Johnson's resignation had not come voluntarily, Roosevelt's praise may have been intended to mollify him. Nevertheless, this particular framing of the mollification would indicate that they both took a living wage seriously.

Roosevelt and a Living Wage

So far in this chapter, I have presented places where Roosevelt and high members of his administration referred to the NIRA as having a goal of providing workers with a living wage. Regarding Roosevelt, his clearest expression of this goal were his statements on the NIRA of June 16, 1933.[31] In his book on the New Deal, Samuel Rosenman, who wrote many of Roosevelt's speeches, tells us that Roosevelt's "speeches as finally delivered were his—and his alone—no matter who his collaborators were."[32] From this perspective, we can conclude that the living wage terminology of his NIRA statements was there because Roosevelt wanted it that way. To be sure, it is possible that Johnson, who wrote speeches for Roosevelt in the early days of the New Deal, might have been a collaborator on the NIRA statements; he had helped draft the NIRA and was slated to be its top administrator. Perhaps he suggested the living wage terminology in the statements. His biographer indicates that Johnson often expressed a sincere but uneven compassion for the problems facing workers.[33]

Regardless, I have found no direct evidence as to why Roosevelt took up a living wage and made it a theme in his administration. It may have been due to the influence of the supporters of the living wage as outlined in Chapter 2. One of those supporters who might have influenced Roosevelt's interest in the living wage was Sam Lewisohn. We saw in Chapter 2 that he was a supporter of a living wage and wrote, "the primary responsibility is upon the employing group to endeavor so to perfect the industrial process that each worker may be provided with a wage that will give him at least all the ordinary comforts of life."[34] Lewisohn apparently had a long relationship with Roosevelt because they attended Columbia University Law School during the same years. As the governor of New York, Roosevelt appointed Lewisohn to two state committees on prison reform. At a conference on parole issues in 1939, in his opening address Roosevelt mentioned the good work done on parole reform by "my old friend, Sam Lewisohn."[35]

More to the point, as described in Chapter 2, there was a great interest in a living wage during the 1920s, much of it based on the experiences of the WIB and the NWLB, and Roosevelt had worked with the WIB. In addition, I would add Ryan to the list of potential influencers of Roosevelt, given the long-term relationship he had with Roosevelt, although there is nothing in Ryan's correspondence to indicate this influence. Raymond Moley, who was Roosevelt's closest advisor in the early years of the New Deal, drafted the message Roosevelt sent to the Congress to ask for the legislation for the NIRA[36] and he might have worked on the NIRA statements.

The Secretary of Labor, Frances Perkins, was a living wage advocate (See Chapter 6) and a long-time associate of Roosevelt who might have been an influence. In her book, *People at Work*, Perkins pointed out that the NIRA was the result of a massive outpouring of messages to the Roosevelt Administration, asking it, among other things, "to fix a living wage as a minimum wage for each person working so that the total wage income and purchasing power would be increased." Once the NRA was established, its administrator asked the industry code writers to produce labor provisions that included the provision of "a minimum wage level which was at least a decent living wage." Finally, after a review of the NRA's first year of operation, Perkins indicated that it had to keep to its mission of "reasonable returns to capital, fair rates to labor, [and] just prices to the consumer."[37] Perkins' comments are consistent with Roosevelt's two statements on the NIRA, but she may have been reflecting those statements rather than having been the author of them. Still, she was well known as the conscience of the New Deal and might have been the one who nudged Roosevelt toward support of a living wage.

Another conscience of the New Deal was the president's wife, Eleanor Roosevelt. She also had an interest in a living wage, as will be described in Chapter 7, and perhaps she prodded him in this direction as a part of her overall sympathy for the poor. Finally, we have seen support for a living wage in the speeches by Roosevelt's two political role models, Theodore Roosevelt (Chapter 1) and Woodrow Wilson (Chapters 1 and 2). There is even a similarity between Wilson's statement of the aim of his post-war reconstruction program, "Labor not only is entitled to an adequate wage, but capital should receive a reasonable return upon its investment ..."[38] and Roosevelt's goal for the NIRA, "the assurance of a reasonable profit to industry and living wages for labor."[39] Given all of these potential influences on Roosevelt's advocacy for a living wage, the real point is that the idea of a living wage was more commonly held during the Progressive Era and the New Deal than has previously been recognized, and Roosevelt was one of those who adhered to the idea, set forth by Ryan, that a living wage was a right of labor. As a result, a living wage was one of many of Roosevelt's objectives for the NIRA in the area of labor reform. In addition, there is evidence that he supported a living wage as a goal of the NIRA in the statements that others, especially administrators of the NRA, made about the living wage. The idea of a living wage was a part of the NRA approach and we will see that persons outside the NRA recognized this attitude.

The US Supreme Court declared the NIRA unconstitutional in 1935 in the Schechter Case. The Court objected to the centralization of economic control that the NRA apparently had put in place, but it disapproved even more of the control it delegated to private businesses.[40] A lingering issue after the Schechter decision, however, was whether the NRA had accomplished its goal of a living wage. The president and his supporters argued that the NRA had started to accomplish its goal of a living wage, but not all proponents of a living wage agreed. There were many *post mortems* on the NIRA after its demise and I will concentrate on the ones with a connection to a living wage.

Clark, Planning, and the NIRA

As described in the previous chapter, for nearly a decade before the New Deal Clark had been an advocate for national economic planning, based on the problems caused by an economic concept he had devised: social overhead costs. Capital investment in productive overhead meant that a small amount of increase in consumer demand could accelerate a larger increase in investment, which, in turn, could expand the purchasing power of workers and set off an economic boom. But then, the increased capacity from the new investments would create overproduction and layoffs, leading to reduced purchasing power and a recession. Since labor was not an overhead, it was let go and unemployment followed. At least that was how Clark argued in the 1920s.

In the early 1930s, he had refined his view of planning in a book, *Strategic Factors in Business Cycles*.[41] His goal was to identify the strategic factors that had brought about the Great Depression. He reached a strong conclusion, "The study of the special features of the present depression seems to indicate that it may have extended past the point at which the usual forces of automatic recovery can be expected to come into operation." In short, the forces that proponents of the market economy believed would bring about the end of the Depression could not be hoped for and "a search for more powerful and positive measures was urgently indicated." Unemployment would remain as an ongoing problem and the government should engage in "long-range planning" to solve the problem.[42] The goal of that planning was a "balanced economy" where all the productive capabilities of the economy were in tune with the needs of society and a proper balance existed between the prices of inputs, including labor, and the prices of final products as well as between the level of savings and the amount of investment.[43]

Armed with this approach, Clark conducted an early review of the NRA in his March 1934 article, "Economics and the National Recovery Administration," published in *The American Economic Review*. Clark reviewed the main features of the NIRA and the objectives behind it. Clark listed the NRA's objectives and categorized them as having a short-run aim of ending the Depression and a long-run aim of ensuring a stable economy with enduring prosperity. One criticism of the NRA was that it focused on the long-run goals and was, therefore, hampering recovery. Clark did see the NRA's efforts to limit production as contrary to a recovery. He also was concerned about efforts to protect inefficient firms through setting prices at levels that made them profitable.[44] The problem was that the philosophy of cooperation of the NRA had to "be converted from a mere philosophy into an organized interest, wide enough to include those who contribute and those who benefit, on a basis somewhat more solid than mutual expressions of good will."[45]

When the US Supreme Court voided the NIRA on April 1, 1935, President Roosevelt issued an executive order creating a Committee of Industrial Analysis to undertake a summary of what results the NRA had produced. Clark was selected as a member of the Committee. Based on what he had learned as a member of the Committee, he revised his attitude toward planning as a way to produce a living wage that covered the social overhead costs of work. He found that planning in the USA contained a contradiction.

Planning was needed for society to meet human needs. The problem for Clark, however, was that the capabilities of workers had not developed to an extent where they could participate in any system of planning. Only business had developed the technical capability for planning. As a result, Clark now argued that under the NIRA businessmen had captured the NRA and used it effectively to raise prices for business without a corresponding increase in wages for labor. Labor participation in the NRA had been weak, while its government administrators had proven ineffective.

The issue for Clark was a big one. He asked, "Can we control business or does it control us?"[46] Under the NIRA, apparently, business was controlling us, and unless the USA went to the extreme of abolishing private property, which Clark certainly doubted, business would control any system of planning to serve its own purposes and not the interest of society as a whole.[47] Planning and a living wage were not compatible with private enterprise and the market economy.

Progressives like Clark, Chase, and Swope had argued that through planning business, government and labor could collaborate effectively. As Clark saw it, labor was not ready to play its part in that system of planning. First, workers were becoming more reliant on union leaders to do their thinking for them, an outcome Clark found to be of doubtful value. Second, modern working conditions in large-scale factories had hindered the capability of workers to do anything more than rely on others to lead them.[48] Clark now saw a flaw in his own case for planning. National economic planning needed input from labor to be effective, but workers could not be relied on when it came to participation in planning and certainly not on a level equal to that of the expert managers of business. As a result of his critical analysis of the failure of planning under the NIRA, Clark greatly diminished his interest in planning and in his subsequent writings began to worry that unions were gaining too much power without the capability to use that power for the good of society.[49]

Clark took a perspective on unions that was very pessimistic at the time. We will see in subsequent chapters that union leaders continued to push for a living wage. In doing so, they often used the consumerist argument that a living wage increased the purchasing power of labor, but they also employed Clark's theory of social overhead costs in support of a living wage, as can be seen in their writings in union publications.

Unions Favor the NIRA

With the New Deal in place, unions should have been staunch supporters of its programs. At the end of the critical first 100 days, however, the AFL was still waiting for some good news about the economy. John Frey (1871–1957) expressed the concerns in the June 1933 issue of the *American Federationist* in an article, "Business Depends on Wages." As Frey saw it, the Roosevelt Administration had spent its early days giving first aid to victims of the crash and was spending many dollars on public works projects, but had done nothing to address the relationship between wages, consumption, and recovery. He wrote, "No legislation has been enacted which deals with the prime cause of the depression, underconsumption."[50] Even public works projects were of little help if the wages earned from working on them were low.

The AFL did not have long to wait for the New Deal to address its concerns. Indeed, in the same issue where Frey was expressing his concerns, William Green (1873–1952), president of the AFL and editor of the *American Federationist*, wrote a lengthy editorial, "New Economic Planning," in support of "the Industrial Recovery Bill." The Bill, when passed, would place a great deal of power over industry with the president. But such "obvious drastic measures are necessary to prevent national bankruptcy." The efforts by business to cut costs to meet competitive price cutting had resulted "in unemployment, low wages and even the dishonesty of sweat shop industries." The proposed Act would set up codes of fair competition to avoid these damaging practices and help the economy recover. Green added, "The fundamental purpose of this measure is to provide employment so that by increased purchasing power, business may revive."[51] In this and other articles, Green adhered to a consumerist perspective on a living wage.

Green amplified the goals of the NIRA in a second editorial, "Control the Disorganizer." The NIRA was giving the president a great deal of power over industry, but it was a power to foster an effective policy of collective action. Green believed that the age of the individual was over and that business and workers now had to join in groups to cooperate in a fight against individuals whose behavior disrupted the economy. Chief among them were sweatshop operators who were practicing a form of "industrial brigand" by imposing their terms of hard work for low pay on all business firms that competed with them. This disruptive behavior had negative side effects for all persons, Green added, echoing Clark (see Chapter 2),

> Since the sweatshop forces society to pay its production costs, society has a right to set up regulatory machinery that will force the industry to pay its own costs. Minimum standards determined jointly by all groups in the industry must be made binding upon all enterprises within the industry.[52]

Workers needed a living wage to keep the society from having to provide some or all of their needs and unions were the way for them to get a living wage is what Green was saying here.

This focus on the cooperative activity to be brought about by the NIRA did not distract the AFL from remembering the primary need in the economy—increased purchasing power for labor. In yet another article in the June issue of the *American Federationist*, "Recovery Program," the writer outlined many of the early New Deal policies, such as going off the gold standard, that were reducing consumption. The NIRA would be different because with it Roosevelt took on "the fundamental obstruction which is holding business down—shortage of buying power." Here, as before, the argument was that most businesses wanted "to maintain wages." But a few "selfish employers" cut wages in order to undersell those businesses. The NIRA would curb these unfair employers and take a big step "toward the maintenance of fair wages." The result would be a better balance "between producing and buying power."[53]

The AFL was in accord with Roosevelt's goal for the NIRA of a living wage for workers. In its next issue, the *American Federationist* published Roosevelt's statement on the NIRA, including its call for living wages, under the title, "An Industrial Covenant."[54] It followed up with another article, "Recovery—Facts for Code Making," which reminded readers and those writing industry codes, "The two chief objectives in a campaign to restore buying power are: Put men to work and raise their wages." Both objectives should be a part of the industry codes. As to the question of how high the wages should be raised, the *American Federationist* answered that they should be at least "a living wage" as defined by budget studies.[55] Green repeated this notion in the August 1933 issue of the *American Federationist* by writing about his desired outcome of code making, "One of our first considerations in fixing wages is to give the worker a living wage. The President left no doubt about this in his statement of policy on signing the Recovery Act on June 16."[56] Here is an example of an important union leader who took Roosevelt's statements about a living wage seriously.

It became clear to the AFL, however, that business was not taking that statement seriously. The *American Federationist* voiced concern about the business approach to the NIRA in a March 1934 article, "Four Labor Problems." The four problems related to labor's participation in the NRA and its lack of influence. The first three were the lack of union representatives on the code-writing authorities, the non-existence of joint industrial relations boards under the NRA, and the continued presence of company unions. The upshot was that without union participation, the NRA was producing the fourth problem, falling real wages.[57]

In an editorial, "Recovery Situation," in December 1934, Green also found that business was seeking to modify the NIRA to suit its needs. The New Deal was trying to establish an economic balance between business and labor and Green believed that this meant that executives and workers "must have parity of participation." This parity was needed to ensure the "balance between the capacity to produce and the capacity to consume." But business, realizing that the voters were supporting the New Deal, was trying to capture the NIRA by proposing new plans of "cooperation in order to gain control." Their goal was to offset the ability of unions to be a force for gaining a balanced economy of "plenty for all."[58]

A similar pattern of support and then concern over the NIRA can be found in the *United Mine Workers Journal*. On June 1, it gave the following headline to a summarization of the provisions of the proposed Act: "Industrial Recovery Bill, About to Become Law, Means Emancipation of the Wage Slave."[59] The next issue was headlined, "Greatest Labor Victory in History Achieved as Industrial Recovery Bill Becomes Law." It was considered a great victory because the NIRA "contained every provision labor had asked for."[60] The plaudits continued with an "Appraisal of the Industrial Recovery Act" that indicated it gave every worker the right to become a member of a union.[61] As had the *American Federationist*, the *United Mine Workers Journal* also published Roosevelt's Statement on the NIRA.[62] Finally, on January 15, 1934, the *United Mine Workers Journal* cited its president, John L. Lewis, as saying about the NIRA, "From the standpoint of human welfare and economic freedom, we are convinced that there has been no legal instrument comparable to it since President Lincoln's Emancipation Proclamation." Moreover, thanks to Section 7 of the Act, economic recovery was going to take place and labor would see "a better economic and social life in the future."[63]

These are very heady rhetorical statements of support for the NIRA from the house of labor to the point that one wonders if they were not being overdone to flatter Roosevelt. They did not last. On April 1, 1934, the *United Mine Workers Journal* reported that Lewis was now supporting legislation that would strengthen the NIRA. The activities of the NRA had not turned out as well as unionists had hoped they would, and business was using its rights under the NIRA to organize itself to cooperate in raising prices while doing everything it could to deny that right of organization to labor.[64] When the US Supreme Court declared the NIRA unconstitutional, the *United Mine Workers Journal* disagreed in part because it thought the NRA had accomplished "a great amount of good" but its enforcement had been too much in favor of business.[65]

The union perspective on a living wage followed a pattern about the social outlook toward the NIRA that can be found in a number of writings at the time: enthusiasm at the start and disillusionment once the USA had some experience with the NIRA. This pattern was expressed with special vehemence by a strong advocate for social justice, whose story comes next.

Father Charles Coughlin and Social Justice

Father Charles E. Coughlin (1891–1979) was a controversial figure during the Great Depression. A Roman Catholic priest from Detroit, Michigan, he pioneered in the methods now used by talk radio hosts, starting his radio broadcasts in 1926. He was bombastic and while he did not take telephone calls on the air, he did read letters from his listeners and respond to them on the air. The key to all his talk was his advocacy of social justice as presented by Pope Leo XIII in his encyclical *Rerum Novarum*, and he used his standard of social justice to judge what politicians and the economy were providing for the USA. In this way, he was part of the same movement of Catholic social activists as Ryan. Ryan supported Coughlin in his early years because of his effectiveness in bringing the message of social justice to a mass audience on the radio.

As did Ryan, in the early 1930s, Coughlin thought he heard a kindred voice in Roosevelt and became an early supporter of the New Deal. He was not a devoted follower of anything but his own views, however. As Brinkley points out, Coughlin was convinced that a crisis in the system of money and banking had caused the Great Depression and favored a policy of expanding the money supply to bring about recovery.[66] He wished for the success of the New Deal and believed that it had two years to prove itself by addressing the issue of "why there is want in the midst of plenty."[67] To be sure, Coughlin had his own answer to this question—increase the money supply. When Roosevelt did not do as much about the money and banking system as he wanted, Coughlin began to sour on him. Ultimately, Coughlin accused Roosevelt of being a communist (See Chapter 7).

As did many other persons, moreover, Coughlin also saw the problem of the Great Depression as one of underconsumption. The appropriate solution to the Great Depression was "a just and living annual wage for all citizens who care to earn their own livelihood."[68] From Coughlin's viewpoint, the living wage was needed for economic as well as for moral reasons. He saw the problem of unemployment as being created when workers were paid low wages while they worked and then were laid off until the products they produced were sold. The idea of a living wage meant that "a new annual wage scale must be adopted," one that led to a "new era where henceforth our problem shall be one of distribution of the profits not only to the owners and stockholders but also to the laborers and mechanics, enabling all to live prosperously even when the wheels of industry have ceased operating."[69]

When Roosevelt seemed to pay less attention to him, in November 1934, Coughlin came up with a new idea and asked his listeners to form a National Union for Social Justice. He then outlined "the principles of social justice" the USA should try to establish. It was a long list and included a living wage, the right of workers to form unions under the protection of the government, a broader tax base with tax cuts for workers, and a preference for "the sanctity of human rights to the sanctity of property rights."[70]

Coughlin had supported Roosevelt in the election of 1932, coining the slogan "Roosevelt or Ruin." When his support for Roosevelt gradually dwindled, he indicated that he could not "praise policies like N.R.A. when criticism is required."[71] Never a wholehearted supporter of the NIRA, he had written to Roosevelt his view that the NIRA could not bring about a recovery. He had hoped that the NIRA would help labor by maintaining wages and controlling prices, but was especially concerned that business influence in the NRA had kept wages low and allowed for price fixing in most industries, with the result that wage increases lagged behind price increases. The point for Coughlin was that the NRA was not bringing about the social justice that he had called for. It had not delivered on the promise of according workers a living wage and had not abandoned the primacy of profits over people. Consequently, Coughlin changed his earlier phrase "Roosevelt or Ruin" to "Roosevelt and Ruin," in a radio address delivered on June 19, 1936.[72]

Coughlin intended that his National Union for Social Justice serve as a lobbying group. When that effort failed, he began electioneering by giving speeches before large groups in major cities. His radio audience may have reached ten million listeners by the mid-1930s and chapters of the National Union for Social Justice were formed around the country. But they were too unwieldy and disorganized to have success in influencing elections.[73] Still, for a time, Coughlin was a popular force in the USA who helped push the New Deal toward its programs of economic security that replaced the NIRA.

Douglas, the NIRA, and Minimum Wages

Coughlin was not the only proponent of a living wage to take this dim view of the accomplishments of the NRA. As noted in Chapter 2, Paul H. Douglas had a strong interest in a living wage. Behind that interest was an economic theory of how wages were determined and, in 1934, Douglas published a lengthy book, *The Theory of Wages*, to evaluate how that economic theory held up in actual practice.

The theory Douglas set forth was the marginal product theory of wages, an explanation of how wages are determined in the market economy, as set forth by John Bates Clark (See Chapter 1). This theory maintains that wages will equal the value of the additional product an incremental worker will add to total output. Its thrust is to link wages to the productivity of workers and to argue that businesses cannot pay wages in excess of what a worker produces. In his book, Douglas examined the underlying assumptions of the theory to consider its strengths and weaknesses.[74]

Douglas was careful to warn his reader that the theory was "merely an explanation of the way in which wages and interest are determined in a competitive and capitalistic society. It is not an ethical justification of what distribution 'ought' to be."[75] Moreover, the theory had a number of implicit assumptions that needed to be considered. Two of them were germane to the idea of a living wage. First, the theory assumed that businesses competed with each other in hiring labor; second, that there was equal bargaining power between business and workers.[76] Douglas questioned the validity of these assumptions. Regarding competition among businesses in hiring workers, he observed that "tacit or organized combinations among employers to depress wages or to prevent their being advanced are common." In addition, at the time he was writing, the recently enacted NIRA had caused these combinations of employers to be "greatly increased and nearly universalized. This increase in employer combinations also violated the assumption that there was equal bargaining power between business and labor."[77] Douglas might have had inside information on this issue; he had worked for the NRA in its Educational Section,[78] and was a member of the Consumer Advisory Board to the NRA.

Even though the NIRA was enhancing the bargaining power that business had over labor, the NRA industry codes were fixing minimum wages and maximum hours in many sectors of the economy. Douglas was not sure how long the NIRA would last but it did mark a departure from the market economy and its replacement by "a partially controlled society."[79]

The question remained: who was in charge of this partially controlled economy? A typical response was that business was still in charge, as we can see from another proponent of planning who was critical of the NRA.

Rexford Tugwell Downplays a Living Wage

Rexford Guy Tugwell (1891–1979) had a long career in government service as part of Roosevelt's brain trust with a title of Assistant Secretary of Agriculture. Before that, during the 1920s, he was a professor of economics at the Columbia University. In 1927, he published a study of the increased productivity of the US economy, *Industry's Coming of Age*. In it, he analyzed the trends in the economy whereby its ability to produce was increasing, which gave the society the potential to solve many of the problems associated with poverty. Tugwell argued that the government was capable of solving those problems by directing the economy as the experience of the WIB showed.[80] In making this argument, he revealed a philosophy of government that would come to the forefront in his New Deal activities, "Governmental controls ought to be brought to bear where voluntary ones break down."[81]

Just as he began working for Roosevelt, Tugwell wrote another book, *The Industrial Discipline*. He intended it to be a philosophical, qualitative look at the new economy that had been ushered in during the 1920s. His main premise was that the new economy relied heavily on mechanization, and the use of machines in industry would continue to grow. Tugwell drew many inferences from this hypothesis, most of which are tangential to the idea of a living wage. He did touch upon a living wage, however, by describing how the machines in industry reduced the skills needed of workers, which meant the typical worker was "presented with the alternative of taking what is offered or not having a job."[82] To be sure, that employment system was part of the market process which determined what standard of living a worker would have, but to Tugwell, the labor market no longer operated under conditions of competition. Business had bargaining power, and for workers that meant that "alertness, organization, expert advice, are all necessary to the maintenance of even a living wage."[83] Indeed, it was necessary for workers to gain more than a living wage. Here, Tugwell brought in the purchasing power argument as linked to high wages for workers to guarantee high levels of consumption. "A nation of well-paid workers, consuming most of the goods it produces," he concluded, "will be as near Utopia as we humans are ever likely to get."[84] To bring us closer to that consumerist utopia, Tugwell went on, the USA would need government intervention in the economy.

The New Deal had answered the need for intervention in 1933 with the NIRA. In 1934, Tugwell co-authored a book, *Our Economic Society and its Problems*, with Howard C. Hill (1878–1940), at the time an assistant professor of the teaching of social science at the University High School of the University of Chicago. In addition to surveying current economic problems in the book, Tugwell and Hill took a look at the NIRA. Overall, the book presented a pattern of an increased standard of living from the earliest days of human life through the 1920s, with the Great Depression being a watershed event that ended this history of economic progress. Moreover, the economic progress was not without social costs of unemployment, poor working conditions, and "levels of living that still yield little by way of comforts and well-being."[85] As long as these negative features of capitalism existed, society faced the issues of how to increase its wealth and how to use that wealth to the greatest benefit to society.

As part of their study of these two issues, Tugwell and Hill reviewed the available data on poverty stating that their basic concern was with how high an income was needed "to buy the minimum of goods that that are necessary for decency and comfort."[86] To answer that question, they devised a graduated standard of well-being in three categories—poverty, comfort, and riches—to consider how many persons fell into each category. They found that the rising real wages during the 1920s had reduced the number of persons living in poverty, but the Great Depression greatly increased it. In analyzing poverty during the Depression, however, instead of looking just at wages, they also looked at total income for all workers. Their argument for using this approach reflected Clark's social overhead approach. They wrote, "Since the wages paid to persons at work must provide for practically the entire wage-earning class, whether busy or idle, we must examine primarily the drop in total earning."[87] Tugwell and Hill determined that a reduction in total payrolls, as took place during the Depression, meant increased poverty for many workers and their families. The number of individuals living in comfort was also influenced by prosperity and its decline. Tugwell and Hill found that in 1918 about 50 percent of the US population lived in comfort; the number rose to about two-thirds of the population in 1929, only to fall back to half in 1933.[88]

Given their use of comfort as a standard of well-being along with their application of Clark's perspective to the issue of poverty, Tugwell and Hill were on the verge of our interest in a living wage, but they never used that term, even though their notions of comfort and decency sound similar. Their eschewing the term, a living wage, was likely due to their dislike for the rights-based approach that went with Ryan's use of the term. They wrote, "Many clergymen insist that injustice is a violation of God's will and that the poor have a *right* to more than they receive." The problem with this appeal to rights was that it was difficult "to prove anyone's inalienable right to anything."[89]

Instead, Tugwell and Hill took an approach that considered consequences instead of rights. To them, the major consequence of large numbers of persons living in poverty was that it led to depressions and a reduction in everyone's income. As they described the case, "Certain authorities maintain that the present distribution of income brings about the downward swing of the business cycle" by preventing a coordination between production and consumption.[90] In short, low pay led to the purchasing power problem that many viewed as the cause of the Great Depression.

The solution Tugwell and Hill proposed for achieving better coordination was the redistribution of income by government policy. Their general approach to the issue was to experiment with national economic planning and they reviewed a number of proposals that had been set forth in the USA. Of particular interest to the theme of the book, they analyzed the Swope Plan (See Chapter 2), including its provision of private insurance to cover workers for unemployment, life and disability losses, and pensions. These insurance provisions were desirable but they were not sufficient to maintain purchasing power when a downturn in the economy took place. In addition, while the Swope plan called for minimum wages, it had "no provision that would raise wages high enough to coordinate production and consumption."[91]

The NIRA, according to Tugwell and Hill, remedied these problems of the Swope Plan. Its primary goal was "to promote industrial coordination" through government regulation of business. In addition, labor was being protected by codes that recognized "the right of collective bargaining," eliminated unfair labor practices, and established a minimum wage scale "assented to by employer and employee."[92] The drawback to the NIRA was that it still relied on profits as a measure of the value a business added to society. This was a hindrance to the NRA's effectiveness because "the social utility of an industry cannot always be determined by its ability to yield private profits." They also thought that "the wage provisions of the act have great possibilities." It was a defect, however, that the NIRA did not set any standards for wages. As a result the NRA administrators had the authority to set them based on their personal "social objectives." By giving administrators this latitude, the NRA would not live up to its potential as a planning agency. Tugwell and Hill described this detrimental approach to labor as follows, "It is one thing to set a minimum wage which provides a subsistence level of living. It is quite another thing to fix wages with a view to coordinating production and consumption."[93]

Tugwell and Hill are arguing that the living wage goal of the NIRA would be easy to accomplish and might take precedence over the more important purchasing power goal. The former required no planning while the latter did, which is why they considered the NIRA to offer a possibility of planning but not really a plan. In his memoirs of the first year of the New Deal, Tugwell indicated that Roosevelt was not interested in the purchasing power argument in the early days of his administration. To be sure, he added, the president believed that the "government had a responsibility for people's welfare" and to alleviate the suffering caused by the Depression, "but he had not admitted that the first necessity was the enlargement of purchasing power."[94]

Tugwell's indication that Roosevelt favored social justice over purchasing power would explain why he and Hill were concerned that a producerist living wage was taking precedence over the consumerist purchasing power approach. To be sure, Roosevelt mentioned the purchasing power argument more often than he talked about a living wage, even in his early years as president, as can be seen through a word search of his presidential papers. Tugwell, of course, had not done a word search, but his insider information led him to suspect that many of his colleagues in the New Deal, including Roosevelt, had not appreciated the need to have consumption in balance with production.

Ryan Speaks Up for the NRA

As the writings of Tugwell indicate, there was doubt among supporters of national planning that the NRA had been able to achieve its goals, including the goal of a living wage. Not everyone in favor of a living wage agreed, however. On October 9, 1934, Ryan made an address to the National Conference of Catholic Charities. He titled his address, "Shall the NRA Be Scrapped?" His answer was a resounding no.

To Ryan, the opponents of the NRA overlooked the good it was doing. Without the regulations contained in the NRA Codes, "workers would no longer be protected by minimum wage rates," which meant that "employers would be free to pay starvation wages." Hours of work would increase without an increase in pay. Workers would find their right to organize into unions taken away and "tyrannous employers would again be in a position to prevent the functioning of genuine and effective labor unions."[95] In short, the NRA had brought the USA closer to the conditions of a living wage and Ryan did not want to see it taken away.

Ryan's support for the NRA did not mean that he found it to be the best that could be done. Rather, he proposed several reforms in its functioning. First, he believed that the code-writing committees of each industry should be expanded to include more consumers and, especially, more workers. Increased labor representation on those committees would "bring about greater self-government in industry" and nurture a guild-like approach that was in "the Catholic economic tradition."[96] He also wanted removal of some of the restrictions the NRA placed on production as well as a further reduction of the work week to 30 hours. Finally, he felt that the NRA could do more to achieve the distributive justice he had written about by shifting income from capital to labor. He wrote, regarding this last reform, "On the assumption that our people are moderately honest, I believe that the NRA is capable of...bringing about this just distribution."[97]

Ryan sent a copy of "Shall the NRA be Scrapped" to Gerard Swope, author of the Swope Plan which served as one of the models for the NIRA. At the time, Swope was chair of the Business Advisory Council to the NRA, a non-governmental organization.[98] Swope responded by telling Ryan, "I read it...with much interest and I think it is very clearly stated."[99] Here is another case where Ryan and another advocate for a better life for workers through government coordination of the economy expressed their common concerns.

Ryan's support for the NIRA continued in another book, *A Better Economic Order*, published in 1935. Ryan sent copies of the book to the Progressives and members of the New Deal. In return he received letters approving of the book from Richard T. Ely,[100] Frances Perkins,[101] Roosevelt,[102] and Senator Robert F. Wagner, who wanted Ryan "to know how highly I value it," calling Ryan "the respected and outstanding authority on our economic problems."[103] At the time he was writing the book, the NIRA had not been struck down by the US Supreme Court and his focus was what the NRA had accomplished and how it could be improved. Of less importance here, Ryan also devoted his attention to business cycle theory and what it said about the causes of the Great Depression. As did many writers at the time, he laid the cause of the Great Depression on the idea of overproduction by business and the low purchasing power of labor. This interpretation added to his argument that workers needed a living wage.

There were a variety of ways to raise wages. A goal of the NIRA was to raise wages by nurturing unions through Section 7A and by having industry NRA Codes specify a minimum wage. By the time he was writing, Ryan observed of this effort to increase wages, "In a moderate degree it has already been accomplished" by the NRA.[104] Another way to improve income for workers was to initiate a 30-hour work week without reducing the weekly wage. The NRA had experienced less success in attaining this goal. Ryan attributed it, in part, to a fear that the NRA was oppressing small businesses. As a member of the NRA Industrial Appeals Board, he had learned that small businesses' complaints about the NRA all centered on labor issues. He noted,

> In other words, the "small man" seems to be the victim of oppression under the NIRA only because he is required to pay decent wages…Neither right reason nor social justice requires that a small number of inefficient and marginal men should continue to function as business men at the expense of humane standards of thousands of wage earners.[105]

Ryan agreed with Roosevelt that businesses that were so inefficient that they could not pay a living wage should be allowed to become bankrupt and disappear from the economy. He approved of what the NRA was trying to accomplish with codes requiring a minimum wage and maximum hours and especially favored the nurturing of unions under Section 7A of the Act. These components of the NRA should have been improving wages.

That was not happening, however, and Ryan counted it as a defect in the NIRA that labor was rarely represented in writing of the NRA Codes. In many industries, the lack of unions and collective bargaining made labor participation in code writing infeasible. As a result, he argued, the codes were leading to increased profits without similar increases in wages. For reasonable profits to become a common goal, he added, businessmen had to accept "the ethical doctrine that there is such a thing as fair profits, and that they are under moral obligation to practice and promote social justice."[106] Instead, business despised Section 7A of the NIRA and opposed unions whenever they could. To Ryan, this meant that Section 7A should be strengthened and he approved of the Wagner Bill that had recently been proposed with a goal of adding some clout to the NIRA. He indicated that to improve the NIRA, a new labor law needed to outlaw company unions, and provide for collective bargaining agents to be determined by a majority vote of workers in a company and for the use of a national labor board.[107]

In the final chapter of the book, Ryan considered whether the NIRA had created a better economic order. His standard was the idea set forth by Pope Pius XI that society should be organized into occupational groups, such as the medieval guilds had done, to plan and control the industry covered by each occupation; there would also be an overarching group to coordinate the various industry groups. The NRA had come close to establishing this approach but its shortfall was the lack of inclusion of labor in the code-writing bodies and its neglect of the minimum wage.[108]

Ryan retained his support for the NRA for the rest of his life. In 1945, just a few months before his death, Ryan repeated his view that the NRA "represented the most comprehensive and fundamental measure for social justice that has been set up in modern times."[109] His continued support of the NRA may have come from the way he saw the NRA as leading to a system of guilds that was still developing. This interpretation of the NRA was consistent with the organic view of society noted in Chapter 1. Organisms can evolve, which was what Ryan was anticipating.

A Brookings Study Criticizes a Living Wage

Up to this point, I have presented criticisms of the NRA made by advocates for a living wage. While these criticisms have been valuable, I also think it useful to look at criticisms from persons not attuned to the quest for a living wage. The first one comes from the Brookings Institution. Originally formed in 1916, the Brookings Institution is one of the oldest "think tanks" in the USA with a mission of investigating national policy issues. In 1935, the Brookings Institution took on the NRA in a lengthy (947 pages) study, *The National Recovery Administration: An Analysis and Appraisal*, written by six policy analysts.[110]

Part I of the study took a look at the overall goal of the NRA as set forth in the NIRA. It quoted Roosevelt as saying the NIRA had a goal of "the assurance of a reasonable profit to industry and living wages for labor."[111] The Brookings scholars took this goal to include the NIRA's labor components of shorter hours and higher pay, a goal they felt had been sought by unions for decades. In the same vein, business had long wanted relief from the antitrust laws and the Brookings scholars gave prominence to the gains to business through the easing of antitrust laws as a fundamental impetus for the NIRA.[112]

Part III of the study dealt with the labor provisions of the NIRA. The purpose of the labor provisions was to reduce unemployment and increase wages with a goal of providing everyone with "living wages."[113] The Brookings scholars cited Roosevelt for the philosophy of the labor codes as he presented them in his statement of the NIRA, "The idea is simply for employers to hire more men to do the existing work by reducing the hours of each man's week at the same time paying a living wage for the shorter work week."[114] The problem the NRA faced in writing labor codes for wages was that the wage structure was more complex than this simple idea seemed to indicate. Differences in wages existed due to geography and in terms of skill level, occupation, and industry standards and once the NRA Codes started changing some wages, the impact would be felt everywhere. The Brookings scholars concluded, "with few exceptions the handling of classes of wages above the minimum was and is inept."[115]

In Part IV on industrial relations, the Brookings scholars pointed out that the NIRA had three goals: minimum wage and maximum hour provisions consistent with fairness, collective bargaining as a legal right for workers, and mutual cooperation between management and labor. The last two goals were connected, with collective bargaining by labor acting as an impetus for better industrial relations and mutual cooperation. Working together, unions and business would bring about reduced work and higher wages under a premise "that prosperity based on higher wages and shorter hours would be an enduring prosperity."[116] The guiding intention was that by bringing about more equality of bargaining power between labor and management, collective bargaining would work in place of government regulation of wages.

The catch was that businesses needed to keep from raising their prices as fast as they raised wages. The Brookings scholars cited Roosevelt as arguing in his statement on the NIRA,

> I am fully aware that wage increases will eventually raise costs, but I ask that managements give first consideration to the improvement of operating figures by greatly increased sales to be expected from the rising purchasing

> power of the public. ... If we now inflate prices as fast and as far as we increase wages, the whole project will be set at naught.[117]

The entire functioning of the NRA required that price increases lag behind wage increases; the expansion of sales would lower costs per unit and reduce the need for price increases.

The Brookings scholars, however, argued that without higher prices businesses would not have the funds to increase wages. They considered how business could pay the higher wages through cutting down other expenses, and found none of their possibilities was feasible. The Brookings scholars then looked at what had happened to wages and prices under the NRA. To do so, they first put the NRA in a context of what had happened to wages and prices in the first four years of the Depression. They found that from 1929 to 1933 prices had declined faster than wages from President Herbert Hoover's exhorting business to hold the line on wages with the result that "average real earnings per hour were higher in the first half of 1933 than in 1929" in most of the industries they surveyed.[118] The problem of the Depression was that many workers were not working full-time at those higher real hourly wages.

Increased wages meant that businesses had to raise their prices. The Brookings scholars found that the control over prices that the NRA gave businesses allowed them to continue to raise prices to pay for higher wages in some cases and in advance of wage increases in other cases. This meant that "the NRA raised hourly wage rates for some classes of employees by more than it raised living costs" but "for other classes it raised the cost of living without any increase in compensation."[119] One group was benefitted at the cost of another, but what was the overall impact? A review of the aggregate data on wages and prices showed that "the codes apparently raised living costs on the whole concurrently with, or even in advance of, the hourly earnings of workers."[120] The Brookings scholars summed up the dilemma of the NRA as follows: "One group of workers may improve its relative position by higher wage rates and one industry may benefit itself by higher prices, but this is merely because wages and prices are not similarly raised elsewhere. When the game is played universally it is self-defeating."[121] The NRA efforts to put a floor under wages and prices very likely reduced production in the economy and prolonged the Depression.

The Brookings study is one of the few examples I have found of a direct criticism of the New Deal's support of a living wage. Its conclusion was that a living wage was not feasible in the economic climate of the 1930s, because higher wages for all workers would only lead to higher prices and the outcome was uncertain as to whether anyone would be better off. That conclusion, however, did not stop economists from considering what it would take to attain a living wage, as the next section will describe.

Mordecai Ezekiel Promises $2500 a Year

In 1936, Mordecai Ezekiel (1899–1974) published a book with a provocative title, *$2,500 A Year: From Poverty to Abundance*. Ezekiel, who had a PhD in economics from the Robert Brookings Graduate School of Economics, spent much of the New Deal era working as an economic advisor to the Secretary of Agriculture. His book promised a new approach to the economy that would build on the NIRA and offer "abundant living" where "each family would have an adequate supply of physical necessities and comforts, and sufficient leisure in which to enjoy them." As a result they "would have the opportunity to share in the finer things in life."[122] As we have seen before in this book and will see again, Ezekiel expressed a definition of "abundant living" comparable to a living wage, but never used the latter term. He calculated that his definition of "abundant living" would require an annual income of $2500.

Ezekiel made it clear that under the conditions existing at the time he wrote, only 29 percent of families in the USA earned $2500 a year or more. To get all families up to that standard, the total output in the economy would have to be increased but he believed that the economy, if properly organized, could achieve the level of output needed to bring incomes up to his standard of $2500 a year. That new economic organization could take place, he argued, by using the full capabilities of all humans. The economy had the potential to greatly increase production not only to the level of the last prosperous year of 1929, but by double that amount. There was a general agreement that the economy had to be changed and Ezekiel quoted approvingly Roosevelt's social objectives of the New Deal, as described in Chapter 1

> To do what any honest Government of any country would do: to try to increase the security and the happiness of a larger number of people in all occupations of life and in all parts of the country; to give them more of the good things of life, to give them a greater distribution not only of wealth in the narrow terms, but of wealth in the wider terms; to give them places to go in the summertime—recreation; to give them assurance that they are

> not going to starve in their old age; to give honest business a chance to go ahead and make a reasonable profit, and to give everyone a chance to earn a living.[123]

Ezekiel followed up this quote by indicating that current levels of income—total national income in 1934 would equate to about $1000 a year per worker—were not nearly adequate to give everyone more of the good things in life.[124]

The reason for the inadequate level of national income was that business was based on profits. To Ezekiel, this meant that business leaders would produce at a level that was profitable for them, regardless of how much they produced. He added, however, that those same business leaders recognized that increased sales would lead to lower costs and an improved profit picture, but they were afraid of starting "price wars" with their competitors. What was needed was a coordinated approach where "every concern all through the business system expanded its operations, employed more men, and paid out more to workers." That approach would result in "larger production, greater employment, and greater buying power" and "would create bigger demands all around."[125] This approach was no longer possible in the market economy, at least, not when Ezekiel was writing, because the "rules of profits no longer insure production." He based this idea on his view that "During the three long years from 1929 to 1932, the modern profit system had a chance to show what it could do to create prosperity."[126] One might wonder at the wisdom of discrediting a system that had raised standards of living for over a century by using only three data points, but that was the prevailing sentiment of the New Deal era. One wonders even more when, later in the book, Ezekiel observed, "The New Deal has corrected many of the flaws in the previous economic machinery … and has produced a substantial degree of recovery. … But business activity is still far below 1929, and even further below our potential capacity."[127]

Ezekiel did not infer from this observation that the New Deal had been no more successful than the profit system in restoring prosperity and bringing in a period of abundance. Rather, he believed that the New Deal had not done enough to coordinate production among all the industries of the US economy and the bulk of his book was devoted to proposing a national blueprint for abundance and setting forth a system of industrial adjustment to carry out the blueprint. His proposals are beyond the scope of this book's interest in a living wage, but Ezekiel remains of interest because he claimed a commonality with Ryan.

Regarding Ryan, Ezekiel reviewed his book, *A Better Economic Order*, as part of a chapter looking at what other writers had proposed as a system of planning. He especially approved of Ryan's use of occupational groups as a way to bring about a form of Industrial Democracy that regulated wages and profits. These proposals were strikingly similar to Ezekiel's program, as he admitted, although he worried that Ryan might be going too far in regulating wages and profits. Indeed, after the Schechter Decision, Ezekiel felt that Ryan's proposals would require an amendment to the US Constitution while his system of industrial adjustment would not.[128] Although he acknowledged that Ryan's proposal stressed higher wages,[129] Ezekiel made no mention of Ryan's support of a living wage.

In doing so, Ezekiel held to a consumerist view in contrast to Ryan's producerist perspective. To Ryan, a living wage meant that workers had a right to share in what they produced and the level of consumption was a side effect, even though it was an important indicator of the benefit of a living wage. Ezekiel wanted business to be encouraged to expand production with the security that production would be balanced with consumption by government planning. His program would ensure the balance between production and consumption that Clark and Tugwell had called for. Whether the government was capable of that type of planning was raised as a vital issue, as the next section will describe.

Charles Roos Looks at Wages under the NRA

In 1937, Charles Roos (1901–1958) produced a lengthy study, *NRA Economic Planning*. At the time the study was completed, he was director of research at the Cowles Commission, having previously been director of research at the NRA (1933–1934). The purpose of his study was to gauge the effectiveness of the NIRA in terms of bringing about an economic recovery. A key part of the NIRA program for economic recovery was to reduce the hours of work of labor and implement minimum wages. These policies were expected to reduce unemployment through the sharing of work and to increase the income and purchasing power of workers to stimulate demand. Roos doubted that the policies had done the job expected of them.

In terms of the minimum wages written in the NRA Codes, Roos found their biggest fault to be a reduction of wage differentials among different industries and in the same industries in different regions of the country. The NRA operated under a philosophy that those differentials should not exist "and proceeded so zealously to eliminate them that few, if any, if its policies upset business interrelation and balances to a greater degree." Hourly wages had always fluctuated in the US economy, especially during business cycles, but "despite such extreme movements in wages, sizable wage differences between large cities and small towns and between the North and South in all industries are of long standing."[130]

Roos maintained that the NRA believed that there were no economic reasons for the differences, as they resulted from a lack of unions among workers and unscrupulous behavior by business. As a result, the NRA Codes aimed at a large reduction in the differential pay. Roos attributed the differences in pay between the North and South to differences in productivity, the lack of urban markets for consumer goods in the South, and a lower cost of living in that region. He observed first hand that many factories in the South, especially in small towns, had to shut down due to the increased cost of paying higher wages brought about by the NRA Codes.[131] Thus, he concluded, "Truly the problems involving minimum wages are enormously difficult."[132]

Roos points to a difficulty in attaining a living wage in the market economy. From his market perspective, government officials, even if they were wise and impartial, would find it difficult to make all the adjustments in wages that the market economy accomplishes. The intricacies of the price system as a method of allocating resources requires careful adjustment beyond the best human capabilities and Roos doubted that government officials reflected the wisdom and impartiality that equaled those best human capabilities. His book is sprinkled with examples of bureaucratic infighting within the NRA and outside political interference with its functioning. The wage and hours policies of the NRA did not measure up to the standards of the market economy and were certainly not up to the standards needed to bring about a living wage. Roos' analysis would make us doubt that national economic planning by the government could take on the more complex problem of balancing consumption with production.

Conclusion

Roosevelt and top officers of the NRA clearly had a goal of a living wage. Things had not worked out the way they had planned, however. Proponents of planning such as Clark were happy to see the NRA go. On the other hand, Tugwell and Ezekiel wanted to see the NRA strengthened into an agency that really did use planning. All of them, however, agreed that the NRA Codes had been dominated by business and used to improve business conditions. Writing in 1947, economic historian Broadus Mitchell (1892–1988) found that 85 percent of the industries covered by the NIRA had written codes with little or no input from labor.[133] More recently, the view that business dominated the NRA Codes has been supported by Barber.[134] Even though he agreed that the short-term impact of the NRA had been to increase business' bargaining power with labor, Douglas was non-committal about the future of the NIRA, but he had not supported its mission of planning. In a similar fashion, Ryan, who was not an advocate of planning, favored continuance of the NRA for the good it had accomplished and could accomplish in bringing about a living wage.

Ryan's support for the NRA went against the logic of his own thinking, however. In his book, *Distributive Justice*, he had objected to socialism because its "expectation that altruistic sentiments" would replace monetary incentives was "based on the very shallow fallacy that what is true of a few" would become true of everyone under the right circumstances. He perhaps recognized this fallacy from his experiences as a cleric, for he noted even Christianity had not been able to persuade very many of its devoted adherents to take up a "life of altruism."[135] The Progressives in the New Deal era did not consider the NRA to equate to socialism.[136] Nevertheless, its success also depended, if not on altruism, at least on a sense of the common good and social justice if it were to achieve the goal of a living wage. To be sure, as described in Chapter 2, there were business leaders who favored the approach of the NRA toward the living wage, such as Henry Kendall, Sam Lewisohn, Edward Filene, and Gerard Swope, but it is unlikely that their spirit was common in the business community. This need for the right spirit may be why the NRA was lacking both as a planning agency and as an agency for social justice.

We can see the business attitude toward the NRA in two articles in *Nation's Business*. The first was in June 1933 titled "Business Agrees to Regulate Itself." The article was a summary of proposals made at the annual meeting of the US Chamber of Commerce. The article summed up the proposals as indicating, "Business has reasserted its right to govern itself through its own organizations subject to the approval of the government." What the proposals at the meeting had in mind was that trade associations in collaboration with government and labor would set up fair practices for each industry; this was a policy the Chamber long espoused.

If the New Deal would follow these proposals, business would accept its policies.[137]

In its next issue, *Nation's Business* expanded on its views of the NIRA in a second article, calling it "the boldest of a series of bold, swift measures to start economic restoration." The article, written by Morris Edwards, a former Associated Press journalist who worked for the Chamber, described what business believed was the deal the NIRA offered it with its title, "The Truce on the Sherman Law." Edwards outlined the deal business was making as follows:

> If business men will agree, voluntarily if possible, by compulsion if necessary, to put men back to work and raise wages, the Government will do two things. It will refrain for the time being from any more drastic form of control to achieve these ends. Furthermore, it will sanction a control over factors affecting prices to a degree sufficient not only to finance such employment and wage increases but to permit resumption of reasonable profits and dividends.[138]

Business could achieve the collaboration needed for maintaining prices with impunity from antitrust prosecution in return for "the partial relinquishment of control over management policies" not to the government but to "a group of proprietors among whom he has one voice."[139] Edwards also had praise for the NRA administration, warning business leaders that they should not try to sidestep the codes set forth under the NIRA. NRA administrators had "experience with this sort of thing in the War Industries Board" and were fully capable of dealing with businesses that did not comply with the NRA Codes.[140] The upshot of the NIRA, from this business perspective, was that it marked a return to the mercantilism that Adam Smith had hoped to defeat with free-market thinking.

I have focused on business because it was the key player in making the NRA work. It did not help, however, that labor, at least in the eyes of Clark, had also not been ready to play the part the NRA required of it. It should also be added that government officials in charge of the NRA were not as astute as they might have been, at least if the findings of the Brookings Study and Roos are credible. It would appear that no group affiliated with the NIRA project was up to the task of meeting its goal of a living wage. As Mitchell observed, "Though the NRA continued to give lip service to the concept of the 'decent living wage,' ideal criteria were not applied."[141] As long as the minimum wage in an industry code increased the income of the covered workers the code was approved. Writing a bit later, labor historian Joseph G. Rayback (1914–1983) concurred with this assessment, noting that while the NRA may have increased employment and wages for workers, it "made no real effort to provide a decent living wage."[142] When two historians who lived during the New Deal complain that the NRA was lackluster in its pursuit of a living wage for workers, they surely believed that it had a goal of a living wage.

When the Supreme Court disapproved of the NIRA, the Roosevelt Administration could have sought to amend the Constitution to permit the NIRA, which was suggested at the time.[143] This approach would have allowed it to experiment with the collaborative efforts of the NRA. The Roosevelt Administration, however, could argue that it would be difficult to write an amendment to cover all its members wanted to do. In a speech on September 17, 1937 to celebrate the 150th anniversary of the Constitution, Roosevelt indicated that the view of the Constitutional role of the government had been changed by "the idea that the resources of the nation can be made to produce a far higher standard of living for the masses of the people if only the government is intelligent and energetic in giving the right direction to economic life."[144] It had been the job of the NRA to give that right direction to the economy, but an amendment to the Constitution could not redeem the NRA.

Instead, the New Deal ended a program of self-regulation by all components of an industry and began a policy of regulation of business by government agencies. Critics of the NRA had argued that government participation in it had been too weak. The approach that followed the NRA strengthened government participation in business by making it the sole regulator. Still, it can be argued that the NIRA paved the way for subsequent reforms by getting business, unions, and the general populace used to the idea of government intervention in the economy on behalf of labor. This made the road easier to follow when the New Deal turned to policies based on the regulation of business such as the NLRA and the FLSA that compelled business to behave "fairly" with regard to its treatment of unions and the minimum wage it paid workers. The New Deal also used the taxation power of the federal government to provide workers with unemployment insurance and old-age pensions under the SSA. These programs would enable the New Deal to pursue its goal of a living wage. They were similar to the obligations of the government for pursuing a living wage that Ryan had called for in 1906 and we will see in Chapter 7 that Ryan approved of them.

Notes

1. Nation's Business, 1932, pp. 29–32.
2. Domhoff and Webber, 2011, p. 2450.
3. Mitchell, 1947, pp. 240–41.
4. Nordlund, 1997, p. 8.
5. Roosevelt, 1932b.
6. Ryan, 1932.
7. Roosevelt, 1933b, p. 1.
8. Roosevelt, 1933c, pp. 118–26.
9. Roosevelt, 1933c, pp. 131–141.
10. Roosevelt, 1933d, pp. 12 and 17.
11. Roosevelt, 1933f.
12. Filene, 1923, p. 412.
13. Roosevelt, 1933h, pp. 239–41.
14. Roosevelt, 1933h, pp. 278–80.
15. Roosevelt, 1933e, p. 1.
16. National Recovery Administration, 1933.
17. Roosevelt, 1933f.
18. Roosevelt, 1933k.
19. Roosevelt, 1933g.
20. Roosevelt, 1933i.
21. Roosevelt, 1935b.
22. Roosevelt, 1933j.
23. Roosevelt, 1933a.
24. Ryan, 1906, p. 261.
25. Kaufman, 2012; Barber, 1996.
26. Cates, 1934, p. 150.
27. Cates, 1934, pp. 137–38.
28. Johnson, 1935, pp. 6–7.
29. Johnson, 1935, p.72.
30. Roosevelt, 1934b.
31. Roosevelt, 1933f and 1933g.
32. Rosenman, 1952, p. 11.
33. Ohl, 1985, p. 195.
34. Lewishon, 1923, p. 219.
35. Roosevelt, 1939.
36. Cohen, 2009, p. 242.
37. Perkins, 1934a, pp. 144, 147 and 184.
38. Wilson, 1919.
39. Roosevelt, 1933g.
40. Schechter, 1935.

41. Clark, 1934a.
42. Clark, 1934a, pp. 121–23.
43. Clark, 1934a, p. 131.
44. Clark, 1934b, pp. 20–21.
45. Clark, 1934b, pp. 23–24.
46. Clark, 1939, p.484.
47. Clark, 1939, pp.427–440.
48. Clark, 1939, p.489.
49. Clark, 1957.
50. Frey, 1933, p. 584.
51. Green, 1933a, p. 565–66.
52. Green, 1933b, p. 569.
53. *American Federationist*, 1933a, p. 629 and 631.
54. *American Federationist*, 1933b, p. 681–3.
55. *American Federationist*, 1933c, pp. 699–70.
56. Green, 1933c, p. 802.
57. *American Federationist*, 1934, pp. 268–78.
58. Green, 1934a, 1289 and 1291.
59. *United Mine Workers Journal*, 1933a, p. 3.
60. *United Mine Workers Journal*, 1933b, p. 3.
61. *United Mine Workers Journal*, 1933c, p. 7.
62. *United Mine Workers Journal*, 1933d, p. 10.
63. *United Mine Workers Journal*, 1934a, pp. 10–11.
64. *United Mine Workers Journal*, 1934b, p. 3.
65. *United Mine Workers Journal*, 1934c, p. 4.
66. Brinkley, 1983, pp. 2550–2562.
67. Coughlin, 1934.
68. Coughlin, 1934.
69. Coughlin, 1934.
70. Coughlin, 1934.
71. Coughlin, 1935.
72. Coughlin, 1936.
73. Brinkley, 1983, pp. 3118–4057.
74. Douglas, 1957 [1934], pp. 17–97.
75. Douglas, 1957 [1934], p. 67.
76. Douglas, 1957 [1934], pp. 69–71.
77. Douglas, 1957 [1934], pp. 77–79.
78. Rutherford, 2011, p. 79.
79. Douglas, 1957 [1934], p. 92.
80. Tugwell, 1927, p. 234.
81. Tugwell, 1927, p.224.
82. Tugwell, 1933, p. 176.

83. Tugwell, 1933, p. 182.
84. Tugwell, 1933, p. 183.
85. Tugwell and Hill, 1934, p. 36.
86. Tugwell and Hill, 1934, p. 42.
87. Tugwell and Hill, 1934, p. 80.
88. Tugwell and Hill, 1934, p. 36.
89. Tugwell and Hill, 1934, p. 383.
90. Tugwell and Hill, 1934, p. 385.
91. Tugwell and Hill, 1934, pp. 536–7.
92. Tugwell and Hill, 1934, pp. 538–39.
93. Tugwell and Hill, 1934, p. 541.
94. Tugwell, 1977, p. 270.
95. Ryan, 1934, p, 4.
96. Ryan, 1934, p. 10.
97. Ryan, 1934, p. 15.
98. Domhoff and Webber, 2011, pp. 2490.
99. Swope, 1934.
100. Ely, 1935.
101. Perkins, 1935a.
102. Roosevelt, 1935c.
103. Wagner, 1935c.
104. Ryan, 1935a, pp. 63–64.
105. Ryan, 1935a, p. 95.
106. Ryan, 1935a, p. 91.
107. Ryan, 1935a, pp. 91.
108. Ryan, 1935a, pp. 179–81.
109. Ryan, 1945, p. 298.
110. Lyon et al., 1935.
111. Lyon et al., 1935, p.3.
112. Lyon et al., 1935, pp.20–21.
113. Lyon et al., 1935, p.303.
114. Lyon et al., 1935, p.343.
115. Lyon et al., 1935, p. 364.
116. Lyon et al., 1935, p.415.
117. Lyon et al., 1935, p.758 from Roosevelt, 1933f.
118. Lyon et al., 1935, p.779.
119. Lyon et al., 1935, p.785.
120. Lyon et al., 1935, p.788.
121. Lyon et al., 1935, p.808.
122. Ezekiel, 1936, p. 3.
123. Ezekiel, 1936, pp. 10–11, from Roosevelt, 1935d.
124. Ezekiel, 1936, p. 11.

125. Ezekiel, 1936, p. 32.
126. Ezekiel, 1936, p. 35.
127. Ezekiel, 1936, p. 296.
128. Ezekiel, 1936, pp. 276–280.
129. Ezekiel, 1936, p. 287.
130. Roos, 1937, pp. 154–5.
131. Roos, 1937, pp. 172–5.
132. Roos, 1937, p. 193.
133. Mitchell, 1947, p. 255.
134. Barber, 1996, pp. 39 and 57.
135. Ryan, 1916, p. 165.
136. Stabile and Kozak, 2012, pp. 137–165.
137. *Nation's Business*, 1933, pp. 13–14.
138. Edwards, 1933, p. 13.
139. Edwards, 1933, p. 13.
140. Edwards, 1933, pp. 13–15.
141. Mitchell, 1947, p. 284.
142. Rayback, 1966, p. 332.
143. Lippmann, 1937, p. 27.
144. Rosenman, 1952, pp. 163–4.

CHAPTER 4

A Useful and Remunerative Job: The National Labor Relations Act

Throughout the history of political economy theorists from Adam Smith and John Stuart Mill to Alfred Marshall and John Bates Clark had argued that bargaining power in labor markets was clearly on the side of business (see Chapter 1). As a result, they went on, unions were essential to redress this imbalance. In the USA, as we have seen in previous chapters, unions had argued that they were an instrument to securing a living wage for workers. Progressive politicians and intellectuals in the USA accepted this argument. John Ryan, for example, made unions and collective bargaining a part of the policies he advocated in support of a living wage, and the NWLB had implemented those policies during World War I. In the early days of the New Deal, the NIRA had included the ideal that fair wages would be part of any industry codes developed to plan an industry and Section 7A of the NIRA aimed at fostering collective bargaining by unions to achieve those fair wages.

With the end of the NIRA and its experiment with industry planning through the writing of codes that included fair wages, the leaders of the New Deal had to develop other strategies for labor. An obvious one was to bolster the ability of workers to form unions. This strategy had been part of the NWLB and the NIRA, and it became a hallmark of the New Deal that remains with us today. The NLRA was a first step in a movement from the more or less voluntary cooperation of the NIRA to government regulation of business. This chapter will examine the NLRA with its aim

D. Stabile, *The Political Economy of a Living Wage*,
DOI 10.1007/978-3-319-32473-9_4

of establishing collective bargaining as a way to provide workers a useful and remunerative job, a key element of a living wage. It will investigate the extent to which a living wage influenced the NLRA, including in the debates in the Congress and will uncover an argument that collective bargaining was the best way to attain a living wage. It will also review business criticisms of the NLRA to highlight how those criticisms overlooked the living wage elements of the NLRA.

The AFL Favors the NLRA

We saw in Chapter 3 that the AFL saw a great opportunity for unions in the NIRA under Section 7A, but they came to see that the law needed to be strengthened. In March 1935, the *American Federationist* in an article, "The National Labor Relations Bill (Wagner Bill)," discussed one of the efforts being made to strengthen the NIRA. The article indicated that union experience under the NIRA convinced them that Section 7A had to be reinforced by the addition of "an independent National Labor Relations Board … with power to enforce its decisions." It was also necessary to outlaw company unions. The Wagner Bill would take these two important steps. Just as important, the Wagner Bill contained language that the AFL approved of, such as its statement of a goal "to promote equality of bargaining power between employers and employees." The article also liked the Bill's goal of providing "for the general welfare by encouraging the practice of collective bargaining."[1] The NLRA would be the beginning of a new approach of Industrial Democracy for unions, which is why the *United Mine Workers Journal* on June 1, 1935, gave the following headline to a summarization of the provisions of the Act: "Passage of Wagner Bill is Great Victory for Workers."[2]

The support for the NLRA from the AFL and its unions should not surprise us. It is a bit surprising more was not written about the NLRA in union publications. Samuel Gompers, however, had warned unions to be wary of government programs to help unions that could readily be reversed and the AFL's experience of enthusiasm and then disillusion with the NIRA may have reminded unionists to curb their enthusiasm. More important, there was enough enthusiasm for the NLRA among supporters of the New Deal.

Robert Wagner Explains the NLRA

As a staunch New Dealer, Senator Robert F. Wagner (1877–1953), Democrat of New York, introduced many of the key reform laws enacted during the 1930s. On February 21, 1935, he gave a speech indicating the need for the NLRA, which was also known as the Wagner Act. Wagner began the speech by pointing out that the New Deal recovery program under the NIRA had been intended to give business and labor the freedom to work together in the struggle to end the Great Depression. The NIRA had exempted business from antitrust laws to allow it to avoid the competition of "the price cutters and wage reducers." To maintain the principle of "equal treatment upon which a just democratic society must rest," the NIRA had granted workers the ability to act cooperatively under union leadership as provided by Section 7A. But the NIRA had not worked out as the Congress had intended. Business had used the NIRA wrongly and "the trade association movement has blanketed the entire country," while it had rebuffed workers who wanted to organize unions under Section 7A. The National Labor Board of the NRA had tried to swing the balance back toward workers but did not have sufficient power to enforce its decisions.[3] Wagner would know. He was chair of the National Labor Board.

As a result, the USA had faced a period of strikes that had not helped business, labor, or the economy. Moreover, because workers were not able to form unions when they wanted to, they could not "participate in our national endeavor to coordinate production and purchasing power," that is, the writing of industry codes under the NIRA. As a result, profits were outstripping wages.[4] To equalize the power between business and labor, Wagner proposed a new national labor relations bill, which he indicated was simply enacting a principle of workers' rights to organize that was generally accepted by the Congress.

In presenting the bill, Wagner argued, "It seeks merely to make the worker a free man in the economic as well as the political field."[5] To do so, the bill would also establish the National Labor Relations Board (NLRB). Wagner defended the NLRB from charges that it "would be invested with arbitrary or dictatorial or even unusual powers." He noted that its powers had been modeled on other government agencies such as the Federal Trade Commission. Like them, its decisions would be enforced by federal courts, with "every affected party entitled to all the safeguards of appeal."[6] As a result, he concluded, the bill, if enacted, would make the legal status of industrial relations much clearer, help to avoid industrial strife, and "improve business by laying the foundations for the amity and fair dealing upon which permanent progress must rest."[7]

We can see elements of the rights-based approach to social justice throughout Wagner's speech. He continually used fairness as the justification for the bill he was then proposing. Indeed, his argument was that the bill would "make the worker a free man in the economic as well as the political field."[8] As Lawrence B. Glickman has described, Gompers had always linked high wages to economic freedom in his advocacy of a living wage.[9] As noted in Chapter 1, Walter Lippmann called for an Industrial Democracy "where every adult is sufficiently insured for the primary needs of life so that he is capable of making some kind of free contract with other men,"[10] and Wagner would have agreed. We might also recall from Chapter 3 that Wagner called Ryan "the respected and outstanding authority on our economic problems."[11] New Dealers such as Wagner agreed with him that business had bargaining power over workers and used it to pay wages below a living wage—a condition that was manifestly unfair from their perspective.

Congress, the NLRA, and a Living Wage

As we might expect, any law as new, complicated, and controversial as the NLRA would experience full scrutiny in the Congress during 1935. The legislative history of the NLRA that was subsequently published by the NLRB in 1949 contained over 1000 pages of hearings, tables, and statements read into the record. The idea of a living wage came up in five different places in those pages. Although there was nothing new said about the living wage in those places, what was said is consistent with my theme that the living wage was an influence on the New Deal program.

The first person we encounter in the NLRA debates to use the term a living wage, Frank P. Walsh, was well known in the Progressive circles for support of a living wage. He was a lawyer and advocate for labor who had served as a co-chair of the NWLB during World War I (see Chapter 2). He began his comments by stating that the NLRA was the "greatest step forward in industrial democracy that has ever been taken."[12] This statement was in line with the Progressives' attitude toward labor that had started during the war. From that context, Walsh cited the experience of the NWLB as indicative of what an Industrial Democracy could accomplish. During the war, efforts to expand production led to the discovery that "conditions in certain industries were at such a low ebb that the men were not getting a living wage."[13] In a paradigm shift, the government and labor unions had remedied those conditions in a precursor of the type of Industrial Democracy that the NLRA was bringing about.

A second witness with a living wage leaning was Louis B. Ward (1891–1941), an attorney from Detroit. In 1933, he had written a biography of Father Charles Coughlin, noted in Chapter 2 as a one-time supporter of the New Deal, a living wage, and social justice. Ward spoke of the need to have the government take a larger role in industrial relations. Specifically, he wanted to amend the NLRA to have the government take the lead in organizing unions; once a union was organized and on its feet it could continue to function on its own. Organized labor was needed, he argued, because he wanted unions "to reach back to the principles of social justice with a living wage as a fundamental principle. This cannot be accomplished without organization."[14] By stating the case this way, Ward was reflecting the hopes that had been expressed regarding the NIRA, where business and labor would organize under an industry code and secure a living wage for workers and reasonable profits for business.

The same sentiment was expressed by Jacob F. Madden (1887–1960), Representative of Employees, Weirton Steel Co. As had many businesses at the time, Weirton Steel had organized its workers into a company union; the NLRA would ban them when it was enacted. Madden opposed the NLRA, in part because of the increased taxes its operations would entail. He argued, "The working class of people in this country does not want any more legislation to put more taxes on our backs. What we want is more dollars so that we can live like human beings." To be sure, the Weirton Steel Co. had sustained operations during the Depression and its employees had kept their jobs. Still, he added, "our wages were far from a living wage." The NLRA would not accomplish that goal of a living wage. Ward continued, "You can pass laws to compel the manufacturers to sign an agreement with organized labor...but you can never satisfy the masses of working men until they are paid a good living wage for their labor."[15] Unions collected dues from their members, which would take away from the potential for a living wage and workers did not want to be forced to join them. Since the NRA under the NIRA Codes had been setting wage standards for labor without the need for union dues, the NIRA represented a better option for workers than the NLRA.

The role of the NRA in securing a living wage was also a part of a statement made by Congressman Terry Carpenter (1900–1978), Democrat from Nebraska. He observed that aside from workers, everyone in the

USA had long held that wages set by the competitive market "were always just and fair." He disagreed, insisting that "remuneration must be sufficient to support the worker in reasonable and frugal comfort," that is, it must be a living wage. To be sure, many persons in the USA had given "at least lip service to the principle of the living wage." Under the New Deal, however, "It is the principle embodied in the NRA. No business whose existence depends on paying less than living wages to its workers has any right to exist in this country."[16]

At this point, Carpenter was reading into the record from President Roosevelt's statement on the NIRA[17] as described in Chapter 3. He added that if the living wage principle had been adhered to in the USA, the Great Depression might have been avoided. It had been caused by a lack of purchasing power due to workers not earning a living wage. Consequently, he concluded, "a living wage is not only ethically right but wise economically."[18] The best way to enable workers to attain a living wage was through the encouragement of unions, much as the NLRA would do. Carpenter was seconded in this view by Congressman William Connery (1888–1937), Democrat from Massachusetts, who believed strongly that only real unions, not company unions, would fight for a living wage.[19]

These few comments about the living wage must certainly be considered as a small part of the many pages included in the legislative history of the NLRA. It is doubtful that they influenced the outcome in terms of the vote on the Act, which passed the Senate by a 63 to 12 vote on May 16, 1935, and by an unrecorded vote in the House a month later. The more important influences in its passage were that Roosevelt finally came around to supporting it after holding out because he preferred the collective bargaining provisions of the NIRA. That preference was moot following nullification of the NIRA by the Supreme Court, on May 27, 1935. [20] Still, these comments indicate that the living wage was included on the agenda among New Dealers. Other members of the New Deal coalition certainly had the living wage in mind when they talked about the economic security unions would bring to workers.

Emil Rieve and Labor's Demands from Government

Emil Rieve (1892–1975) was a long-time leader of unions related to the textile industry. In 1935, when he published an article, "What Labor Demands of Government," in the *Annals of the American Academy of Political and Social Science*, he was president of the American Federation of Hosiery Workers, an affiliate of the AFL. When the newly formed Congress of Industrial Organizations (CIO) began organizing workers into the Textile Workers Union of America, he joined with them and served as the president of the new union for over two decades.

At the time Rieve was writing, Wagner was in the process of pushing for Congressional approval of what eventually was enacted as the NLRA. To Rieve, it appeared that "every one agrees that labor's right to organize must be protected." Still, he felt that while the Roosevelt Administration was on the side of labor, it was losing the initiative in the propaganda war with business over labor policy. He made it clear, moreover, "The American wage earners are for the New Deal." But labor was concerned that the Administration's labor policy under the NIRA had aroused "a real feeling of discontent" among workers "as a result of the slow and feeble workings of the Labor Boards." Promises of "justice" for workers were not good enough. Workers who might be fired for union membership needed "immediate redress" to keep their faith in the Administration's labor policies from being "completely shattered."[21] Management's power over labor was much stronger than the Roosevelt Administration recognized. Rieve added, "Economic justice cannot be assured workers by society until the worker is able to secure economic power through organization as potent as that which the employer group has had in the past."[22]

Economic justice in the form of a living wage for labor was not possible until unions were strong enough to counter the power of business. Unions had experienced what they saw as business' capture of the NIRA and a reduction in their chances for getting a living wage. Rieve worried that the same might happen with the NLRA. Still, support for collective bargaining as a means for attaining a living wage was a long-held position of union leaders and if the NLRA truly increased their ability to bargain with business over wages, the AFL was for it.

The Details of the NLRA

Selig Perlman (1888–1959), the preeminent historian of labor and unions during the period of the New Deal, argued that throughout history collective bargaining had been a way for workers to gain "more welfare, security, and liberty."[23] During that time, he found that governments first tried to suppress unions, then had entered a stage of grudging toleration for them. At the beginning of the twentieth century, government began a stage of benevolent toleration which removed many of the criminal sanctions against unions. The latest stage was government promotion of unions, which, Perlman wrote, "arrived with the New Deal."[24]

The New Deal promotion of unions aimed to change the balance where equal treatment of two parties of unequal strength tilted power toward the stronger party, that is, employers. The NIRA had included Section 7A, which had strengthened workers' ability to form unions. Just as the Supreme Court declared the NIRA unconstitutional in May 1935, the Congress was enacting the NLRA to address the shortcomings in Section 7A of the NIRA. The new law set up specific procedures for elections to recognize that workers wanted to form a union, establish penalties for businesses that did not follow the election procedures or that committed a set of unfair labor practices, and require that businesses bargain in good faith with duly elected unions in a system of collective bargaining. The NLRA also set up the NLRB to oversee that the procedures of the law were followed by business and labor and to take legal action where the procedures were not followed.

In this way, the advocates for the use of collective bargaining as a vehicle for attaining a living wage got what they wanted—a national labor policy.

When the NLRA was made a federal law, many observers, especially in the business community, anticipated that the US Supreme Court would determine that it was unconstitutional. In a series of cases brought before the Court immediately after the NLRA went into effect, however, a narrow majority of the justices (usually 5-4) upheld the Act. The most important decision was in the case of *National Labor Relations Board v. Jones & Laughlin Steel Corporation* announced on April 12, 1937. In reaching its decision, the majority relied on what had become a generally accepted belief, labor's unequal bargaining power compared to business. The decision indicated that the Court had long held that unions "were organized out of the necessities of the situation; that a single employee was helpless in dealing with an employer; ... that union was essential to give laborers opportunity to deal on an equality with their employer."[25]

While I am tempted to place the Court among our proponents of fairness and a living wage, we must remember that its recognition of the need for labor to organize unions to take collective action when bargaining with management was common to advocates of the market economy. The foremost exponent of the market economy, Adam Smith, worried about the same unequal bargaining power, noting, "Whenever the legislature attempts to regulate the differences between masters and their workmen, its counsellors are always the masters" with the result that "masters are always and every where in a sort of tacit, but constant and uniform combination, not to raise the wages of labour." As a result, he added, that when the regulation helped workers, "it is always just and equitable."[26] As the Court saw it, the Congress had enacted the NLRA, perhaps with labor as its counselors, although it was more likely to have been industrial relations experts, in an effort to make bargaining between management and labor equal. Following Smith, it would be "just and equitable" for unions to increase wages as part of a quest for a living wage.

Frances Perkins and a National Labor Policy

As Secretary of Labor in the Roosevelt Administration, Frances Perkins (1880–1965) held an important responsibility in developing the policy for dealing with the issues related to labor and industrial relations. Her expressed view on that policy, however, was that "labor policy in a democracy is not a program conceived by government." It was up to workers and management to create a labor policy that would serve their needs, with government serving as "a stimulating agent to facilitate the formation of such a policy, which will be just and fair to all the people and in line with human progress."[27]

The notion that a labor policy had to be "just and fair" and consistent with "human progress" suggested that Perkins was writing from the perspective of a living wage and I will explore her perspective in Chapter 6. To her, the labor policy at the time she was writing was far from this perspective, but it was developing along the lines that "a growing sense of justice make possible." Still, it was heading toward a policy that would be "realistic, flexible, practical, and based on the habits of people and the prevailing necessities of production and distribution."[28] Perkins then outlined several ways the government could facilitate this developing labor policy. It should establish standards for minimum wages, maximum hours, and healthy working conditions. It should influence workers and managers to develop an industrial relations system that eliminated strikes. It should encourage unions that would give labor status in society but which also encouraged "mutuality between labor and employers." This last facilitating role for government was especially important, because, Perkins noted, "If labor's rights are defined by law and by government, then certain obligations will of course be expected of wage earners." These expected obligations meant that labor must develop an attitude that was consistent with "all professional ethics in modern society."[29]

Under the New Deal, the federal government was doing its part to bring about the elevation of labor's status in society and put it on the road to a living wage. It had settled the issue of workers being able to join unions of their own choosing and not be compelled to become members of company unions. The NLRA established the NLRB to set up "impartial tribunals" to adjudicate alleged violations of the NLRA. And the work of the NLRB had resulted in the process whereby unions gained recognition through election, with a majority vote determining which union, if any, would represent workers, which Perkins called "a significant step in the history of American labor policy."[30]

The overall aim of the NLRA, however, according to Perkins, was to usher in an era of better industrial relations and thereby reduce the number of strikes that were such an economic waste. Through the work of the NLRB, Perkins wrote, "We should be able to look forward confidently to a fairer and more scientific handling of the relationships between employers and employees." That handling of industrial relations through the agency of the NLRB might eventually resolve the root causes of industrial conflict. Government agencies charged with carrying out labor policy, such as the NLRB, would gain more authority as time went on and "as the spirit of cooperation between employers and employees continues to grow" and both sides came to recognize that the use of government agencies as a way to avoid strikes was "in their interest and in the interest of the public as well."[31]

Perkins was speaking the language of Industrial Democracy as envisioned by the Progressives as bringing about the type of economy they had experienced during World War I. Business, government, and unions would all participate in this Industrial Democracy through the NLRA.

William Green and Organized Labor's Goals

As the president of the AFL, William Green could truly say he was the authorized spokesman for organized labor. That was especially so in 1936, before the rise to prominence of the CIO with its new breed of labor leaders. In that year, Green contributed an article "The Goals of Organized Labor" to the *Annals of the American Academy of Political and Social Science*. Green's article was part of an issue of the *Annals* on "Problems of Organized Labor."

In that article, he took a moral view of unions, stating, "the purpose of the organized labor movement is justice for the underprivileged." The bulk of the population in society, Green called them “common people,” had seldom been able to count on the legal system “to secure justice or redress injury.” Instead, they had recognized that they had to unite to achieve their goals. Unions were one way for them to unite and gain “redress of wrong at the hands of business and society.” Hence unions always endeavored “to get justice in daily living for those who work for others.”[32] By taking this moral high ground of organized labor’s goals as the pursuit of justice, Green argued that unionism was essential to fairness.

In the market economy, according to Green, labor was considered as just another component of the costs of using resources to produce a good or service. In this system, workers had to accept whatever jobs or working conditions they were offered or else go without work and starve. Organized labor wanted to end this system and replace it with a system based on mutual obligations. Green wrote, “Organized wage earners believe that employment ought to rest on a contract mutually satisfactory to the parties concerned. To arrive at a mutual contract, the parties must have equal bargaining power.”[33] At the present time, labor did not have this equal bargaining power with employers. Instead, employers opposed the concept of collective bargaining.

Green appeared optimistic that the NLRA would hasten management’s acceptance of collective bargaining. If it did, then collective bargaining would provide “methods and machinery for dealing with work problems so that there is developed the spirit and the channels for cooperation between workers and management for efficient production.” It would also serve “to develop mutual responsibility and decisions upon the basis of facts.” Moreover, the time was right for collective bargaining. Unions had fought for better pay, improved working conditions, and a shorter work week for labor. The AFL had helped to decease the work week, giving workers more time “for other interests and for participation in civic and social undertakings.” It would continue the fight, because “in 1936 we need and seek a thirty-hour week.”[34]

The need for a continually reducing work week was based on Green’s understanding of technological innovation. On his account, technological innovation during the 1920s had greatly reduced employment in a number of manufacturing industries. The 30-hour week was needed to improve employment, with an underlying goal of giving workers security through “equity in the job.” Business had a responsibility to provide continual employment for its workers. Green wrote,

> Labor performs a work essential in carrying on industries and wages should be a fixed and inescapable charge on the industry to which the workers are attached. No industry has a right to lay off a portion of production staff to be supported by society.[35]

Here Green is using the argument developed by John Maurice Clark through his concept of social overhead costs (See Chapter 2). He made it a matter of a moral right of labor and believed that it could be brought about through collective bargaining. The implication of Green's argument was that a living wage could be brought about by unions through collective bargaining.

Paul Douglas and Unions

Paul Douglas, as noted in Chapter 2, had a long interest in labor issues and a living wage. In December 1937 he published an article, "American Labor Relations Acts," in *The American Economic Review*. His goal was to describe a series of labor laws that had altered the situation where "the employed workers of this country had the legal right to seek collective bargaining by lawful means, but there was no reciprocal duty for the employers to accord it."[36]

Because of this situation, employers could refrain from recognizing unions and the unions had to rely on their economic strength to gain that recognition. New Deal legislation such as Section 7A of the NIRA, the Railway Act of 1934, and the NLRA had brought about a new era by outlawing many of the tactics business had used in its efforts to keep from recognizing unions as agents for collective bargaining by labor. The NLRA specifically made it mandatory that when a majority of workers acted collectively through a union, management had to bargain with that union. Douglas saw the law as having two objectives, a reduction in the number of recognition strikes and "to strengthen unionism as an agency for improving the conditions of workers."[37] This second objective was Douglas' unspoken recognition of the role unions could play in bringing about a living wage. We should recall from Chapter 2 that Douglas was a committed advocate for a living wage.

Despite the NLRA's favorable treatment of unions, he observed, business still had ways to combat unions and to sidestep the NLRB. To him, this indicated that unions would have to "participate actively in politics." They would have to give up the non-partisan stance that Gompers had promoted as the best course for unions. The only issue was whether their political action would take place through the formation of a labor party that rested "more solidly upon labor than do the present parties" or whether it would "take place within the framework of the present two-party system."[38]

Gompers had always cautioned unions to avoid tying themselves to one political party. Instead, unions should support whichever politicians were willing to enact laws that helped unions. On Douglas' account, unions had changed this perspective. To be sure, their support for the New Deal was in return for the aid it was giving them but it ultimately tied them to the Democrat Party.

Collective Bargaining and a Living Wage

Up to now in this chapter the relationship between the NLRA and the living wage has mainly been implicit; few of the persons I have considered so far stated this relationship directly, but their statements were consistent with the idea that by negotiating for wages through collective bargaining unions would be able to secure at least a living wage for their members. The AFL had often made this argument. In this section, I present one writer, Max Rheinstein (1899–1977), who explicitly made the link between collective bargaining and a living wage. Rheinstein was a student of the German social thinker, Max Weber, and spent part of his career as the Max Pam Professor of Comparative Law at the University of Chicago. He presented his perspective on the living wage in an article, "Methods of Wage Policy," in the June 1939 issue of *The University of Chicago Law Review*.

By wage policy, Rheinstein meant the approach any government took toward the wages that were in place under its jurisdiction. The New Deal was adopting a wage policy so an evaluation of its approach was in order. In any country where the market economy took hold, government had to decide whether to let the forces of supply and demand determine wages or whether to adopt a wage policy. On Rheinstein's account, there were economic theories that argued that because of an abundance of unskilled labor, wages "will never rise above the minimum necessary for subsistence and physical reproduction." There was no need to justify that theory because most economic studies showed that even though "the standard of living of the majority of the working class had been rising during the last one hundred and fifty years," wages were still too low.[39] Governments had two options to addressing this problem, promotion of collective bargaining or setting up a legal minimum wage.

The New Deal was promoting collective bargaining through the NLRA. Rheinstein approved of this approach to securing a living wage. He wrote, "When labor is strong enough to compel employers to bargain collectively, it will, normally, also be strong enough to obtain terms at the level of a decent living wage." That wage, however, would not be higher than that paid by the most efficient firms in an industry. In this way, collective bargaining would get wages to the right level. It would eliminate sweatshop wages without having wages undermine the profitability of business. The advantage of this approach to Rheinstein was that it would take place without the ambiguity of "the systems of immediate governmental wage fixing," which left "the determination of the minimum wage to administration or judicial arbitrariness or guesswork as to what constitutes a 'fair' wage in a given industry."[40] This outcome would be consistent with Roosevelt's goal of "reasonable profits for business and a living wage for workers."[41] To be sure, Rheinstein added, the wages set by collective bargaining might have the result that "weaker firms are eliminated."[42] But that result was also consistent with Roosevelt's view that "any firm that cannot pay a living wage in this country should not be allowed to exist."[43]

Rheinstein represents a culmination among the Progressive intellectuals of the idea that unions and collective bargaining could bring about a living wage for union members, an idea that had long been present among union leaders. While I have reviewed others in this chapter who implicitly believed that the NLRA and collective bargaining were adequate to bring about a living wage, he stated this belief directly. This belief was not widespread in the business community, where opposition to the NLRA was stronger than it was to the other reforms I cover in this book. I now turn to those opponents and the criticisms they made against the NLRA.

Business Criticizes the NLRA

By the 1930s, collegiate business programs had grown in number and size and offered a place for professors who had an interest in scholarly research about business and who identified with the problems business faced, such as with the NLRA. One example of this research was a book by William H. Spencer, professor of business law and dean of the business school at the University of Chicago. Spencer called his study, *The National Labor*

Relations Act: Its Scope, Purposes and Implications. His starting point was with the assumptions underlying the NLRA. The most prominent one was the inequality of bargaining power between management and labor. Spencer agreed that employers had advantages in bargaining with individual workers. The federal government had in the past aided management in gaining this advantage and some businesses had gone too far by exploiting their workers. Still, Spencer argued, remedial action by the government to help labor should not go to the point of putting "all employers under the yoke of collective bargaining because some employers took advantage of the necessities of their employees."[44]

Another important assumption implicit in the NLRA and related to the first one was that "we are in a collectivist era." Since business was organized into large collections of capital, New Deal legislators believed that labor must be supported in its efforts to organize and "the possibility of returning to a regime of competition is remote, if not entirely out of the question." Spencer, however, thought it "premature to assume that we have come to the end of a competitive regime."[45] The market economy was not quite dead and there was no need to rush into an economy of collective action.

For the rest of the book, Spencer subjected the NLRA to a searching examination as to what many of its provisions meant. For example, the NLRA prohibited lockouts where a business closed down to preempt a strike as being an unfair labor practice. He worried how far the NLRB would go to support this provision. Could an employer close down operations to keep striking workers from damaging a factory? If management moved the factory to another location to avoid a union organization drive would that constitute an unfair labor practice? To what extent could management respond to misinformation being disseminated by union organizers without being guilty of an unfair labor practice? These were some of the many issues the NLRB would have to grapple with, and from Spencer's analysis of the NRA Labor Board's handling of them, business was in for a rough time. In the case of workers being fired for union organizing activities, the NRA Labor Board had shifted the burden of proof from the worker to the management and he feared the NLRB would do the same.[46]

Spencer's analysis, however, missed the point about the living wage movement. Ryan had argued that profits, dividends, and interest were "subordinate to the laborer's right to a Living Wage"[47] and New Dealers at the NRA had agreed with him (See Chapter 3). The NLRA followed this argument at least far enough to want to place the rights of workers on par with the rights of capital.

Neglect of this argument about the need to place a living wage above the rights of property was common in business circles. In June 1938, *Nation's Business* looked closely at the NLRA by presenting a discussion on "Needs in the Field of Labor" that had taken place at a US Chamber of Commerce convention. The goal of the discussion was to consider what could be done about "the unworkable National Labor Relations (Wagner) Act." The overriding concern of the discussants was the "bias and prejudice" of the NLRB "against employers, against unorganized workers and against certain unions as against favored unions."[48] One discussant, William S. Knudsen of General Motors, stated his concerns bluntly:

> The largest drawback to good industrial relations is, of course, the Wagner Act. The National Labor Relations Board makes no pretense of even paying any attention to the employer's side of the case. He can be heard only when he is summoned and he knows before he goes there that there is no record of a single decision where he had a ghost-of-a-show.[49]

Knudsen counseled his fellow executives to maintain their good tempers and keep working to have the NLRA modified in ways that would be more fruitful to business.

Knudsen also reported on the recent sit-down strikes that had taken place at General Motors, where workers had unlawfully seized the company's plants to force it to bargain with them and neither the local nor the federal government had prosecuted the workers. He referred to the strike as "mob hysteria employed by the C.I.O." and "fed by vacillation at Washington." Public opinion was against the strike, he added. Knudsen then related how he had been called to testify before a Senate Committee and "mildly castigated for having laid people off" when General Motors had a surplus of $400 million. He defended the company by explaining that not all of that surplus was cash and that General Motors "had more motor cars than the public would buy." To be sure, the company regretted having to make the difficult decision to lay workers off, but it had no alternative.[50]

The tone of these discussions indicated that business leaders believed that government officials and politicians did not understand the type of decisions businesses had to make and why they made them. A system of economic security where everyone was taken care of might seem feasible in the rarefied air of Washington, but it did not work on the ground in Detroit where the rules of the market economy held sway.

We can see this tone when, in 1939, Orme W. Phelps and John E. Jeuck compiled a survey of the criticisms business made of the NLRA in an article in *The Journal of Business of the University of Chicago*. From their perspective, the NLRA had brought about more criticism than any other act of labor legislation in the USA. Management specifically objected to the basic premise of the NLRA that there was a "conflict of interests as between management and labor." That was the union position, but the government should not base public policy on a special interest group such as unions were. Business also questioned a second assumption of the NLRA that "union development under government patronage" would eliminate strikes. Rather, unions would increase the number of strikes. Phelps and Jeuck indicated, however, that many strikes were for union recognition and the NLRA should surely eliminate them.[51]

A more trenchant criticism from business, according to Phelps and Jeuck, was that the NLRA did not provide for management to lodge complaints with the NLRB regarding unfair practices by union members. This deficiency made the law one-sided and pro-union. To be sure, Phelps and Jeuck added, management might abuse the ability to lodge complaints and use it to oppose unions. But they had confidence that the NLRB would investigate the complaints and discover cases where management took advantage of their ability to complain about unfair tactics to the detriment of union organizing campaigns. This same approach would hold with respect to another business complaint, that the NLRA provided safeguards against "employer coercion" but contained "no penalties for the excesses of labor organizations." Phelps and Jeuck indicated that the problem was that "persuasion must be distinguished from coercion," which was not an easy task for the NLRB. Still, they thought that an addition to the NLRA that put limits on what unions could do "would exert some moral force on labor leaders."[52] Phelps and Jeuck's statement that labor leaders needed to have a "moral force" imposed on them indicated that they had not accepted arguments such as given by Rieve and Green (see above) that labor unions were a moral force that could lead to a fairer economy.

As noted earlier, this business criticism of the NLRA missed the point about the living wage movement. Its position, as stated by Ryan, was that labor's right to a living wage trumped a business' rights to manage its operations as it saw fit. The purpose of the NLRA from this perspective was to clarify and codify those rights of labor as they pertained to the formation of unions as a vehicle for securing a living wage.

Conclusion

Part of the Progressive vision captured in the NLRA was to address the imbalance of bargaining power between management and labor. The road to economic security was through strengthening labor's ability to bargain for a living wage by way of fostering a more favorable union environment. Emil Rieve and William Green, two labor leaders of the time, viewed the NLRA as a means for bringing "justice for the underprivileged."[53] Robert Wagner, a political force whose name is often associated with the NLRA, viewed the NLRA as a means for "making the worker a free man in the economic as well as the political field."[54]

Roosevelt seconded these statements about what the New Deal was accomplishing. In his Labor Day address on September 6, 1936, he outlined that one of his goals was

> To achieve and maintain a national economy whose factors are so finely balanced that the worker is always sure of a job which will guarantee a living wage. By a living wage I mean a wage which will insure the worker and the worker's dependents a living in accordance with American standards of decency, happiness and self-respect. The wage earners of America do not ask for more. They will not be satisfied with less.[55]

He repeated this goal in his next Labor Day message on September 5, 1937, referring to "the urgent need to insure all able-bodied working men and women a living wage for a fair day's work."[56] By equalizing the balance of power between business and labor, the NLRA was part of the plan for a balanced economy that produced a living wage and social justice.

Inherent in these calls for justice for labor was the idea that justice included a living wage. Whereas most proponents of collective bargaining by unions, as sanctioned by the NLRA, assumed that a living wage would be the result of their policy, Rheinstein made that assumption clear. Unions and collective bargaining were a path to a living wage and a living wage took precedence over managerial prerogatives. As a result, there was a real sense that the NLRA with its legitimization of collective action on the part of labor was inevitable and a concrete sign that the nation under the New Deal was on its way to establishing economic security through a living wage.

In 1942, two union advocates, Clinton S. Golden (1888–1961) and Harold J. Ruttenberg (1914–1998), looked at the relationship between the NLRA and Industrial Democracy in their book, *The Dynamics of Industrial Democracy*. Golden and Ruttenberg believed that the USA was "on the threshold of a new era in industrial relations" where management and labor would "work together as a unit."[57] In 1947, however, a Congress controlled by the Republican Party with bipartisan support from southern Democrats amended the NLRA through the Taft–Hartley Act which added a group of unfair labor practices by unions to US labor law. The changes were one of the few cases where New Deal legislation was reversed in a way that reduced the chances for workers to get a living wage.

Unions grew to about 30 percent of the labor force in the USA by the mid-1950s. Since then they have been in decline with membership now at about 10 percent of the private workforce. It is arguable, however, whether the Taft–Hartley Act was a significant factor in the decline of unions that began a decade after it was enacted. Changes in the structure of the economy such as the transition from a base in manufacturing to a growing service sector and increased global trade created difficulties for unions in terms of their gaining new members. Technological innovation contributed to this transition. The result was a bifurcated economy captured in the dual labor market theory that became popular among labor economists in the 1970s. Under that theory, the economy divided into a primary sector with large corporations and unions agreeing on high wages and a secondary sector of smaller, non-unionized firms and low wages. The result was an economy that Ryan had worried about with some union workers receiving more than a living wage while other workers got less than a living wage. As the primary sector declined as a percentage of the economy, union membership also fell to the point where presence of unions in the primary sector became very small. As a result, the median real wages for workers entered a long decline. The New Deal policy of using unions and collective bargaining as a means for achieving a living wage proved unsustainable.

Notes

1. *American Federationist*, 1935b, p. 263.
2. *United Mine Workers Journal*, 1935, p. 5.
3. Wagner, 1935a, p. 2371.

4. Wagner, 1935a, p. 2371.
5. Wagner, 1935a, p. 2371.
6. Wagner, 1935a, p. 2372.
7. Wagner, 1935a, p. 2372.
8. Wagner, 1935a, p. 2371.
9. Glickman, 1997, p. 4.
10. Goodwin, 2014, p. 205.
11. Wagner, 1935c.
12. NLRB, 1949, p. 190.
13. NLRB, 1949, p. 192.
14. NLRB, 1949, p. 491.
15. NLRB, 1949, p. 908.
16. NLRB, 1949, p. 1146.
17. Roosevelt, 1933f.
18. NLRB, 1949, p. 1149.
19. NLRB, 1949, p. 1152.
20. Domhoff and Webber, 2011, pp. 2952–2959 and 3030–3034.
21. Rieve, 1935, p. 124.
22. Rieve, 1935, p. 128.
23. Perlman, 1936, p. 154.
24. Perlman, 1936, p. 158.
25. Supreme Court, 1937b, p. 55.
26. Smith, 1976 [1776], vol. I., pp. 74–6.
27. Perkins, 1936, p. 1.
28. Perkins, 1936, p. 1.
29. Perkins, 1936, p. 1.
30. Perkins, 1936, p. 2.
31. Perkins, 1936, p. 3.
32. Green, 1936, p. 147.
33. Green, 1936, p. 148.
34. Green, 1936, pp. 149–50.
35. Green, 1936, p. 151.
36. Douglas, 1937, p. 735.
37. Douglas, 1937, p. 741.
38. Douglas, 1937, pp. 760–61.
39. Rheinstein, 1939, p. 554.
40. Rheinstein, 1939, p. 575.
41. Roosevelt, 1933g.
42. Rheinstein, 1939, p. 575.
43. Roosevelt, 1933f.
44. Spencer, 1935, pp. 3–4.
45. Spencer, 1935, pp. 3–5.

46. Spencer, 1935, pp. 9, 12 and 25.
47. Ryan, 1906, p. 261.
48. *Nation's Business*, 1938, p. 37.
49. *Nation's Business*, 1938, p. 38.
50. *Nation's Business*, 1938, p. 38.
51. Phelps and Jeuck, 1939, pp. 31–2.
52. Phelps and Jeuck, 1939, pp. 32–33.
53. Green, 1936, p. 147.
54. Wagner, 1935a, p. 2371.
55. Roosevelt, 1936c.
56. Roosevelt, 1937b.
57. Golden and Ruttenberg, 1942, p. xxi.

CHAPTER 5

Social Security: Protection from Poverty in Old Age and Unemployment

The goal of economic security through a living wage is only attainable in an affluent society. The Great Depression of the 1930s saw a significant reduction in affluence in the USA, however, and providing economic security through social insurance for all members of the USA in the midst of it would be a daunting challenge. In addition, the provision of social insurance by the federal government was something new. There had been programs for pensions for the elderly and for unemployment insurance in a small number of the US states, but they provided a limited amount of data on which to base a new, national program of social insurance.

Instead, the leaders in the movement for social insurance relied on the European experience for guidance; two of them, Barbara Armstrong and Abraham Epstein (see below) provided histories of the European social insurance systems in their books advocating for social insurance in the USA. The systems provided by France, Germany, and Great Britain, as well as in the rest of Europe, however, had an uneven development. There were differences in the compulsory aspects of the coverage as well as who was covered and who would pay and how. Germany started off with compulsory health insurance in 1883 and workers' compensation in 1884. In the UK, workers' compensation began in 1880 and health insurance in 1911. France initiated voluntary unemployment insurance in 1905, but delayed compulsory health insurance until 1930. Pensions were added in Germany in 1889, with the cost being shared by workers, employers,

D. Stabile, *The Political Economy of a Living Wage*,
DOI 10.1007/978-3-319-32473-9_5

and the government. In most of Europe, social insurance was subsidized by the general tax revenue. The system implemented in the USA would use approaches similar to Europe, but with provisions that would also be unique.[1]

In this chapter, we will look at two New Deal programs that used the tax system to fund unemployment insurance and old-age pensions as part of a program dubbed "social security." They were part of a large plan set forth in the SSA of 1935. My focus in the first part of this chapter will be on the views of the supporters of the SSA; the second part will deal with its critics. In both parts, the discussion will revolve around a living wage. To be sure, these two elements of the SSA—unemployment insurance and old-age pensions —were also a part of the New Deal program to increase purchasing power and I will touch on that aspect of the SSA. Still, my interest is in telling the story of a living wage and that will be the main focus of this chapter.

Armstrong, Social Insurance, and a Living Wage

As indicated in Chapter 2, Barbara Armstrong focused on social insurance and the minimum wage as essential to a living wage program. In this chapter, I will present her views on two elements of social insurance, pensions and unemployment insurance. She also included workers' compensation insurance for accidents and health insurance for sickness as part of her program, but the former had been put in place in many states of the USA when she wrote and the latter did not become part of the New Deal agenda.

Pensions were an essential element to a living wage program, because nearly every worker reached an age where work was no longer possible. For some workers that age may come earlier than the typical retirement age, due to a disability. Others might carry on past the typical retirement age. Regardless, workers needed to make a provision for when they could no longer work. Unfortunately, according to Armstrong, workers were unable to save for their retirement, due to low wages, and even life insurance was beyond their means. Many writers and politicians in the USA operated under the premise that rising wages among workers would take care of this issue, but Armstrong noted that "reliable evidence refutes the claim that American workers have been achieving large increases in their incomes in the past thirty years."[2] She presented some of that data and added in data on the extent to which there was discrimination against older workers, which added to their difficulties.

To be sure, some businesses did offer pensions to their employees, but studies showed that fewer than 10 percent of workers stayed employed with those businesses long enough to become eligible for a pension. Unions also provided pensions for their members but the number who collected them was small and the amounts collected were meager. Some states provided homes for elderly workers but "the majority of states in the United States make no systematic provision for the security of the citizen who arrives at economic old age without income sufficient for his maintenance."[3] The USA stood alone among industrial economies by its lack of provision of help for the elderly. Those other countries provided pensions for their workers and the USA should follow suit. She reviewed what types of pensions those countries offered as examples for the USA to follow. Her conclusion was that the USA should use a national system of pensions based on insurance principles where workers contributed to their retirement benefits.[4]

Every economic system experienced some form of unemployment, according to Armstrong, because even early-age hunters would return empty-handed from their hunt. The type of unemployment experienced in the modern world, however, was tied to the market economy "wherein each individual is responsible for finding his own work."[5] Unemployment resulted from seasonal changes in production, the business cycle, and technological innovation. Seasonal unemployment could be taken care of by better management of production by business. Public works projects could alleviate cyclical unemployment to some degree, but there remained many workers who had "to weather the hardship of having no work for long periods when business is at low ebb."[6] The most crucial type of unemployment was from technological innovation, which many in the USA thought was an enduring problem. Regardless of the source, the USA would always have some level of unemployment and something must be done to help workers without a job.

As usual, Armstrong surveyed the countries of Europe to describe how they handled the unemployment problem. She then analyzed efforts in the USA in the private sector to provide some form of unemployment insurance. Unions offered some coverage for their members, and advanced corporations such as General Electric offered workers unemployment insurance where both the company and the workers contributed to an unemployment insurance fund.[7] The potential coverage by such private programs was limited, however, due to the small percent of the workforce that belonged to a union or that worked for a large firm. Government provision of unemployment insurance was needed and Armstrong noted two potential approaches, compulsory unemployment insurance paid for entirely by business or paid for by business and workers combined. Whichever approach was taken, Armstrong ended by advocating for a system operated by the federal government.[8]

Only the federal government could mandate social insurance at the level of a living wage. This would be a big step for the federal government to take, however, because it would be controversial. While Armstrong's arguments may have been cogent, it took an obscure figure from California to prod the New Deal to take that step.

The Townsend Plan

At first glance, Francis Townsend (1867–1960) would not appear to have the makings of a social activist. Born in Illinois and raised in Nebraska, he spent his early adulthood as an unsuccessful small-business entrepreneur. At age 31, he entered medical school and for the remainder of his life alternated between work as a physician and efforts to operate a variety of business ventures in southern California. His life as an activist began on September 30, 1933, when he wrote a letter to the editor of the *Long Beach Press-Gazette* outlining a plan to provide pensions for the elderly. The paper gave his letter a good deal of play, printing it in banner format and including an editorial analysis of the plan Townsend proposed.

The basics of the plan were simple enough. Every person over the age of 60 in the USA would be given a pension of $200 a month by the federal government, to be funded by a national sales tax of 2 percent. The recipients of the pension, that Townsend called the Old Age Revolving Pension Plan, had to be retired and not have a criminal record; they also had to agree to spend the entire proceeds of their monthly pension within 30 days after they received it (Townsend 1933). The importance of the plan and, especially, its last condition in terms of the theme of this book was that Townsend saw his plan as helping the economy. He indicated that there were over ten million individuals in the USA who would qualify for his pension, and they would contribute $2 billion a month to spending on consumption. This amount, he wrote, would be "Enough to raise the standard of living very materially above the present low level but quite within the nation's ability to provide." Business sought to improve its profitability by increasing efficiency, but it did so by eliminating jobs. When the resulting technological unemployment reduced total buying power in the economy, total consumption would decline. As a result, even business leaders were beginning to see the necessity of keeping up the buying power of the people by some such plan as the Old Age Revolving Pensions.[9] The rest of the letter concerned itself with answers to critics of the plan and an explanation of the impact of its implementation in terms of taxes and increased prices in the economy.

The newspaper led off its publication of Townsend's plan with an editorial and analysis of the plan. That foreword also stressed the benefits of the plan for helping out the economy. It began by characterizing Townsend's proposal as a "plan for combining liberal retirement compensation for the aged with national financial recovery and permanent prosperity." The editorial added,

> *It will put about two billions of dollars more in circulation than has ever circulated before by creating important buying centers of poor communities that have never had buying power, thus insuring brisk trade in every section of the country.*

The plan would allow its recipients who were among the employed elderly to retire and open up jobs for younger persons who were unemployed and create more jobs through the spending of the pensions, with a total estimated eight million new persons being employed. It would also save the working elderly who would otherwise someday have to retire without a pension "from the humiliation of accepting charity in some form, either from relatives or from the state."[10]

The publicity given to Townsend's plan created a grassroots movement that brought about 7000 Townsend Clubs with over 750,000 paid members by 1939. The movement surely added to the pressure to create a system of social insurance that was building at the time.[11] Its desire to eliminate the need for the elderly to accept charity or government relief bore kinship to the living wage movement's goal of allowing all workers to have a life of dignity. Townsend once expressed this similarity in explaining that he came up with the figure of $200 a month for his plan because a lower income level would not provide a living standard that gave recipients the possibility to experience the religious and cultural facets of existence in a way that brought about their full potential as humans and as citizens.[12] This description compares to the definition of a living wage given by unions nearly two decades earlier (see Chapter 2).

Equally important, the Townsend Plan added to the view that consumption was more important as a catalyst for production than had previously been considered by advocates for a living wage as a vehicle for increasing the purchasing power of labor through higher wages. Instead of relying on higher wages to increase consumption, the government could give direct money to the elderly as a reward for their previous work lives. The editorial in the *Long Beach Press-Gazette* stated this new theory of the government as follows:

> We say that one of the chief functions of government should be the exercise of its power to insure a steady and sufficient flow of money through the channels of trade and commerce adequate to keep that trade at an even tempo free from fear of panic or boom. We say that our government must assume this function and adopt a system whereby money shall flow in a constant volume into the coffers of the U. S. Treasury and immediately start on a return flow back into the avenue of commerce whence it came.[13]

Government needed to spend to bring about an economic recovery and spending on the needs of the elderly was a good way to do it. This approach represents the consumerist approach that eventually came to forefront in the USA after World War II.

It would take a break from the linkage between a producerist and consumerist thinking for that change to take place. Supporters of a living wage consistently argued from a producerist viewpoint that workers were entitled to a living wage because they worked hard. Unions added the idea that the higher pay they earned would enable them to be better consumers and help the economy. The Townsend Plan offered the elderly a living wage because they were elderly. They might be entitled to it as a reward for their life's work, but it remained an entitlement that was plainly a welfare program. Because supporters of a living wage placed a high value on the dignity to be accorded to a worker who earned it, they objected to welfare as harmful to that dignity. As a result, when they contributed to the development of the social insurance component of the SSA, supporters of a living wage made sure it was not an entitlement. We can see the beginning of the approach in an article intended for business.

The *Nation's Business* Examines Unemployment Insurance

The US Chamber of Commerce as the peak association for business often offered a venue, *Nation's Business*, for business leaders to speak out on social issues. In October 1934, for example, H.W. Story, vice-president of the Allis Chalmers Manufacturing Co., took up the problem of unemployment protection that was then becoming a pressing matter as states were adopting their plans and the federal government was looking forward to its own system for taking care of the unemployed. To Story, a key question was how the funds to cover the unemployed should be pooled.

In answering this question, Story found a debate between advocates of a European Plan of using general tax collections to provide adequate benefits for all unemployed workers for as long as they needed them versus proponents of an American Plan of employing a reserve insurance fund for unemployment benefits. Story sided with the American Plan because it gave businesses an incentive to maintain steady levels of employment; their contributions to the insurance fund would depend on their employment levels while the European Plan would impose penalties on them since they would pay taxes even if they maintained employment. He bolstered his support for the American Plan by using John Maurice Clark's theory of social overhead costs (See Chapter 2), writing,

> The industry or plan with widely fluctuating unemployment repeatedly dumps some or all of its workers upon the community. Unless these workers can be utilized at such times in other concerns or industries, they must be supported by somebody. Correct social cost-accounting requires that this be done by the concern or industry for which they are, in effect, a labor reserve. Otherwise such a concern or industry is not paying the full cost of its production. Instead it is in effect receiving a subsidy.[14]

An unemployment insurance system that based premiums on the level of employment of an individual firm would be using proper social cost accounting, while payment of unemployment benefits from general taxes would not.

By using Clark's social overhead theory to justify social insurance, Story, perhaps unwittingly, made himself at least a fellow-traveler in the living wage movement. Someone had to take care of workers when they were out of work. He proposed that business should be responsible through its payment into an unemployment insurance plan. His thinking on this issue was consistent with the plan set forth by Roosevelt.

Roosevelt Promises Social Security

On June 29, 1934, Roosevelt established, through an executive order, the Committee on Economic Security (CES), a short-term organization, with a task of formulating a system to provide social security. The Committee was chaired by the Secretary of Labor, Frances Perkins, with several other cabinet officers as members; its staff members included many experts on social insurance such as Edwin Witte (see below) and Barbara Armstrong, who produced four of the Committee's staff reports; Domhoff and Webber explore her contributions to the SSA in great detail.[15] Other individuals discussed in earlier chapters as advocates for a living wage, John Ryan, Sam Lewisohn, Gerard Swope, and William Green, served as members of the President's Advisory Council to the CES.[16]

Once the CES formulated its approach to social security, Roosevelt sent a message to the Congress on January 14, 1935, that was exceptional in its use of the rhetoric of social justice. He told the Congress that a political change was sweeping the world as economic problems that had been accumulating for years were beginning to be taken care of by government. As a result, he said, "In most nations social justice, no longer a distant idea, has become a definite goal, and ancient governments are beginning to heed the call."[17] In outlining the reason for the mounting economic problems, Roosevelt put technological innovation at the heart of the need for social reform. He spoke thusly about it, "Thinking people in almost every country of the world have come to realize certain fundamental difficulties with which civilization must reckon. Rapid changes—the machine, the advent of universal and rapid communication, and many other factors—have brought new problems."[18] Piecemeal efforts to solve these problems had not succeeded and "we have not weeded out the overprivileged and we have not effectively uplifted the underprivileged."[19]

Roosevelt insisted that he did not want to "destroy ambition" or to "divide wealth into equal shares." Rather, he accepted "the greater ability of some to earn more than others." There should be limits on that ability, however, and the desire for security from an acceptable level of income was "an ambition to be preferred to the appetite for great wealth." For this reason he proposed unemployment insurance and old-age pensions as "the security against the major hazards and vicissitudes of life."[20] Unemployment insurance would provide protection to workers who lost their jobs during the business cycle, while old-age pensions would take care of them when their work lives were finished.

Roosevelt's statement reflects his approach to social justice as described in Chapter 1. Under that approach, he argued that it was acceptable for income to be unequal as long as the "overprivileged" did their social duty of helping those who did not have a living wage and thus experienced economic insecurity. It was also acceptable for the government to make sure that this social duty was performed, even if it involved mandating premiums for social insurance under the guise of a payroll tax.

The proposed bill that the president sent to the Congress did not use the term "living wage." But the spirit of the term was present in the draft of the bill. It stated, "As used in this title, old-age assistance shall mean financial assistance assuring a reasonable subsistence compatible with decency and health to persons not less than sixty-five years of age," and the phrase was repeated several times.[21] In keeping with its goal of economic security, the Roosevelt Administration was promising a living wage to the elderly who needed help.

The AFL and the SSA

Having fought for social insurance for years, the AFL was in accord with Roosevelt when he brought his social insurance program to the Congress. In an editorial in the December 1934 issue of the *American Federationist*, William Green gave his views on "Unemployment Insurance." He recommended that all the unions that were members of the AFL support the passage of a system of unemployment insurance. To be sure, there needed to be some experimentation with the "national-state cooperative measure to provide incomes for the unemployed" but those experiments should be confined to "standards that assure real protection for wage-earners."[22] To that end, Green provided a list of such standards. Unemployment insurance should be made compulsory. Its coverage should be extended to as many workers as possible. The funds for the program should be based on a tax levied on employers only. Although the unemployed should have to be willing to look for work and take a job for which they were qualified, they should not have to take a job when the opening was caused by a strike, if the wages offered by the job were lower than the local wage rates, or if the wages offered would tend to reduce wages in general.[23]

The *American Federationist* considered the entire SSA in a March 1935 article, "Economic Security for the Worker." The article began with a depiction of what it was like to get a job and gain some economic security, because "insecurity has hung heavily over wage-earners" for a long time during the Depression and even before it. The proposed SSA would end this long-term insecurity. Not only would the unemployment insurance component of the SSA give workers security of income, it would maintain workers' incomes and "exert a stabilizing effect upon our industrial system." It would also "bring about a more equitable distribution of income."[24] In looking at the specifics of the unemployment program, the *American Federationist* felt that many changes in the law were needed. Among the most important were that it should be a national program, especially since businesses operated in many states and workers often crossed state borders to find work. There should also be a labor representative on the board who would oversee the program. And the federal government should directly subsidize the program.[25]

With regard to the pension program of the SSA, the *American Federationist* argued that its provisions of starting out with a low payroll tax and gradually increasing it was an "over modest beginning." It suggested higher payroll tax rates be implemented to meet "the imperative need for bringing the old-age insurance plan into operation in the shortest possible time." It also recommended that "a larger relative pension be made available to the lower paid worker." Finally, the article indicated that the AFL believed that the retirement age should be reduced to 60 years.[26]

The union approach to social insurance was a bit different from what was enacted in the SSA. With the pensions, unions wanted them to be higher than the SSA put in place and their preferred retirement age was certainly lower than the Act permitted. With unemployment, insurance unions wanted a national plan subsidized by the government and done in a way that did not interfere with collective bargaining. To be sure, their approach in both cases added in the idea that the increased benefits they wanted would add to overall consumption. By relying on government subsidies for some of those increased benefits, the union perspective weakened the connection between a living wage and consumption that they had often made. Subsidized unemployment insurance might indeed increase consumption but only through welfare. The union view did not prevail in the SSA as can be seen through consideration of the approach to unemployment insurance of a member of one of the SSA Advisory Committees.

Lewisohn Analyzes Unemployment Insurance

As described in Chapter 2, Sam Lewisohn was a financier who had a long career in the investment business his father had started. But he also took an interest in the social problems of labor and supported a living wage. In keeping with that interest, he and his father, Adolph Lewisohn, were longtime members of the AALL. The father was the organization's treasurer for many years and the son served as its president in 1928. As noted above, he was on an advisory board to the CES.

With this background it is not surprising that in 1935, in the period when the SSA was being developed, Lewisohn presented two articles on social insurance at political science conferences. In presenting the papers, he was a staunch supporter of unemployment insurance. Still, he felt a need to discuss alternative methods for dealing with the issues surrounding it. First, should unemployment insurance be provided at all instead of relief programs? Second, when should benefits be paid? Third, who should contribute to the fund? Fourth, where should the insurance reserve funds be held? And fifth, what should happen if the insurance reserve funds were exhausted?[27] His overall perspective was that the Great Depression had made unemployment insurance an essential program because it had made government "assume the burden of preventing starvation."[28]

The government had a variety of ways to prevent starvation, however, from outright relief to employing workers on public works projects. Relief from charity or from government welfare involved the loss of dignity for its recipient, and public works projects were expensive and often wasteful. It was thus better to utilize "an organized, dignified reserve fund to which employees are entitled because they have participated in building it up."[29]

Because workers and their employers had built up this reserve, it was important to use it properly. Lewisohn believed that there were two ways to sustain the reserve fund—one, which requires a relatively long waiting period before workers could collect their benefits and the other, where the funds can be only utilized during especially difficult periods. Under the issue of the waiting period, he argued that by making the workers support themselves during an initial period of unemployment, there would be more funds available for the later phase of a long period of unemployment. Moreover, during periods of mild unemployment the duration of joblessness would be short. Lewisohn even argued that unemployment insurance should not be paid for unemployment during periods of prosperity in order to preserve the funds for really high periods of unemployment. He considered this approach to be using sound insurance methods of only insuring against large losses.[30]

Insurance principles should also be applied to the issue of who should contribute to the reserve fund. It was important to retain mutual support as part of the program, which meant that employees and employers should both contribute to the fund. Employees would attain a sense of ownership and want the funds to be used as sparingly as possible, while employers would want to have smaller premiums by having fewer claims.[31] Once the reserve fund was built up, there were alternatives as to where it should be held. Lewisohn considered the alternatives of having it held by the individual employer, the industry, or the government. Each alternative had advantages and disadvantages and he favored experimentation with each to determine which worked best.[32] In the event that the insurance fund was exhausted, as was likely during an exceptionally long period of unemployment, the government should provide for backup relief.[33]

Lewisohn did not mention his previous support for a living wage in his analysis of unemployment insurance and we might wonder how workers who did not earn a living wage would be able to save enough to survive the waiting period before unemployment insurance would be paid. At the same time, he indicated that "unemployment insurance is no longer to be classed as a social humanitarian problem. It is a link in the chain of governmental business and finance."[34] By making unemployment an economic issue, Lewisohn reflected the economic rights approach that underpinned the idea of a living wage, which means he had not forgotten his earlier support for that idea. A living wage offered workers the dignity of earning their own way rather than being the beneficiaries of someone's humanitarian impulse.

Wagner Proposes Social Security

That Robert Wagner was a mainstay of the New Deal legislation should not surprise us, since he and Roosevelt had been political allies in New York for over two decades. Wagner was responsible for proposing the legislation that became the SSA. In the May 1935 issue of *The Forum and Century* he explained the need for the legislation in an article titled "Toward Security."

The push for social security had been going on for almost a decade, but the time had come for it because public opinion now accepted that "men may become unemployed without having been shiftless and indolent" and "the aged may be reduced to destitution without having been squanderers." Of the two main goals of the Act, unemployment insurance and old age pensions, unemployment insurance was the most important because unemployment was the primary result of the Depression and the unemployment insurance system would serve "to minimize, if not to abolish, the likelihood of depressions." The payment of unemployment benefits in the early stages of an economic downturn would "release floods of purchasing power to check the decline and swing the cycle more quickly back to the prosperity level." If unemployment insurance had been put into place a decade earlier, the payment of benefits might have reduced the severity of the Great Depression.[35]

Old age pensions also had a role to play in preventing depressions and could also offset the problems caused by technological innovation. In the economy of the 1920s and 1930s, technological innovation meant that young workers were constantly being replaced by machines. It was "infinitely wiser," Wagner argued, "to make openings for these young men, who are entitled to jobs, by retiring older workers who are entitled to rest." In addition, the pensions provided to the elderly would add to purchasing power.[36]

These economic advantages of social security might appear to be based on "cold logic" as to the benefits the program would offer society. Wagner insisted, however, that the program aimed at the social justice of a living wage. He wrote, "Justice does not exist when the man unemployed through no fault of his own is more neglected than machinery... Humanitarianism is made a mockery when a worker who has worn himself out in the service of industry is given less consideration than a retired race horse."[37]

Wagner strikes a note more along the lines of the union approach than the living wage as dignity approach. Workers without a job and the elderly without income needed to be helped on humanitarian grounds. Social insurance was also good for the economy through the increase in purchasing power it would bring about, even if it hinted at poor relief. This perspective was different from Lewisohn's approach of using social insurance as a backup relief. Both sides were presented in the debates in the Congress over the SSA.

Congress, Social Security, and a Living Wage

The proposed SSA was a far-reaching step in US history and all the parties to the new law recognized its importance. Both houses of the Congress held lengthy hearings where they listened to the testimony of many witnesses, expert and otherwise; they then subjected the bill to a lengthy debate. The legislative fights over the SSA were long and complicated.[38] Here, I will stick with my focus on a living wage.

There are two pertinent examples of the use of the idea of a living wage from members of the Roosevelt Administration. First, in his opening comments Edwin Witte, the director of the CES, mentioned the language of the bill about assistance to the elderly meaning, "financial assistance assuring a reasonable subsistence compatible with decency and health" and he repeated the phrase three times.[39] The Secretary of Labor, Frances Perkins, who chaired the CES, indicated that the proposed bill included a pension "high enough to ensure a decent standard of living" for the elderly. She added that for persons aged 30–60 who would not contribute fully to the pension system, it would be an obligation of the government to subsidize them "up to a sum upon which they can reasonably hope to live according to a good standard of life."[40] Today, it is often argued that social security pensions were intended as a supplemental retirement income. For Roosevelt, Witte, and Perkins those pensions were supposed to secure a living wage. As noted in Chapter 1, Ryan had quoted Pope Leo's encyclical on the condition of labor "that the remuneration must be enough to support the wage earner in *reasonable and frugal comfort.*"[41] Witte came close to the same quotation in his remarks on the SSA.

The need for unemployment insurance was brought up in testimony by William Green, president of the AFL and member of an advisory committee to the CES. He argued that unemployment insurance was needed because many workers were not able save enough money to tide them over when they were hit by the loss of their job, with the result that they suffered from a lack of economic security. Studies showed, he went on, that one-third of workers in the prosperous years of 1928–1929 "earned below the minimum subsistence level."[42] Without a living wage workers could not save. From this perspective, Green shared with the members of the House the notion that social insurance in the form of unemployment insurance was an ingredient in a living wage.

The debates over social security in the House of Representatives took place during April 5–19, 1935. In those debates, the idea of a living wage was presented in a small degree. The phrase in the bill about "financial assistance assuring a reasonable subsistence compatible with decency and health" was cited favorably at least 12 times during the debates.[43] In addition, the idea of a living wage was set forth with phrases such as "the right to earn a normal living," "fair and honorable living," "little comforts which will make life worth living," "security and a comfortable living," "decent living and comfortable existence," and "means of comfort and decent living."[44]

Those debates contain a few direct uses of the term "living wage," however. On April 16, 1935, Congressman Joseph Gray (1884–1966), Democrat from Pennsylvania, used a living wage as an argument against the bill. He was concerned that once pensions were adopted they would be changed to allow more people to get them, such as by lowering the retirement age. A better way to take care of the elderly was "to provide a proper return to the man who labors." It would take great changes in the economy to provide "the laboring man and worker by skill or brawn a living wage," especially since workers had rarely gotten such a wage in the past. Gray went on, "If a man be given a living wage during his productive years, he can provide against the vicissitudes of old age by his own thrift." Without it, a worker would barely be able to afford a family, much less to save for retirement.[45] John Ryan had favored Gray's approach as an ultimate goal of a living wage, but thought government programs such as social security were necessary until society accepted the idea of a living wage. Gray apparently thought the time was right.

While Gray used the concept of a living wage to oppose the bill, Congressman Fred Vinson (1890–1953), a Democrat from Kentucky, who would later be the Secretary of the Treasury and Chief Justice of the United States, found that unemployment insurance might help workers get a living wage. He argued that if employment agencies knew that a worker was covered by unemployment insurance, "they might be able to provide a job for that man so that he earns a living wage."[46] He apparently meant that unemployment insurance would give workers time to look for the best and highest-paying job possible rather than settle for a job at any pay scale.

As had the House, the Senate held hearings on the SSA. Green testified that workers could not afford to contribute toward their unemployment insurance because their wages were so low. To him, "employee contributions would literally have to come out of the bread and butter of workers." It was wrong to ask workers to pay for insurance against a risk they had no responsibility for. It would be better to make the cost of unemployment insurance "a legitimate on the cost of production" because it was like "any other overhead cost which employers must meet."[47] Here, Green is echoing the social overhead cost argument set forth by Clark (see Chapter 2).

A different perspective on who should bear the costs of social security was presented by Earl Browder (1891–1973) of the Communist Party. To him, social security was something the federal government should provide. He testified, "It is the responsibility of the National Government to provide, against all those vicissitudes of life which are beyond individual or group control, a guaranty of a minimum standard of decent livelihood equal to the average of the individual or group when normally employed."

Here, we have a definition of a living wage although Browder did not use the term. The bill being proposed had to "maintain the living standards of the masses unimpaired." If it did not, it would amount to "social insecurity." Finally, he insisted, the "costs of social insurance must be paid out of the accumulated and current surplus of society, and not by further reducing the living standards of those still employed."[48] Income redistribution was the way to pay for social insurance, much as had been argued by more moderate proponents such as Abraham Epstein, who did not like the idea of collecting premiums for social insurance (see below).

The debates in the Senate lasted from May 20 to June 19, 1935, with most of it taking place on June 14–19. The only part of the debates pertinent to our interest in a living wage took place on June 15. An amendment was proposed by the Committee on Finance to change the language that had figured so prominently in Roosevelt's version of the bill, "financial assistance assuring a reasonable subsistence compatible with decency and health," to "assistance, as far as is practical." The change was approved with regard to aid to the elderly from the individual states and for aid for children.[49] The House Ways and Means Committee had already imposed enough restrictions on that language to make it meaningless.[50] The hint of a living wage in social security thus ended.

It is doubtful that the idea of a living wage had much impact on the final outcome. The Act passed both houses of the Congress with bipartisan support, especially when the support of Southern Democrats was assured by leaving out agricultural and domestic workers from coverage by the SSA.[51] In the House of Representatives, the vote was 372 in favor, 33 opposed, and 27 who did not vote. On party lines it was 284 to 15 in favor for Democrats and 81 to 15 in favor for Republicans. In the Senate, the overall vote was 77 in favor and 6 opposed, with Democrats supporting the Act by 60 to 1 and Republicans in favor by 16 to 5.[52]

The Details of the SSA

Both unemployment insurance and old-age pensions were a part of a multifaceted SSA that went into effect on August 14, 1935. The Act was divided into eight titles that contained provisions for relief aid for the elderly and for children, old-age pensions, and unemployment insurance; it had a funding section that included contributions from those to be covered by the unemployment insurance and the pensions in the form of payroll taxes on wages, paid by both workers and employers in part because

Roosevelt wanted the system to be funded on insurance principles and not be an outright welfare.[53] These taxes would go into the general funds of the US Treasury and in the case of old-age pensions the Congress would appropriate an annual amount to pay benefits and to build up a reserve fund—in this way it was hoped to avoid the Constitutional issues a direct mandatory contribution might entail. The writers of the law carefully named the compulsory contributions of the pension program as taxes so that the Supreme Court would be more favorable toward them as being a part of the taxing authority of the federal government.

With old-age pensions, the tax would start in 1937 at 1 percent of wages payable by workers and employers and would increase by 0.5 percent every three years until 1949 when each side would contribute 3 percent of wages. Because of exemptions of persons such as the self-employed, domestic workers, agricultural laborers, employees of state, local, and federal governments and those employed by non-profit organizations, about half the workforce would be covered. Benefits would be provided to workers at age of 65 if they were not in an exempt occupation and if they had worked for at least five years based on a formula tied to earnings.

With unemployment insurance, the federal government did not establish its own system of unemployment insurance but used a tax-offset plan where the federal government imposed a tax upon employers based on the total they paid in wages and salaries. Small firms were exempted as were certain job categories similar to those excluded from the pension program. If a state enacted an unemployment insurance law that met the criteria established by the federal government, the contributions made by employers would serve as an offset against the federal tax which they would otherwise pay. States that did not enact such a law would see their employers paying the tax to the federal government. In this way, states that did not set up an unemployment insurance plan could not gain a competitive advantage over states that did set one up. The taxes would be sent for holding to the federal government by the states.

As noted earlier, Roosevelt did not get all he wanted in the SSA. One change in the original proposed law is pertinent to our interest in the living wage. As originally drafted, the law contained a statement that it aimed at "a reasonable subsistence compatible with decency and health," that is, a living wage. The Southern members of the Roosevelt coalition worried that this phrase would cause problems for their states and eliminated it from the final legislation in terms of state pensions for those who were already past the retirement age.[54] They were also responsible for some of the categories of work that were excluded from coverage by the Act. Paul Douglas attributed the Southerners' opposition to this language to a fear that the federal government might force Southern states to pay higher pensions to elderly blacks than would be politically tolerable. He also observed that the states outside the South had a similar bias against other ethnic groups.[55]

As with all the new programs of the New Deal, the provisions of the SSA were quickly challenged on Constitutional grounds. In a decision announced on May 24, 1937, Charles *C. Steward v. Harwell G. Davis*, the US Supreme Court decided on a 5-4 vote that unemployment insurance was within the Constitution. The Court based its opinion on the argument that the high unemployment of the Great Depression had gone on for over seven years and it was too late to make an argument that the use of federal money to help the unemployed was "a use for any purpose narrower than the promotion of the general welfare."[56] On May 24, 1937, the Supreme Court also announced a 7-2 vote in favor of the old-age pension portion of the SSA in the case of Guy *T. Helvering v. George P. Davis.* The decision of the Court was based on the premise that the Congress could spend tax collections to promote "general welfare." The issue was in drawing the line between whether a program promoted the general welfare or was for the welfare of a particular group or person. In drawing that line, while the Court had a part to play, "discretion belongs to Congress."[57] If the Congress wished to enact laws because it doubted the ability of the market economy to produce the results that led to the promotion of the general welfare, it had the power to begin replacing it with the provision of economic security.

Perkins on the Benefits of Security

Secretary of Labor, Frances Perkins, spent much of her life as a social worker helping the poor in their struggles in life. Consequently, in a radio address on Labor Day, September 2, 1935, she celebrated the passage of the SSA's unemployment insurance as a "substitute for the haphazard methods of assistance in periods of time when men and women willing and able to work are without jobs." She also favored its old-age pensions as "great progress over the measures we have hitherto depended on in caring for those who have been unable to provide for the years when they can no longer work."[58]

Perkins then explained some of the provisions of the Act, including examples of how much money recipients of the old-age pension would get from their contributions. She also defended the use of states for handling the unemployment insurance program and the federal government for the old-age pension system. Her conclusion was that while the Act was not "a complete solution of the problem of economic security" it did provide "protection for the individual against future economic vicissitudes."[59] It also provided economic security in another form, that is, it maintained "mass purchasing power through a system of protection of the individual against major economic hazards."[60]

Perkins was referring to what economists now call automatic stabilizers, government programs such as unemployment insurance that increase government spending when a recession takes place and, therefore, keep declines in consumption spending from being too large. This approach is consistent with the consumerist idea that policy should encourage consumption in every way possible. Even the unemployed would be able to help the economy to recover.

Douglas Explains Social Security

Paul H. Douglas, as we have seen in Chapters 2 and 3, was a keen and sympathetic observer of programs to help workers. In March 1936, he displayed these traits by offering his explanations for the new US social security system to economists worldwide in an article in the prominent English publication, *The Economic Journal*, titled "The United States Social Security Act."

Douglas began the article by indicating that the enactment of the US system of social security was "evidence of a great change in American public opinion." Because of the lengthy nature of the Great Depression, a majority of the US population had become convinced "that the system of individualism had failed to provide the masses with adequate protection against indigent old age and unemployment."[61] The Roosevelt New Deal was a result of this new conviction in favor of economic security. The measures it used were dramatically different because they expanded the role of the federal government. As a result, the New Deal developed a social security system that was a combination of using taxes to raise the money needed to fund the program and then separately using a system of defined benefits to disburse those funds.

Douglas was also concerned with the impact social security would have on purchasing power. On the one hand, the surplus funds collected for the pension program were put into a reserve fund, which would "undoubtedly serve to decrease the total purchasing power available for the purchase of consumers' goods and may aggravate cyclical depressions." To offset this impact, the federal government might spend those reserves "on grandiose but economically unproductive public works and thus leave the country saddled with a large interest burden."[62] On the other hand, the unemployment insurance program would "be more effective as a means of reducing depressions through the purchasing power which will be released at such times to the unemployed in the form of benefits and which will be used to help sustain consumption and consequently production."[63] The underconsumption view of the Depression influenced every economic program of the New Deal and probably to a greater extent than did the idea of a living wage. Still, the impact of social insurance on a living wage for workers was part of Douglas' criticism of it. He observed that since the states were not as adept as the federal government in engaging in progressive taxation, "the tax-offset system [of unemployment insurance] necessarily makes the poor pay for the cost of relieving the poorest."[64] This was not the type of income redistribution that the Progressives should favor and was certainly not consistent with the ideals of a living wage.

A Business Perspective on Social Security

On November 20, 1936, P.W. Litchfield, president of the Goodyear Tire & Rubber Co., offered his thoughts on the SSA to the New England Conference in Boston. Litchfield was a mainstay of the Industrial Democracy/welfare capitalism movement, having written a book in 1919 titled *The Industrial Republic*.[65] In his talk, he was concerned to make clear to his audience that when high taxes were placed on business the higher prices that resulted did not please consumers.

The social security taxes were a different matter, however. In an argument similar to that made by Clark (see Chapter 2), Litchfield believed that "unemployment insurance as well as old-age pensions should be included in the cost of production, just as wages, interest, depreciation, and such items as fire and theft insurance."[66] Since individual firms could not risk paying these social overhead costs, to use Clark's term, when their competitors did not pay them, government should impose them on all firms as it was doing with the social security taxes. In that way the public (consumers) would be charged the full cost of production by all firms without anyone gaining a competitive edge from giving workers low benefits.

The Committee on Economic Security

When the SSA was put in place on August 14, 1935, much of the early work to accomplish it had been undertaken by the CES. Roosevelt had established the CES through an executive order on June 29, 1934. It was a short-term organization, with a task of writing a report formulating a system to provide social security. Its ten-volume report was never published, and the Congress altered its proposed version of social security in legislating the final form of the SSA.

In 1937, the Committee produced a book to summarize its work, *Social Security in America*, published by the Social Security Board. In nearly 600 pages, the report covered many aspects of social insurance including historical comparisons with social insurance programs in Europe and the background of state programs in the USA. Here, I am concerned with the underlying point of view the Committee expressed in support of the key aspects of the social security program.

Let us start with unemployment insurance. The Committee's report indicated in its first lines that "the hazard of unemployment is one of the most serious and disastrous of the many risks which confront wage earners in an industrial society." That risk had become especially acute during the Great Depression and private charity had not been adequate to alleviate the plight of the unemployed. Moreover, private charity was "demoralizing to both the donor and recipient." A system of unemployment insurance, however, was not demoralizing because it was "received as a right."[67] By basing unemployment compensation on insurance principles, the SSA established its payments as a contractual obligation from the government to the unemployed worker and not as a benefit based on need. The argument that in a market economy voluntary charity was the best way to help the poor was replaced by a system of compulsory contractual rights consistent with Ryan's view that a living wage was a right to be accorded to workers (see Chapter 1).

The Committee report then turned to the issues surrounding old-age pensions. Without some provision for retirement income, elderly workers either continued to work or became dependent on charity, family, or friends. This dependency resulted from the "conditions of modern society, especially in highly urbanized and industrial areas" which did "not permit the wage earner, unaided, to provide for his old age." For a comfortable existence a worker needed "assurance that each day's work builds up an investment for his old age, permitting independence of the charity of the community or financial aid from sons and daughters" with their own financial requirements.[68] In addition, due to an increased lifespan, the percentage of the population that reached retirement age was growing.

The Committee considered whether help for the elderly should be provided from general tax revenue or from a system of compulsory retirement insurance. It determined that the tax increases necessary to fund a system of welfare for the elderly would be more than the economy could tolerate. It settled on a system of contributory old-age insurance to provide "some form of cooperative thrift."[69] Under this system, benefits would be based on the amount paid in by workers and "individual need would not be a determinant." In this way "insurance benefits would be conceived of as a matter of right, based on contributions related to wages."[70] An insurance system would also offer the elderly the assurance that they would get an established amount that did not depend on political decisions or carry the taint of welfare or charity. Old-age pensions would also be consistent with the living wage ideals.

The contributions to the old-age insurance system would be made through a tax on employers and employees. The Committee recognized that in early years the pension insurance system would not have the funds to provide benefits at "a rate approximating 50 per cent of previous average earnings," which it felt was "socially desirable." It was unfair to place the burden for those benefits on "the present younger generation of contributors." Consequently, the SSA had a provision that "no benefits should be paid during the first 5 years in which the system was in effect." Even though the benefits should be based on contributions, the "system should be adjusted to the relative needs of various classes of beneficiaries even though need is not a determinant in the individual case." Lower-income workers should get a bit more in benefits than was warranted by their contributions. At the same time, to make clear that the system was "geared to the needs of person of small or moderate income" the program set a ceiling on the income "upon which benefits and contributions are based."[71]

Nevertheless, the Committee believed that worker contributions to the system were justified because "benefits under an insurance system would be received as a matter of right without a test of means."[72] Not every worker would be covered because some industries such as agriculture and domestic service presented problems in collecting the tax while small businesses also raised collection difficulties. Regarding the tax on employers, the Committee indicated, following Clark's theory, that "the cost of maintaining industrial employees in old age after years of productive employment has long been accepted as a charge against production." The costs of retirement benefits were "considered proper additions to the cost of production."[73] Businesses could pass those costs on to consumers through higher prices and might also cover some of the costs through reduced wages. The Committee believed that in a national system the changes in wages and prices would not burden any particular income group.

The CES started out with a compromise between a living wage approach that stressed the right of workers to unemployment insurance and pensions because they contributed to funds that paid out the benefits and a system based on welfare. Lower-paid workers would get a bit more than their contributions allowed and higher-paid workers would get a bit less. It could have gone further in this regard, but instead placed a limit on the contributions of higher-paid workers to keep them from getting a level of pension that would be politically unacceptable. The Committee could have omitted the cap on income subject to the payroll tax and used the money to subsidize lower-income pensioners, as is now often suggested. To have done so, however, would have turned the pension program into a welfare system with a means test and the CES was not willing to go that far.

Edwin Witte Defends Social Security

Edwin E. Witte (1887–1960) was one of the chief architects of the SSA through his service as executive director of the CES. A long and active member of the Progressive movement, he studied economics and earned a PhD in 1927 at the University of Wisconsin, where he eventually became professor of economics in 1933. Previously, he had held several state government positions where he participated in many of the Progressive reforms implemented in Wisconsin during the first three decades of the twentieth century.

In February 1937, he published an article, "Old Age Security in the Social Security Act," in *The Journal of Political Economy*, to explain the new pension system and defend it from criticisms that had been made of it. One criticism was that employers would pay for their share of the payroll tax by reducing the wages of their workers. To Witte, the argument was based on theoretical issues of the incidence of taxes and the ability of employers to shift those taxes back to workers or forward to consumers. Who would ultimately bear the burden of the tax would depend on the industry and its product. Some critics contended that the taxes would hurt business. Witte found it "natural that employers should be worried about the new taxes."[74] But he believed that it was fair for businesses to pay the taxes, using the social overhead cost argument developed by Clark (see Chapter 2). He wrote, "That employers should contribute something to the costs of retirement allowances for their employees is generally conceded. Such contributions are quite similar to the amounts which employers include in their costs to cover depreciation of machinery and equipment. A charge for the depreciation of the labor element in production is just as proper as is a charge for depreciation of capital."[75]

The idea that businesses had an obligation to take care of their employees either during periods of unemployment or when they could no longer work was consistent with the notion of Industrial Democracy that had become popular among forward-looking business leaders in the 1920s. It was also consistent with the ideology of a living wage. These business leaders and their living wage compatriots had recognized that providing benefits to employees placed them at a competitive disadvantage in comparison to competitors who did not offer benefits. They had hoped that the NIRA would impose the provision of benefits for workers on all firms. The SSA answered that hope.

Criticisms of Social Security

The SSA remains as an enduring legacy of the Roosevelt New Deal and its promotion of a living wage. The remainder of this chapter will consider the criticisms made by those who disagreed with the social security program as proposed and enacted in the New Deal, including critics among the Progressives who felt that it did not go far enough in providing a living wage.

Many of the criticisms made about the SSA are not germane to our interest in the living wage. For example, one of the most controversial features of the old-age pension program was its use of the reserve fund. Under the SSA, payroll taxes would be deposited in a reserve fund and then be used to fund current government spending. As a result, future taxpayers would be on the hook to redeem those funds. This criticism was levied by enemies of the New Deal, such as the 1936 Republican nominee for president, Alfred M. Landon[76] as well as its friends such as Hugh Johnson,[77] *The Nation*,[78] and *The New Republic*.[79] These last criticisms were meant to be friendly, however.

Another criticism of the SSA came from a book, *An Economic Program for American Democracy*, jointly written by seven economics professors at the Harvard University and the Tufts University. The book argued that the experience of the downturn in 1937 made it clear that government spending was vital to economic recovery and the authors outlined a permanent spending program for the USA that would keep the economy on track. A potential problem in their program was the payroll taxes. They wrote, "The present old-age insurance law needs fundamental revision if it is to serve within the next decade as an instrument for increasing mass consumption." The social security law called for payments into the reserve fund for five years, without any benefits being paid out. The payroll tax rate would then increase gradually, while only small benefits would be paid out. The authors wrote, "This relationship between income and outgo must be changed if the system is not to be a continuing drag on prosperity." It would also help if the benefit payments began earlier and if the method of determining benefits for early beneficiaries of the system be changed to give them "equal treatment with those becoming eligible later on."[80] In this way, the old-age pension program would contribute to the economic security of retirees by paying them benefits while avoiding the negative impact the payroll taxes might have on the economy. Here was another friendly criticism of the SSA that tied in with the purchasing power explanation of the Great Depression. More important to the concern of this book, friendly criticisms extended to areas of social security related to a living wage.

The Nation Examines Social Security

As a magazine of Progressive reform, *The Nation* would be expected to support a program of economic security. It did offer its support to the proposed SSA, but that support was mixed. It agreed that the Act was filling a social need, but was not doing enough to meet that need. We can see this in an editorial on January 30, 1935, titled, "Where is Security, Mr. Roosevelt?" The editorial praised the proposed bill for social security as "a historic act in the whole social outlook in this country." But given the magnitude of the problem of unemployment in the country, the Act was defective in its "fundamental principles." The unemployment provisions were weak in terms of who was covered and in putting them in the care of the individual states; it was better to have a national plan to spread the risks of unemployment as widely as possible. Moreover, the benefits of "half pay for from fifteen to twenty-five weeks" was certainly not "protection against the hazard of unemployment."[81] A better approach would be to pay workers the average wage for their occupation.

The problem of unemployment insurance received further analysis in *The Nation* in an article by Maxwell S. Stewart (1900–1990) on January 16, 1935, "Security versus Mathematics." Stewart noted that the need for economic security had been growing over the previous five years and the Roosevelt plan for meeting it was much better than the plan "of local self-help" of Herbert Hoover. There were alternative approaches that might be better, however. One alternative favored by business was to base the system on individual firms, with each firm having its own unemployment insurance fund. That approach had the benefit of giving business "a special incentive to avoid needless shutdowns and to lessen unemployment" but it did not take into account "the inequality of risks" of individual business. Another approach was to pay out average wages to the unemployed with funding from taxes on incomes above $500 a year. That approach, however, was not based on "actuarial principles." Still, Stewart preferred it, because it was doubtful that the risks of working in modern industry could "be reduced to mathematical formulas." Instead, the unemployed should be given a job on a public works project or unemployment compensation and the level of benefits of the latter should not be "less than a full living wage."[82] Stewart repeated his argument for a broader coverage and higher benefits in unemployment insurance in a second article on February 27, 1935, "Congress Discovers the Class Struggle."[83]

The New Republic on Social Security

As did *The Nation*, the other prominent magazine of Progressive thought, *The New Republic*, also supported the program for social security. In both cases, however, that support was tempered by the problem many liberals found with the proposed SSA: it did not offer sufficient benefits. This problem was highlighted in an editorial, "Inching Toward Social Security," on May 1, 1935. The editorial observed that "a law acknowledging a definite federal responsibility for helping the aged and the unemployed" was "an important milestone." Nevertheless, passing the milestone did not mean the USA had reached economic security. The fundamental problem was that under the payroll tax, employers would find ways to pass their share to consumers. Since workers were consumers, they would bear the full burden of social security and "the wealthy will avoid even the burden they now bear through local taxation on property for local aid."[84]

A month later, on June 3, 1935, the problem of the fairness of social security was raised in an editorial, "How Much Social Security?" The editorial emphasized the same point as in the previous one that a major defect in social security was that it was to be paid for by the poor, with the wealthy escaping much of the burden of paying for it. For this reason, the editors concluded, "the measure is one of which the Roosevelt administration will have little reason to be proud as time passes and the country begins the slow task of rectifying the mistakes that have now been made."[85]

Abraham Epstein and the Failure of Social Insurance

Abraham Epstein (1892–1942) was a long-time advocate for social insurance in the USA. As director of the Pennsylvania Old Age Pension Commission he was the primary drafter of the Pennsylvania pension plan for the elderly in 1921. In the 1920s, he helped to form the American Association for Old Age Security and recruited Ryan to be on its board.[86] In 1933, Epstein published a monumental book, *Insecurity: A Challenge to America*, as a study of social insurance in the USA and other countries. His book, along with Barbara Armstrong's book described earlier, was influential in the drafting of the SSA. Of interest in this chapter, Epstein authored a second revised edition of the book in 1936 to add chapters that criticized the Act.

In his foreword to the revised edition, Epstein expressed his reluctance to be critical of the first social insurance plan implemented at the national level in the USA. He was told that he should accept the SSA as the best that the New Deal could get in the political climate it faced. In addition, his criticisms would offer solace to the enemies of social security and encourage them to try to repeal it. But feeling as he did that "honeyed phrases will not lead us to genuine social security,"[87] Epstein added chapters to his book to deal with what he called the failure of the SSA to meet the challenge of insecurity.

From Epstein's perspective, social insurance was a way to extend private insurance "to its logical limits." Private insurance spread risk among the individuals who purchased a policy to cover their risks. Social insurance spread the risk to the entire population of a region or a country to help those who needed it the most. To Epstein, it was "a relatively inexpensive form of insurance devised by the state to guarantee the wage-earner and his dependents a minimum of income" when they were not able to work. Its goal was to "establish a minimum of economic sustenance below which no one must fall."[88] In other words, such as Armstrong had used, it would provide a living wage to end poverty and in a way that avoided the indignity of charity or public relief. Social insurance gave workers the right to file a claim that was in place before they became indigent.

The social insurance plans that existed in the world offered several lessons to the USA. First, they had to be compulsory to ensure the entire population was covered. Second, he argued that workers should not pay anything toward their social insurance, with employers and the government paying for it all. Employers were responsible for the insecurity of the market economy as was the government. The use of business profits to pay for a part of social insurance was sound economics, he added, using an argument similar to Clark's social overhead cost approach (see Chapter 2). The government's portion of social insurance should be paid for through a progressive income tax and high inheritance taxes.[89] Third, the benefits paid out by social insurance had an objective of providing "a minimum of security" to those who needed it. In theory, it should cover all aspects of the worker's standard of living, but in practice it would have to be less to give workers an incentive "in finding a job during unemployment or in old age."[90]

Having presented the basic principles of social insurance, Epstein argued that the need for social insurance in the USA was predicated on the prevalence of low wages. He argued that workers wanted more from their work, writing, "The wage-earner today demands to be treated as a full-fledged member of the community." As members of the community they wanted not just a minimum standard of living but a livelihood that includes items once considered "unnecessary luxuries," but which were now "real necessities."[91] They wanted, in other words, a living wage as defined by Ryan (see Chapter 1). They were not able to secure this living wage, especially during periods of unemployment and when they became elderly.

Under the New Deal, the plight of the unemployed and the elderly had been recognized and had resulted in the passage of the SSA. Epstein outlined in great detail the procedures, politics, and choices that had resulted in the SSA. He acknowledged that it was a turning point in US history by establishing the federal government's responsibility for social welfare and making the need for social insurance acceptable. But the SSA was flawed.

Perhaps the biggest flaw to Epstein was the way unemployment insurance and pensions for the elderly were financed by collecting taxes and putting the money into a reserve fund. This might be sound principles for private insurance, but social insurance needed something more. He wrote,

> In social insurance it does not matter whether the people bearing the risk pay contributions themselves. On the contrary, what matters most in social insurance is that those who suffer most should not be made to bear the heaviest burden. The important thing is that relief should be given as a matter of right in a dignified manner.[92]

Social insurance was still insurance even if the recipients contributed nothing in the way of "premiums." The idea that relief was a right was consistent with Ryan's approach.

There was also a problem in the payment of benefits under unemployment insurance and pensions for the elderly. In both cases, the benefits were based on previous wages. This approach gave inadequate benefits to low-wage workers—the ones who needed help the most. As a result, the main objective of social insurance, "the establishment of a minimum of subsistence protection for the insured," that is, a living wage, could not be attained.[93] Instead, as with private insurance, those who paid in the most got the most in terms of benefits. Regarding pensions for the elderly, this meant that low-wage workers would not be provided a living wage by their pensions and would still face the indignity of seeking additional relief. It would have been better, Epstein argued, to fund the pension plan with general tax receipts as increased by progressive income taxes and inheritance taxes.[94] Social insurance was a system of income redistribution and Epstein was unabashed in saying so.

Epstein leveled similar criticisms against the unemployment insurance program. Its two biggest flaws were the level of wages covered and the duration of the coverage. The plan called for coverage for workers for a limited time period. As a result, it did little for those permanently unemployed due to technological innovation. At the same time, the benefits offered were based on previous wages which ignored the basic principle of social insurance of establishing "benefit rates on the basis of the minimum subsistence needs of the unemployed,"[95] that is, on a living wage. As in the pensions, unemployment benefits should be based on the subsistence needs of workers and Epstein was certain this could be done without subjecting them to the indignity of a means test.[96]

In a way similar to Armstrong, Epstein maintained that social insurance was part of the guarantee of a living wage—he just did not use the term. The social insurance system set up in the USA under the SSA did not provide this guarantee and had to be changed in ways that made this guarantee real. He concluded, "This change is of primary importance if we are to accomplish any social purpose with our system."[97]

Epstein was also critical of the impact social security would have on purchasing power in the economy as can be seen in his December 1938 article, "Why Cheer for Social Security?" in the *Nation's Business*. His article noted that there were statistics to show that the pension system and unemployment insurance were withdrawing more money from the economy in taxes than was being paid out for benefits, at least through 1938, which caused a negative impact on consumer purchasing power.[98] The economy went into a recession during 1937–1938 and Epstein blamed the SSA. He argued that the New Deal had long argued that increased purchasing power was the key to recovery. With the SSA, the government instead had removed "large sums from mass buying power."[99] To prevent this problem, Epstein insisted that the SSA needed to be amended in a way that helped the elderly and the unemployed receive higher benefits but also led to a more robust economic recovery.

In his criticisms of social security, Epstein was a compatriot to Townsend in the sense that neither of them believed that benefits should be matched to earlier contributions. Instead, benefits should be paid through higher taxes on the affluent. By arguing this way, they both helped to break the link between a living wage and consumption, and helped pave the way for the consumerist policies that began after World War II. The same can be said about the next writer to be considered.

William Withers and the Social Security Compromise

Once the system of pensions and unemployment insurance was put in place, economists began assessing its nature and effects. One of them was William Withers (1906–1987). Withers had a PhD from the Columbia

University and in 1939 was assistant professor of economics at Queens College, where he remained until he retired. He gave a broad-based assessment of social security in his book, *Financing Economic Security in the United States.* Withers recognized that for the first time the federal government was taking a greater share of the burden of providing economic security.

According to Withers, the underlying philosophy of federal programs for economic security had to be considered in light of the difficulty where the government had to determine if it would provide economic security on a "need principle" or on an "ability principle."[100] Withers argued, "Under capitalism governments may be expected to emphasize the ability principle, rather than the need principle, in financing relief and social security." The ability principle needed lower levels of government spending to implement and required "the ability of the insecure to contribute to their own support,"[101] He wrote,

> The Roosevelt Administration tended, therefore, to perpetuate the ability principle in the Social Security Act, since it reverted to an emphasis upon what it regarded as insurance features and the concept of individual responsibility. Benefits were to be paid according to the amount of money contributed by the beneficiary. Payments were to be received as a right, not in relation to need.[102]

The contributions may have been called a tax for legal reasons, but those taxes and the way benefits were paid out were based on the "ability principle." Since the "need principle" was consistent with a living wage, Withers can be seen as viewing the New Deal as inadequately providing that living wage.

The result of the adherence to the "ability principle" in the SSA was that it was paid for through a regressive tax that hit the poor harder than it hit the wealthy. Withers believed that the provision of programs for economic security would not hurt the economy as long as progressive income taxes replaced the payroll tax.[103] The failure to move in that direction showed the "considerable timidity" which had "marked the framing of American social security legislation."[104] The New Deal had not gone far enough in finding a fair way to ensure the economic security of a living wage in the SSA.

The SSA was also being counterproductive in terms of the economy, because it reduced the purchasing power of the lower-income groups. The problem in determining whether payroll taxes for old-age benefits and unemployment insurance reduced the purchasing power of wage earners depended on the extent to which the businesses that collected and paid parts of the tax were able to shift the tax to someone else. Withers concluded "that pay-roll taxes, as well as sales and commodity taxes, will be borne mainly by labor, through lower wages or increased prices."[105]

From this perspective, Withers considered the social security taxes to be a reduction of consumer purchasing power and they would likely reduce overall consumption in the economy. Consequently, he favored the view "that if the security payments were financed out of progressive taxes or borrowing ... an increase in purchasing power would result and the distribution of the lower incomes might be altered in ways profitable to business."[106] Without such a change in the funding of the SSA, it would be bad for a living wage and for consumer purchasing power.

Carl Shoup on Clark's Approach

There is one unfriendly criticism of the SSA that needs to be included here. As mentioned several times in this chapter, the proponents of the SSA used Clark's social overhead cost approach (see Chapter 2) to justify social insurance as part of a living wage. In March 1939, the *Annals of the American Academy of Political and Social Science* published a special issue on appraising social security and that approach was challenged in an article, "Taxing for Social Security," by Carl Shoup (1902–2000), associate professor of economics at Columbia University. Shoup was a long-time professor at Columbia and used his expertise in taxation to help craft a tax code for Japan after World War II. In considering what the best tax would be to pay for social security, Shoup concluded that the payroll tax could be shifted to other persons as readily as any other tax and that it thus had no inherent advantage in matching contributions to benefits.[107]

Shoup then considered the argument, related to the social overhead cost approach of Clark, as requiring businesses to contribute to the social security of their workers based on the idea that workers had to be supported by society when they were unemployed or retired.[108] From this approach, social security should be funded through a tax that would be added to a business' costs and then be passed on to the consumer through higher prices. Shoup did not agree with this approach, arguing that finding a tax that would work and not alter the competitive balance among different industries with different cost structures would be difficult. He also believed that it was difficult to know the extent to which businesses "were not already covering the old-age cost."[109] The idea that there was a social overhead cost of labor that had to be covered by wages was a key ingredient in the quest for a living wage and Shoup did not find it appealing or economically sensible.

The point Shoup was making is crucial to economic justification of a living wage. The idea expressed by Clark and advocated by others such as Ryan was that a living wage should be incorporated into the cost structure of business and then passed on to consumers with prices that reflected all the costs of producing the product. The problem Shoup raised was that businesses were not all equal in their ability to pass costs on to consumers with higher prices. If they were not able to raise their prices due to competition and a highly elastic demand for their product, their profits might suffer and they might even become bankrupt. Here, as with other critics of the New Deal approach, Shoup missed seeing the perspective that a living wage came before profits and that firms that could not pay a living wage should not be allowed to exist. Instead, they were being subsidized by the society at large when workers who did not earn a living wage were helped out by government or charity. To living wage proponents, a firm that needed this type of a subsidy to exist was not acceptable.

Conclusion

One interesting finding of the review of the persons surveyed in this chapter is that the SSA had a wide range of support. There was agreement among politicians, business leaders, unions, and economists that the provision of unemployment insurance and pensions was a critical part of economic security. Although it was rarely stated openly, social security was also an essential ingredient of a living wage. The arguments in this chapter mirrored those of Ryan and Clark, presented in Chapters 1 and 2. Ryan believed that a living wage was a right and the proponents of social security presented unemployment insurance and pensions as a contractual right between the government and its citizens. Clark had added the idea that the use of labor in production included a social overhead cost that should be made part of the wage package and we have seen his argument employed several times as justification for social security.

There were critics who believed that the SSA went too far in terms of creating a paternalistic federal government.[110] The USA had long been based on a spirit of individualism whereby the fit took care of themselves and added to the charities that provided a modicum of support to the unfit. Roosevelt offered an answer to these critics in his acceptance speech after his renomination for the presidency on June 27, 1936. His view of the situation was, “Liberty requires opportunity to make a living—a living decent according to the standard of the time, a living which gives man not only enough to live by, but something to live for.” Instead, in the USA the control over the standard of living—a living wage—was concentrated in the hands of a small group of businessmen. To redress this wrong, “the American citizen could appeal only to the organized power of Government.”[111] Liberty required a living wage and the federal government should attain it for labor.

Despite this claim by the president, critics such as Withers and Epstein, insisted that the Act did not go far enough in providing a living wage. To be sure, the SSA had established the benefits of social insurance as a right that was consistent with the dignity of the living wage. But those benefits were meager and were paid for by their recipients. The living wage movement believed that benefits provided by social insurance should be paid for by the community as a whole, and especially by the wealthy, through income redistribution. Instead, it was taxes levied on workers and taxes shifted to them through higher prices and lower wages that paid for their benefits. This was hardly an effective way to attain a living wage. Armstrong’s formula for a living wage was that it had to consist of social insurance plus a minimum wage. If social insurance was paid for by lower wages or higher prices to workers, the formula would not work out.

Roosevelt had an answer to these critics as well. On the third anniversary of the signing of the SSA he acknowledged,

> The Social Security Act offers to all our citizens a workable and working method of meeting urgent present needs and of forestalling future needs. It utilizes the familiar machinery of our Federal-State government to promote the common welfare and the economic stability of the nation. The Act does not offer anyone, either individually or collectively, an easy life-nor was it ever intended so to do. None of the sums of money paid out to individuals in assistance or insurance will spell anything approaching abundance. But they will furnish that minimum necessary to keep a foothold; and that is the kind of protection Americans want.[112]

Here we can see the problem of defining a living wage. Roosevelt’s critics believed that the workers, the unemployed, and the retirees, all should have a living wage. Roosevelt agreed, but his definition of a living wage differed from that of his critics.

These critics also took the consumerist approach of gauging the impact of social security on consumption. Townsend had led off the consumerist approach by arguing that pensions for the elderly would revive the economy. The authors of the book, *An Economic Program for American Democracy*, along with Epstein worried that payment of payroll taxes by workers into a reserve fund at a time when no benefits were being paid would reduce consumption spending. They overlooked the fact that the federal government would be loaning the money in the reserve fund to itself and spending it. Douglas also recognized that payroll taxes would reduce consumption spending, but appreciated that federal government might spend the reserve fund on wasteful projects which would simply shift consumption spending to another form.

The history of the old-age pension plan and the unemployment insurance program since the passage of the SSA has been one of increased coverage, increased benefits, and the resulting increased costs. We can see this pattern by considering the pension plan. Even before it was to begin its payments, the Congress amended the Act in 1939 to change the reserve fund into a trust fund with the payroll tax paid directly into the fund. It also kept the payroll tax at its initial level of 1 percent for two years longer and extended the period for the gradual increase of the tax. The old-age pension benefits were increased and the beginning of the payment of benefits was moved up from January 1, 1942, to January 1, 1940.[113] In addition, the amendments expanded the benefits for children of widows and single mothers and added to spousal benefits. Allan Carlson interprets these changes as "constructed to undergird a family wage economy."[114] Since then, benefits have been expanded in terms of more persons being covered and new benefits added, such as disability coverage starting in 1956. Automatic cost-of-living adjustments for retirees on social security pensions were approved by the Congress in 1972, to begin in 1975. The payroll tax has gradually increased to 6.2 percent, payable by both workers and employers and the ceiling on the amount of income subject to the tax has also increased. The same pattern of increased coverage and benefits has taken place with unemployment insurance.

Throughout this chapter, we have seen several individuals such as Epstein and Stewart who argued that the benefits were too low, certainly too low to qualify as equivalent to a living wage. The idea behind a living wage was that it had to be based on meeting the needs of a decent standard of living. If we use Barbara Armstrong's rough definition of a living wage as "a wage sufficient to obviate the need for public charity,"[115] however, we can identify an inadequacy of the social security pensions. Starting in 1972, the Congress recognized that a number of elderly persons received social security pensions that were too low for a bare standard of living. It added in a program of Supplemental Security Income (SSI) as an entitlement to lift some of the elderly out of extreme poverty. While an entitlement is not quite public charity, the SSI program comes close enough to Armstrong's definition to indicate that not all retirees have a living wage.

The second concern is with a key component of the pension plan, the reserve fund, now referred to as the Old-Age, Survivors, and Disability Insurance Trust Funds.

The key to the solvency of this fund is the ratio of workers to retirees. With the retirement of the baby boom generation that ratio will fall. As opponents of the Trust Fund pointed out during the 1930s, the bonds in the Trust Fund must somehow be turned into cash if they are to be used to pay benefits for the large number of baby boomers who will retire in the next two decades. Turning those bonds into cash will only be feasible through increased taxes or reduced spending such that the federal government runs a surplus in its budget. The federal government may be effective in doing what is right in terms of providing a living income to retirees, but its leaders have not yet figured out how to make its programs such as social security economically sustainable.

Notes

1. Bortz, 2015.
2. Armstrong, 1932, p. 381.
3. Armstrong, 1932, p. 394.
4. Armstrong, 1932, p. 437.
5. Armstrong, 1932, p. 462.
6. Armstrong, 1932, p. 463.
7. Armstrong, 1932, pp. 465–537.
8. Armstrong, 1932, p. 548.
9. Townsend, 1933.
10. *Long Beach Press-Gazette*, 1933, italics in the original.
11. Holtzman, 1963, 17, 49 and 87.
12. Holtzman, 1963, p. 37.
13. *Long Beach Press-Gazette*, 1933.
14. Story, 1934, p. 17.
15. Domhoff and Webber, 2011, pp. 3662–3683.
16. Committee on Economic Security Appendix, 2014.

17. Roosevelt, 1935a, p. 226.
18. Roosevelt, 1935a, p. 226.
19. Roosevelt, 1935a, p. 226.
20. Roosevelt, 1935a, p. 227.
21. Social Security Administration, 2014a, pp. 2, 4, 10, and 11.
22. Green, 1934b, p. 1292.
23. Green, 1934b, p. 1292–3.
24. *American Federationist*, 1935a, pp. 254–5.
25. *American Federationist*, 1935a, pp. 255–7.
26. *American Federationist*, 1935a, pp. 259–60.
27. Lewisohn, 1935a, p. 14.
28. Lewisohn, 1935a, p. 2.
29. Lewisohn, 1935a, p. 6.
30. Lewisohn, 1935b, pp. 67–69.
31. Lewisohn, 1935a, pp. 11–12.
32. Lewisohn, 1935a, p. 12–13.
33. Lewisohn, 1935b, p. 72.
34. Lewisohn, 1935a, p. 3.
35. Wagner, 1935b, p. 294.
36. Wagner, 1935b, p. 295.
37. Wagner, 1935b, p. 296.
38. Domhoff and Webber, 2011, pp. 3858–4016.
39. Social Security Administration, 2014b, p. 41.
40. Social Security Administration, 2014c, pp. 172 and 178.
41. Ryan, 1906, p. 33, italics in the original.
42. Social Security Administration, 2014d, p. 385.
43. Social Security Administration, 2014e, pp. 5471, 5529, 5535, 5700, 5858, 5909, 5956, 5996, 5982, 6038 and 6042.
44. Social Security Administration, 2014e, pp. 5561, 57704, 5714, 5886, 6074 and 6075.
45. Social Security Administration, 2014f, p, 5815.
46. Social Security Administration, 2014f, p. 5961.
47. Social Security Administration, 2014g, p. 164.
48. Social Security Administration, 2014h, pp. 1217 and 1218.
49. Social Security Administration, 2014i, pp. 9354–9355.
50. Douglas, 1939, p. 100.
51. Domhoff and Webber, 2011, pp. 4060–4062.
52. Social Security Administration, 2014j.
53. Schieber and Shoven, 1999, pp. 34 and 37.
54. Poole, 2006, p. 46.
55. Douglas, 1939, pp. 100 and 110.
56. Supreme Court, 1937c, pp. 70–71.

57. Supreme Court, 1937d, p. 73.
58. Perkins, 1935b, p. 792.
59. Perkins, 1935b, p. 793–4.
60. Perkins, 1935b, pp. 793–4.
61. Douglas, 1936, p. 1.
62. Douglas, 1936, p. 8.
63. Douglas, 1936, p. 13.
64. Douglas, 1936, p. 14.
65. Kaufman, 2008, p. 182.
66. Litchfield, 1936, p. 149.
67. Committee on Economic Security, 1937, p. 3.
68. Committee on Economic Security, 1937, p. 139.
69. Committee on Economic Security, 1937, p. 197.
70. Committee on Economic Security, 1937, p. 198.
71. Committee on Economic Security, 1937, pp. 202–203.
72. Committee on Economic Security, 1937, p. 204.
73. Committee on Economic Security, 1937, p. 205.
74. Witte, 1937, p. 26.
75. Witte, 1937, p. 27.
76. Landon, 1936, p. 27.
77. Johnson, 1937, p. 116.
78. *The Nation*, 1936, p. 408.
79. *The New Republic*, 1935c, p. 268.
80. Gilbert et al., 1938, pp. 49–50.
81. *The Nation*, 1935, p. 116.
82. Stewart, 1935a, p. 67–9.
83. Stewart, 1935b, p. 247–8.
84. *The New Republic*, 1935a, p. 327.
85. *The New Republic*, 1935b, p. 210.
86. Ryan, 1927.
87. Epstein, 1936a, pp. v–vii.
88. Epstein, 1936a, p. 23.
89. Epstein, 1936a, pp. 34–43.
90. Epstein, 1936a, p. 57.
91. Epstein, 1936a, p. 94.
92. Epstein, 1936a, p. 719.
93. Epstein, 1936a, p. 779.
94. Epstein, 1936a, p. 789.
95. Epstein, 1936a, pp. 818–819.
96. Epstein, 1936a, p. 845.
97. Epstein, 1936a, p. 845.
98. Epstein, 1938, p. 68.

99. Epstein, 1938, 16.
100. Withers, 1939, pp. 16–17.
101. Withers, 1939, pp. 17–18.
102. Withers, 1939, p. 41.
103. Withers, 1939, p. 137.
104. Withers, 1939, pp. 188–89.
105. Withers, 1939, p. 127.
106. Withers, 1939, p. 131.
107. Shoup, 1939, p. 165.
108. Shoup, 1939, p. 170–171.
109. Shoup, 1939, p. 165.
110. Pollack, 1936, p. 385; Nock, 1936, p. 484.
111. Roosevelt, 1936b.
112. Roosevelt, 1938c.
113. Blakey and Blakey, 1939, pp. 705–6.
114. Carlson, 1988, p. 26.
115. Armstrong, 1932, p. xiii.

CHAPTER 6

The Right to Earn Enough: The Fair Labor Standards Act

The NIRA had a goal of "living wages for labor."[1] Proponents of a living wage believed that the NIRA as a system of planning would lead to the collaboration of business and labor in writing codes of fair prices and wages. Industry code writers would determine what an acceptable living wage would be for each industry and establish a minimum wage for the industry consistent with that living wage. When the NIRA was eliminated by the US Supreme Court, the Roosevelt Administration endeavored to reach the same result by other means, such as collective bargaining under the NLRA and the social insurance of the SSA. Although it took until 1938, the New Deal eventually enacted the FLSA to establish a minimum wage, and the living wage agenda of John Ryan and the Progressive reformers was complete.

Roosevelt's message to the Congress on May 27, 1937, asking it to legislate a minimum wage was emphatic on the need to require business to pay a living wage. He stated what he was seeking from the law as follows:

> To protect the fundamental interests of free labor and a free people we propose that only goods which have been produced under conditions which meet the minimum standards of free labor shall be admitted to interstate commerce. Goods produced under conditions which do not meet rudimentary standards of decency should be regarded as contraband and ought not to be allowed to pollute the channels of interstate trade.[2]

D. Stabile, *The Political Economy of a Living Wage*,
DOI 10.1007/978-3-319-32473-9_6

This statement parallels Roosevelt's statement on the NIRA that "no business which depends for existence on paying less than living wages to its workers has any right to continue in this country."[3] Interestingly, as we will see in this chapter, the initial version of the FLSA retained the approach of the NIRA to some extent by giving flexibility to industry boards to set the minimum wages for their industry within certain ranges.

Before getting to the FLSA, this chapter will first survey thc obstacles that had to be overcome to pass minimum wage legislation in the USA and review the arguments that overcame those obstacles. It will also describe the legislative history of the FLSA and the way it produced a minimum wage that did not equate to a living wage. Unions were especially in favor of a living minimum wage as the chapter will describe. The AFL, however, did not want the FLSA to interfere with collective bargaining, while the CIO saw it with a consumerist perspective that higher wages would increase consumption and bring a recovery.

Economic, Political, and Legal Problems of Minimum Wage Legislation

The persons in charge of establishing a minimum wage faced the same daunting task of how to define a living wage. To be sure, a minimum wage aims at giving workers who receive it the bare essentials of life, while a living wage has a goal of a decent life. In both cases, the issue is that the cost of living that a worker experiences is determined by a number of variables, such as family size and region of the country. There is also an issue of whether a mandated wage will represent an individual's income or a household income. Wage increases can affect the profitability of the firms in the industry as well as employment levels. Because of these complexities, advocates for the market economy often express reservations about minimum wage laws.

To give an example of an economic analysis of the problems the minimum wage or a living wage might cause, let us consider Arthur Cecil Pigou (1877–1954). Pigou's contribution to economics resulted from his development of welfare economics in his highly regarded book, *The Economics of Welfare*.[4] In that book, he argued that when wages were fair, that is, equal to the worker's marginal product, there should be no intervention in labor markets. With this argument, he directly challenged the notion of the living wage. He indicated this by considering the claim that when fair wages (equal to value added) were low they "ought to be raised far enough to yield a decent subsistence to the average worker." This claim, he went on, was confused by a poor definition what a living wage meant. He wrote, "A living wage implies, for workmen of normal capacity in any industry which enjoys it, a 'living income.'" This conception of a living wage, however, was based on a male worker who had good health and a typical family to support. It would not apply to persons with poor health, many children, and perhaps parents to support. Not could it take into account that some spouses of workers earned an income while others did not.[5] A living wage was not easy to define in terms of all the complexities of life that it must account for.

Moreover, proponents of a minimum wage faced a hostile legal climate because the US Supreme Court had overruled attempts by state legislatures to regulate the wages and hours of work. In the *Lochner Case* in 1905, the Court overturned a New York law limiting the hours an individual could work in a day on the basis that it interfered with the workers' freedom of contract. Justice Rufus Peckham felt that workers might want to earn the extra money the additional hours would bring but the law kept them from contracting to do so. In the *Adkins Case* in 1923, the Court overturned a District of Columbia minimum wage law for women and children, enacted by the US Congress, because an elevator operator lost her job when the higher wage imposed by the law caused her employer to shift to a self-service elevator; here again, she was not allowed to contract for a wage low enough to keep her from being displaced by technology. Justice George Sutherland made it clear that "the right to contract one's affairs is part of the liberty of the individual."[6] At the same time, over one-third of the states had minimum wage laws on the books at the time of the *Adkins Case*,[7] indicating that the Court's view was countered by voters in many areas of the country.

Efforts to mandate a federal minimum wage during the New Deal also encountered political problems. At first glance, these political problems appear surprising. In 1936, Roosevelt won reelection in a landslide that should have been taken as a mandate for his programs and their continuation. Instead, he became embroiled in a fight over his plan to expand the size of the US Supreme Court. It was a fight he lost, partly because it was unpopular with the public and partly because a bi-partisan coalition of Republicans and conservative Democrats, mostly from the South, were able to defeat the plan in the Congress. Roosevelt spent too much of his political capital in the fight and that coalition learned that they could take him on with a good chance of winning. Roosevelt was also hampered by the recession of 1937–1938, which took many members of the New Deal by surprise and undermined further the image that the president and his team were astute policymakers.

This chapter will describe how these factors played out in the legislative history of the FLSA, which legislated a minimum wage as a way to attain a living wage. It will also describe how the US Supreme Court altered its legal position on minimum wage laws in a way that was consistent with the political economy of a living wage. But before the FLSA was passed in 1938, proponents of a living wage would counter the arguments of the market view. I will focus on arguments that were made during the Great Depression and that related to a living wage.

Herbert J. Weber Proposes a Rising Minimum Wage

Our starting point is an obscure work with an important point. In 1930, Herbert J. Weber published an interesting nine-page booklet with a seductive title, *A Living Wage*.[8] Weber and the background of his pamphlet are not known, but one of the most interesting things about it is that it had introductions by Thomas Nixon Carver (1865–1961), a long-time professor of economics at Harvard University, and Paul Douglas. Both economists endorsed the proposal Weber set forth, that the minimum wage should be "raised constantly, little by little and with plenty of advance notice but with unending persistency."[9]

There were a number of ideas contained in Weber's proposal. First, the idea of a slow and steady but well-known pattern of advance in the minimum wage would give businesses time to adjust and cause minimal impact on labor markets. The primary way business would adjust would be to replace workers with machines, thereby increasing labor's productivity and attaining economic progress. Weber recognized that the use of machines in production was an important part of economic development and he argued that a rising minimum wage would motivate business to speed up technological innovation of labor-saving methods.[10]

Because he believed that the federal government would have to legislate a rising minimum wage, Weber's next idea related to how it would do so. He first proposed an amendment to the US Constitution that would allow the federal government to take action despite previous cases where the US Supreme Court had struck down minimum wage laws. Once the amendment was in place, the Congress could enact "a minimum wage law in general terms." A "temporary national commission" would then be selected to define industries and create a "trade board" for each industry made up of employees and employers. The "trade boards" would set a minimum wage for each industry, following the guidelines set by the general law. In setting the minimum wage, the board for each industry would base it on "not upon the cost of living but upon the ability of industry to pay."[11] He added,

> The living wage of classical social reform, a wage based upon the cost of living under a standard which is at least just above the poverty line, may be the ideal, but it can never be the actual criterion of any particular minimum wage order. The least that could be considered a real living wage is altogether beyond the per worker income of any country in the world.[12]

The only way to attain a living wage was for the economy to grow and the best way to secure that growth was through the speeding up of technology that would be motivated by the rising minimum wage.

For the approach to work effectively, it would be important to set the minimum wage for each industry at a level that most firms in the industry could afford to pay. The minimum wage would have to be high enough to give business an incentive to adopt labor-saving equipment, but low enough so that the business had enough funds to pay for the equipment. The money for the increased wages thus had to be the result of cost savings from greater efficiency and not from a reduction of profits. Weber had confidence that the industry boards setting the minimum wage would gain the expertise to find that proper wage level and suggested that "what the better employers pay of their own accord ordinarily furnishes the best criterion of what all the employers can pay if they have to."[13] He also indicated that "at frequent intervals the minimum wage is to be translated into current dollars" to keep it from being eroded by inflation.[14]

The minimum wage also had to be supplemented by "a thoroughgoing social insurance system." The purpose of a minimum wage was "to give everyone the means to the enjoyment of the highest possible standard of life." The wage-earner needed income when unemployed but could not afford to save for that possibility with only a minimum wage. Unemployment insurance would take care of that problem, but here, too, a worker earning a minimum wage could not afford premiums for it, so it was up to the government to provide social insurance in the form of "unemployment, disability, old age, and death benefits," with the disability benefits including "extensive medical and hospital care."[15]

Weber's booklet brings out a number of points regarding a living wage. Weber argued that the national income would have to grow considerably before a living wage could be paid to everyone and he was proposing a gradual approach for bringing it about. His approach also took a dynamic perspective. The free market view of the minimum wage is a static view that an increased wage would reduce the demand for labor, holding everything constant. Weber was arguing that other things would not remain constant. In his view, a gradually rising minimum wage would cause the economy to grow and increase the demand for labor. We will see later in this chapter that many of Weber's proposals were discussed and some of them incorporated in the FLSA. Finally, Weber's proposal is another example of the formula reflecting the theme of this book, that is, a minimum wage plus social insurance yielded a living wage. He left out collective bargaining because he believed it would apply only to workers earning well above his minimum standard.

Armstrong and the Minimum Wage as a Living Wage

As indicated in Chapter 2, Barbara Armstrong focused on social insurance and the minimum wage as essential to a living wage program. In this chapter, we will present her views on the minimum wage as a living wage. Her starting point was with the presumed public indifference to the problems of low-paid workers. Most citizens of the USA had become inured to the problems of low-wage workers and they were additionally comforted by the idea that workers in the modern economy were much better off than workers in the dark ages of medievalism. The complacency thus generated had to "be broken through before the story of the Legislative Living Wage will find a general audience."[16]

To break through that complacency Armstrong took her readers through a history of wage regulation from medieval times to the present society. In the present society, technological change had created large firms and workers with low skills. As a result, bargaining power had shifted to the side of business almost exclusively. Efforts to establish minimum wages by legislation had foundered in the USA, because the Supreme Court had found minimum wage laws to be unconstitutional. Armstrong used her law degree to give a long, detailed analysis of those constitutional issues and to argue that the Court had decided wrongly.[17] The result of what she felt to be the Court's erroneous decisions meant that many workers in the USA experienced wages below a living wage.

Armstrong then presented an economic analysis of the minimum wage. Definition of the living wage that a minimum wage should put in place was difficult because the standard of living varied by location. The spread of the modern industrial economy, however, was closing the differentials based on locality and a national standard for a living wage might eventually be possible. Meanwhile, efforts to establish a minimum wage might not bring about a living wage initially. The first efforts would more likely center on bringing "the worst paying firms in the industry up to the standards of the better concerns," at least for unskilled labor. That might not result in a living wage. Moreover, wage increases would have to ensure that business would still earn a profit. To be sure, she added, "an industry which cannot survive with wages at the level of most of its contemporaries is so undesirable an industry as to merit extinction."[18] This view, as we have seen throughout this book, was commonly held by the Progressives and the unionists and was reflected in discussions of the New Deal. Armstrong, however, indicated that it would take considerable courage to let businesses go out of existence during a period of high unemployment, such as the 1930s.

Some businesses could pay for the higher wages by raising prices, depending on the price elasticity of demand for their product. If they faced a highly inelastic demand such that prices increases would cost them few sales, they might raise prices and do nothing else. Firms with a lesser capability to raise prices might make their employees work more intensely to increase their productivity. Or they might use technological innovation to replace workers with machines to cut costs. Armstrong acknowledged that "some speeding up of the mechanization that has been taking place throughout industry should be expected to result from the minimum wage." That might cause unemployment, but mechanization was "taking place quite independent of stimulation by legal wage regulations." Technological unemployment was a looming social problem that would one day need to be addressed and "the slight hastening of its arrival which a legal minimum wage may cause could scarcely be deemed a social detriment."[19] Regardless of its impact on employment, minimum wage legislation was the hallmark of every industrial country but the USA. The most widely accepted standard for that minimum wage, Armstrong concluded, was "the standard of living that the laborers' wage of the better firms provides."[20]

By placing the minimum wage at a level of the most efficient firms, Armstrong was repeating the message of living wage advocates such as Ryan, Clark, and Filene. None of them were concerned that the result might be bankruptcy among the least efficient firms. Rather, it was a result to be welcomed. Instead of the inefficient being weeded out by low or negative profits, as economists had typically argued for over a century, they would be eliminated by their inability to pay a living wage.

Perkins and the Need for a Minimum Wage Law

In July 1933, the Secretary of Labor, Frances Perkins, made a case for a minimum wage law in a surprising place, the pages of *Nation's Business*. She based the need for a minimum wage on the existence of sweatshops that were coming into existence during the Depression to produce items, in her example clothing, at the lowest possible cost through the payment of low wages. Most clothing retailers were moral enough to want to buy from manufacturers who paid workers a living wage, but if the store down the street was buying clothes from a sweatshop and selling them for a lower price, our moral clothing retailer would be at a competitive disadvantage. He would have to buy from sweatshops to keep his prices low in order to remain competitive. The result would be that the moral manufacturer would lose sales and be compelled to operate under sweatshop rules. Perkins summarized her case as follows: "As wages in these shops fall, it means an increased pressure for lower wages throughout the industry," which would result in "lower wages in every other industry."[21]

A minimum wage law would stop this race to the bottom of reduced wages. Business leaders should not fear a minimum wage because it was aimed at unscrupulous sweatshop operators and not them. "If the ten per cent of business men who are willing to exploit labor can be controlled," Perkins wrote, "I feel that the others can be depended upon to fix fair standards of wages." The NIRA was taking care of a part of the problem through the development of codes of fair wages and prices. In particular, it was making enforcement of a minimum wage more feasible by preventing the problem of "runaway" sweatshops, low-wage manufacturers of clothing that relocated as soon as they were discovered. A minimum wage law would protect both the exploited worker and the "responsible manufacturer" who was still "trying to pay a living wage."[22]

In his brief history of the living family wage, Allan Carlson calls Perkins a key person in the Roosevelt Administration in the movement for a living wage.[23] Her use of the term "living wage" in her article in *Nation's Business* would indicate that Carlson's designation was justified. As further evidence, I can cite the direct contact between Perkins and Ryan noted in Chapter 1. It turned into a very close relationship. In her biography of Perkins, Kirstin Downey reports that during the 1936 presidential election, Perkins secured a plank in the Democratic Party's platform calling for a minimum wage defined as a living wage, with the definition derived from Ryan's work.[24] In addition, at the end of her career as the Secretary of Labor, Perkins wrote to Ryan to thank him for his help over the years she was in office. She told him, "We have had, I think, a common objective in which we felt a moral purpose and the cooperative effort has therefore been of great constructive benefit to the wage earners of America."[25] Moreover, in arguing as she did in *Nation's Business*, Perkins was following the social overhead cost argument of Clark (see Chapter 2). Clark had argued that government intervention was needed to enable all firms in an industry to increase wages without suffering a competitive disadvantage. Perkins agreed and she was not the only one to do so.

The US Supreme Court Approves Minimum Wage Laws

For over three decades the US Supreme Court had declared efforts by states to enact minimum wage laws for women unconstitutional, usually on the grounds that the laws interfered with the right of all persons to negotiate contracts freely as in the case of the making of a wage contract between an employer and an employee. In 1936, in a 5-4 decision, it had held a New York minimum wage law for women unconstitutional, using its previous decision in the *Adkins Case* as a precedent. The fact that minimum wage laws kept coming to the Court indicated that they had attained popular support.

When the issue of the minimum wage came to the Court again in 1937 through a challenge to the law of Washington State, the Court approved it by a 5-4 vote in the case, *West Coast Hotel Company v. Parrish*. The hotel relied on the precedent of the *Adkins Case* in its legal arguments. To the US Supreme Court, this situation meant a review of the *Adkins Case* was in order. In making that review, the US Supreme Court held that while the *Adkins Case* had been based on the principle that "the violation alleged by those attacking minimum wage regulation for women is deprivation of freedom of contract," the Constitution placed many restrictions on the freedom of contract and the argument that these restrictions could be "exercised in the public interest with respect to contracts between employer and employee is undeniable."[26] To be sure, it could be argued that workers were adults and should be capable of making their own labor contracts. But in a number of cases, the Court had recognized "the inequality in the footing of the parties."[27]

In addition, the minimum wage law of Washington had been agreed upon after lengthy discussion among persons representing workers, management, and the public. In short, the community had agreed to the law. Moreover, the law did not compel any business to pay the minimum wage or any other wage because it could merely close, although it was assumed under the laws that it might have to accept lower profits when it chose to stay in business and pay the minimum wage to women. As a result, its freedom was not impaired and the Court indicated the impact of its ruling as follows:

> The legislature was entitled to adopt measures to reduce the evils of the "sweating system," the exploiting of workers at wages so low as to be insufficient to meet the bare cost of living thus making their very helplessness the occasion of a most injurious competition. The legislature had the right to consider that its minimum wage requirements could be an important aid in carrying out its policy of protection. The adoption of similar requirements by many states evidences a deep-seated conviction both as to the presence of an evil and as to the means adapted to check it.[28]

Cass Sunstein considers the *Parrish Case* to be a tipping point in the provision of economic rights. To make his point, he uses two diametrically opposed statements by Supreme Court justices. The first statement, by Justice George Sutherland, is from the *Adkins Case.* Sutherland argued as follows, "To the extent that the sum fixed [by the minimum wage statute] exceeds the fair value of the services rendered, it amounts to a compulsory exaction from the employer for the support of a partially indigent person, for whose condition there rests upon him no peculiar responsibility and therefore, in effect, arbitrarily shifts to his shoulders a burden which, if it belongs to anybody, belongs to society as a whole."[29] In economic terms, this statement mirrors the thinking of John Bates Clark and the competitive version of his marginal product theory. As described in Chapter 1, he argued that under the ideal conditions of competition a worker's wage equaled what she contributed to production and employers could not pay her any more than that. Sutherland followed this laissez-faire approach and applied it to the need for freedom of contract between employers and workers.

To be sure, Sutherland was not opposed to a living wage for workers, but only if they were the outcome of the market process, not through government legislation. He indicated this position in the Adkins Case thusly, "The ethical right of every worker, man or woman, to a living wage may be conceded."[30] Following Gompers, Sutherland believed that unions were the best way to attain a living wage for workers, but only as done through market negotiations.

In contrast, in the *Parrish Case*, Chief Justice Charles Evans Hughes argued, "The exploitation of a class of workers who are in an unequal position with respect to bargaining and are thus relatively defenseless against the denial of a living wage…casts a burden for their support upon the community. What these workers lose in wages the taxpayers are called upon to pay."[31] Hughes has entered the world of John Bates Clark's son, John Maurice Clark. As noted in Chapter 2, the younger Clark had argued that there was a social overhead cost of maintaining the workforce and used his argument in support of a living wage. Firms that did not pay a living wage were being subsidized by society and Hughes gave Clark's approach constitutional sanction. Instead of society wrongly shifting the burden of those costs on the business, as Sutherland believed, Hughes saw it as proper to shift the burden from society to business.

In reaching its opinion, the Court was relying on a community approach that fit more readily with a living wage than with a market economy. Its decisions on state minimum wage laws also meant that the FLSA was on solid constitutional grounds when it was passed by the Congress and signed by the president on June 25, 1938, to set minimum wages for workers and to place limits on the hours workers could work in a pay period. To be sure, it took two additional cases at the Supreme Court in 1940 to establish that the federal government had the authority to regulate wages, but the *Parrish Case* had set a strong precedent to make the decisions in those cases easy.

Douglas Reexamines a Living Wage

As noted in the earlier chapters and as we will see in the next section, Paul Douglas took a keen interest in the issues surrounding a government-mandated living wage. In the February 1938 issue of *The University of Chicago Law Review*, he renewed his interest in a living wage in an article, "The Economic Theory of Wage Regulation." Douglas offered four reasons why the government might regulate wages. The one pertinent to this chapter was that wage regulation was needed to establish "a minimum below which the pressure of competition and of employers should not force labor." He attributed this reasoning to Sidney and Beatrice Webb, the English Fabian Socialists, and characterized it in a way that was similar to the argument advanced by Frances Perkins earlier in this chapter. Because of competition and the need to reduce prices, some businesses cut wages below a living level giving them "a competitive advantage over their more scrupulous fellows." In this way, the "meaner" firms would capture the market and maintain low wage standards.[32]

One way to address this problem was through collective bargaining. When unions could not organize a large portion of an industry, however, it was up to the government to regulate wages. The justification for government regulation of wages, Douglas added, was based on the premise that "the vast mass of workers actually produce enough to support and reproduce themselves and that if they are paid less" it was due to their unequal bargaining power. Using an argument similar to that of Clark (see Chapter 2), Douglas characterized the justification for government regulation of wages as follows: "To compel the industry to pay a living wage is, therefore, regarded as being merely a measure which compels employers and consumers to restore to those who produce the articles in question at least as much physical energy as has been expended upon their production."[33] Opponents of this justification might argue that workers earned low wages because they had poor skills, which meant that a living wage would cause unemployment. Douglas argued that they only way to find out was to put a living wage in place and look at its results.

Once the notion of a living wage gained popularity, there remained the daunting tasks of defining the standard of living it implied in terms of goods and services and the number of persons dependent upon the worker. The standard of living could be calculated to some degree, as long as local standards were used. The issue of how many dependents to use was more problematic and Douglas once again weighed in against one standard being used, that is, a family of five (See Chapter 2). By paying a living wage based on that standard, "vast surpluses would be poured into the pockets of the majority" of workers who had fewer dependents.[34]

Another tough problem was determining how high a wage businesses in an industry could afford to pay. The assumption of living wage advocates was that if some firms in an industry could pay a living wage, all of them could. That assumption meant that all firms in an industry were equally efficient, and Douglas questioned that inference. He also considered that if firms were earning low profits and on the edge of bankruptcy wage increases should be used cautiously. It all depended on the ability of firms to pass on higher labor costs to consumers through higher prices. He found "strong evidence" that under the NRA business did pass their higher labor costs to consumers with higher prices, leaving business and labor in an unchanged situation.[35]

Despite all the concerns he raised regarding a living wage, Douglas ended up supporting it. He argued that there were times and places where "competition fails to work perfectly" in a way "as to make one skeptical about wages being fixed by natural law." This alone justified government regulation of wages and the need to fix a living wage in industries where "employers are able to drive the wage scale down to grossly inadequate levels."[36] In promoting a living wage, the government should start in industries where wages were low. It should also base its living wage on the standard of living for a family with fewer than five members. That would make the living wage too high for most workers. Instead, workers with large families should be given an allowance by the government to support their extra children and pay for them by a tax on monopoly profits. The difficulties in determining a complete wage structure for all workers and all family sizes were so daunting that Douglas concluded that "the government should primarily confine itself to the fixation of basic wages in substandard industries."[37]

Implicit in Douglas' approach was a view, consistent with the NIRA approach, that each industry should have a customized minimum wage. Instead of an overall, national minimum wage as we have today, the minimum wage would have to take into account the conditions that existed in each industry. This approach received serious consideration in the debates over the FLSA.

Douglas and Hackman Give the Details of the FLSA

In December 1938 and March 1939, Paul Douglas and Joseph Hackman published a two-part article on the FLSA in the *Political Science Quarterly*. The first article dealt with the legislative history of the Act. According to Douglas and Hackman, the supporters of the FLSA were motivated to enact a minimum wage by a desire to shelter labor from excessive competition, to eliminate the harmful effects of downward spirals of wage reductions, and to increase some wages as a way to restore purchasing power.

They also wanted to use the legal system to enforce shorter hours as part of the program to "share-the-work."[38] The politics of the legislation, however, did not permit a simple proposal to codify these objectives.

The summary that Douglas and Hackman provide of the maneuverings in the Congress over the drafting and final passing of the FLSA pointed to the key problem that a uniform national minimum wage was not acceptable to anyone in the Congress or to all the interest groups engaged in lobbying for or against the bill. Regional differences in the impact of the law had to be included, especially regarding the South. Congressmen from that region succeeded in keeping the House of Representatives from voting on the minimum wage bill until regional differences were implicitly included in it. Finally, someone had to determine where to establish the minimum wage and the maximum hours, since the two were related in defining the total income a worker would receive.

The FLSA solved this regional problem by setting a minimum flat rate of 25 cents an hour in the first year and 30 cents in the second with flexibility for mandated wages to be higher. An administrator in the US Department of Labor would oversee the law and could form advisory committees to establish wages above the absolute minimum in an industry as long as that minimum did not exceed 40 cents per hour. This approach allowed the advisory committees to place wages above the absolute minimum in some regions and keep the wage level at that absolute minimum in others, thereby creating regional differences.[39]

In their second article on the FLSA, Douglas and Hackman looked more closely at the final version of the law. They noted the exclusion of agriculture from the Act as well as parts of transportation and communication. Because of these exclusions as well as others that had not been decided, such as exemption for the disabled and for persons just starting to work in a job, it was difficult to discern how many workers would be affected by the FLSA.[40]

Douglas and Hackman presented an analysis of the work of the administrator of the FLSA in the Department of Labor and the advisory committees established to advise the administrator about what was best for each industry. The committees along with the FLSA administrator had the power to set the minimum wage in an industry somewhere between the minimum hourly rate and the maximum level the Congress had set, that is, between 30 and 40 cents an hour. They also had the discretion for seven years to keep revising the minimum wage they set for an industry if they believed a lower minimum was needed to avoid a decline in employment; the wage differential would be gradually phased out by 1945 when 40 cents an hour would become the national standard.[41]

The FLSA administrator and the advisory committee were charged with getting the minimum wage as close to 40 cents an hour as possible, subject to avoiding unemployment. They also had to take into consideration the wages for similar work set by collective bargaining, wages set by employers who voluntarily paid fair wages, the effect of transportation costs on the cost structure of the firm, which permitted a lower minimum wage in the South with its higher transportation costs, and the cost of living in the locality of a firm, another way to justify lower minimum wages in the South and in small towns versus metropolitan areas. The FLSA, moreover, required the minimum wage set for each industry to take a firm's production costs into account and set a lower minimum wage for higher-cost firms; this requirement was intended to avoid unemployment should higher-cost firms be bankrupted by a minimum wage and to protect latecomers to an industry who had not become efficient enough to reduce their costs. Douglas and Hackman objected to this last policy, because it kept inefficient firms in operation at a higher price to consumers when they should be weeded out.[42] To the extent that these potential problems posed by the FLSA were resolved, Douglas and Hackman were optimistic that the FLSA would be administered effectively.

Congress, a Living Wage, and the FLSA

Douglas and Hackman did not comment on the living wage aspects of the FLSA, which is surprising given Douglas' previous interest in a living wage. Another analyst, John S. Forsythe, did bring up the living wage elements in the FLSA. Writing in the summer 1939 issue of *Law and Contemporary Problems*, Forsythe provided a legislative history of the FLSA that documented the rise and fall of the living wage in the various versions of the FLSA that were considered by the Congress.

The initial impetus for the Congress to act on a minimum wage law was the US Supreme Court decision ending the NIRA with its provisions on minimum wages. When the Court upheld minimum wage laws at the state level, pressure for a federal minimum wage law increased further. Following Roosevelt's speech on May 24, 1937, calling for action on minimum wages, bills were introduced in the House and Senate. The legislative process for getting the bills passed was long and arduous. It took 13 months for the bill to become law, including a special session. During that time, the Congress heard over 1200 pages of testimony by labor leaders, business executives, and other experts. In all, ten versions of the bill were considered; the House was not able to vote on some of those bills because a coalition of Republicans and Southern Democrats on the House Rules Committee kept the bill from being voted on for a long period. The result of this process was that the final bill differed greatly from what Roosevelt had wanted.[43]

An important component in the changes in the different bills was the role the law would have in bringing about a living wage. The original bills called for a Fair Labor Standards Board (FLSB) of five members to take charge of implementing the Act. Its mandate would be to "keep goods produced under substandard labor conditions from entering interstate commerce." The Congress would fix minimum wages by law, but the FLSB would be able to change those wage levels. The idea was to give the FLSB flexibility. It could order wage and hour provision that would be binding and "had authority to fix a minimum 'fair' wage and a maximum 'reasonable' workweek." The FLSB was to be given guidelines by the law such that "it could not establish minimum wages of more than $1200 a year or 80 cents per hour except for overtime, night and extra-shift work."[44] The flexibility the FLSB had to set minimum wages at that level meant that it could give workers a pay rate close to a living wage. Wage boards had been a common feature of minimum wage laws enacted in Australia, New Zealand, and the UK[45] and had been recommended by Weber (see above).

In a changed attitude since the days of Samuel Gompers, who opposed social legislation,[46] labor leaders generally favored this version of the bill in the Senate hearings but wanted it changed in ways that kept government from supplanting unions as the vehicle for getter higher wages for workers. John L. Lewis of the United Mine Workers of America worried that if the FLSB set minimum wages and maximum hours that it considered "fair" and "reasonable," unions would have a hard time getting higher wages; as Figart, Mutari, and Power point out, Lewis did not want the minimum wage to be a living wage because it was the job of unions to attain a living wage.[47] William Green, president of the AFL, wanted collective bargaining protected and sought an amendment that would keep the FLSB from setting wage standards once an industry was unionized, insisting that it was a goal of the AFL to bargain for "a living wage as a minimum."[48] Sidney Hillman of the Amalgamated Clothing Workers of America wanted the FLSB to be able to fix high wage standards because his industry had many small firms and a higher minimum wage would allow unionized firms to compete with non-union firms. A group of business trade associations also testified against the original bill.[49]

The bill that was produced from the Senate hearings had elements that gave the FLSB more flexibility in some areas compared to the original bill. The FLSB, for example, was given greater authority to set wage and hour standards, as long as the minimum wage did not exceed 40 cents an hour and the maximum hours were not less than 40 hours a week. Senators from the South opposed the bill mainly because that region had a lower standard of living that would not be accounted for in the bill.[50] This version of the bill passed in the Senate.

The House version of the bill was amended in committee to satisfy Green's concerns by keeping the FLSB from setting minimum wages "in occupations where collective bargaining facilities were adequate."[51] As noted earlier, this version of the bill was not sent to the full House for a vote. As a result, the bill kept being altered in an effort to get it out for a vote. When the House did vote to approve the bill, it left out regional differences. The Senate did not favor this version of the bill. The bill was only approved when regional differences, as described earlier by Douglas and Hackman, were permitted by the language of the bill. The Senate approved the final version of the bill on June 13, 1938, with the House following the next day. Roosevelt signed the approved bill on June 25, 1938, and the FLSA was put in place.

Forsythe then presented an analysis of the changes that took place from the original bill to the final Act. The hardest fight was over the flexibility in the setting of the minimum wage. The first bill had contained "a somewhat complicated wage and hour schedule centered around the concepts of 'oppressive wage,' 'oppressive workweek,' 'substandard wage,' and 'substandard workweek'." The Congress would define what these terms meant, but the FLSB would still be able to modify the Congress' definitions as far as wages were concerned if change was needed "to prevent the depression of general wage levels below those consistent with the maintenance of a minimum standard of living necessary for health and efficiency, without unreasonably curtailing opportunities for employment." Regarding hours, the FLSB could redefine the Congress' standards by "considering the physical and economic health, efficiency, and well-being of the employees."[52] In essence, the FLSB would have the power to establish a living wage by setting a minimum wage and maximum hours that gave workers a weekly pay package "consistent with the maintenance of a minimum standard of living necessary for health and efficiency," that is, a living wage.

This was all something advocates for a living wage could support. Nevertheless, as Forsythe observes, the changes in the original bill made after the initial Senate committee hearings put a ceiling of 40 cents an hour on where the FLSB could set its minimum wage and the "concept of 'substandard' wages and hours did not again appear."[53] Instead, the House-Senate conference on the bill compromised further to produce the use of an administrator in the Labor Department and an advisory committee to set a minimum wage within a given range, as described previously by Douglas and Hackman.

As was the case with the SSA (see Chapter 5), the Roosevelt Administration sent the Congress a draft bill with a language that was consistent with a living wage, but the Congress removed that language from the final law that was passed. Writing in 1940, economist Walter E. Boles described the attitude of the Congress as follows: "The dominant motive which has long been recognized as a sound justification for wage and hour legislation, that of protecting the health and morals of workers, seemed not to have played a dominant part in the enactment of the Fair Labor Standards Act."[54] Boles characterized this approach as being based on a fear of competition from the South in the traditional industrial states. He also viewed the Act as a continuation of the NIRA with its goal of raising wages to enhance the purchasing power of labor to bring about a recovery.[55] William Leuchtenburg, in his history of the New Deal, made the same point.[56]

With the FLSA, however, the Congress included a finding touching on a living wage in Section 202 of the Act. The Section reads as follows: "The Congress finds that the existence... of labor conditions detrimental to the maintenance of the minimum standard of living necessary for health, efficiency, and general well-being of workers...spread and perpetuate such labor conditions ... burdens commerce...constitutes an unfair method of competition...leads to labor disputes...and interferes with the orderly and fair marketing of goods..."[57] Wages below a living wage had detrimental effects throughout the economy and the FLSA was a remedy.

Although the FLSA did not enact a living wage, it did set off a system where the federal government gained the power to mandate a minimum standard of wages. Many workers saw pay raises as a result. Proponents of a living wage most likely believed that they were beginning a process that would lead to continual increases in a minimum wage until it reached a level of a living wage, much as Weber had argued. Unionists certainly saw the minimum wage as a key element in the fight for a living wage but added that it was also a key to economic recovery.

The AFL, the CIO, and the FLSA

As indicated in the last two sections, the FLSA had a long and twisted legislative history. When the provisions of the bill changed during that time, organized labor had to shift its support as well. Still, it remained steadfast in its backing of a minimum wage. For example, in July 1937 the *American Federationist* supported the version of the bill that was then under discussion in the Congress. It paraphrased Roosevelt's statement that the law "would make it unlawful to ship goods in interstate commerce made under substandard conditions" and supported having a board that would prevent those conditions from arising. The article then presented the testimony before the Congress of several supporters of the bill, including Perkins.[58]

The most important testimony for the unions was the statement of William Green. Green began his testimony by indicating that the AFL supported the 1937 version of the FLSA. He pointed out that the bill was intended to provide a minimum wage for all workers, men and women, under special circumstances but these were not to be construed as a general minimum wage. The AFL did not support a minimum wage that went against its own efforts to establish wages for unionized workers. The key was the level at which the minimum wage was to be set. Green continued as follows: "The American Federation of Labor has insisted from the beginning on the establishment of a living wage as a minimum." Moreover, "through the force of organized effort" it had secured wages for its members "at a higher minimum than would be if fixed by legal enactment." Still, the AFL had also "fought for a living wage and higher standards of pay for unorganized workers." These workers toiled under circumstances that made organizing them into unions difficult. They would be helped by the law. Therefore, "a fair standard of wages—a living wage" for all workers should be the goal of the FLSA. Green added that an industry that did not pay its workers "a living wage is unfit and should not be permitted to exist."[59] While this statement appears to be repeating Roosevelt's similar maxim, we must recall that unions had held this view for at least two decades before Roosevelt expressed it.

When the FLSA was finally enacted, the *American Federationist* continued to analyze how it was working. In an editorial on July 1938, Green observed that while the FLSA did not provide what the AFL had wanted, it did take a step in the right direction in terms of outlawing sweatshops.[60] A month later, he saw the FLSA as giving unions an opportunity to serve on the advisory boards the Act required, because they were experts on the conditions in the industry each board would advise on.[61] Indeed, the *American Federationist* started a monthly feature article, "The Wage and Hour Law."[62] Its coverage was factual, but unenthusiastic.

The CIO was more vociferous in its support of the FLSA. The CIO had originally been formed as an offshoot of the AFL to organize industrial workers who did not fit into the craft union framework of the AFL. Eventually, the CIO would split from the AFL. It started publishing its own newspaper, the *CIO News*, in 1937. Unlike the *American Federationist*, a monthly publication which had an almost academic journal quality and appearance, the *CIO News* took a weekly tabloid approach. Still, it raised important issues. For example, on December 15, 1937, it ran an article supporting the FLSA to give workers a right to decent pay, because sweatshop conditions were driving down wages, which reduced consumption and was "driving this country into another depression."[63] A week later the *CIO News* saw the failure of that year's version of the FLSA as "defeating legislation directed against starvation wages." The defeat was a sign of the reaction against the New Deal programs that had led to the recession of 1937 "when government spending" was vital "to give purchasing power to those who need it most and can do the most good with it." Instead, the federal government had cut its spending in the pursuit of a balanced budget and brought on the recession.[64]

In its consumerist views, the approach of the CIO toward government spending was far in advance of what other writers on economic conditions had thought. It saw workers as consumers and their spending could enable the economy to recover. This approach was stated clearly in an article in the *CIO News* on February 19, 1938. The article was titled "CIO has Plan to Fight Business Depression." The most important part of the plan was to give each worker a job with "sufficient income to permit him to maintain his family on a decent standard of living," that is, a living wage. If private industry could not provide those good-paying jobs, the federal government should provide them through an extension of programs such as had been done by the Works Progress Administration. Equally important, the FLSA must be enacted to eliminate the "lowered purchasing power of sweatshop wages."[65] The *CIO News* felt that delay in passing the FLSA was making the 1937 recession worse.[66]

When the FLSA was enacted, the *CIO News* was enthusiastic about the impact it would have on workers and on the economy. An article on June 18, 1938, quoted Sidney Hillman, a spearhead of the CIO, as follows: "The bill is a sincere effort to raise the standard of living of underpaid and overworked labor." He added, "It is a modest beginning to improve the purchasing power of the American worker and thereby to strengthen and improve the markets for products of the American factory and the American farm."[67] The same sentiment was expressed in a later article that considered how the FLSA would impact workers in the South, even with their lower minimum wage. The *CIO News* believed that the minimum wage law would benefit that region more than any other. Its workers would gain higher wages, which would make them "better customers for the merchants of their towns."[68]

In maintaining this theme, the *CIO News* took a very strong stand in the consumerist camp by seeing workers in their role as consumers. It also saw consumption spending as an important component of economic recovery and progress. To be sure, we have seen other individuals and organizations in this book that had argued for increased wages as a way to increase the purchasing power of labor and improve the economy. But they often forgot that approach. For example, so far in this chapter I have shown no other examples of the centrality of the relationship between the FLSA and consumption spending put forth with such force as was done by *CIO News*. Perhaps because its members were industrial workers without the identity that came from the producerist practice of a craft, the CIO thought it best to give them a social identity as consumers.

Solomon Barkin's Union Perspective

Solomon Barkin (1907–2000) brought a unique perspective to the issue of the minimum wage, based on his multifaceted experiences. While working on his doctoral dissertation at the Columbia University, he went to Washington, DC, to meet his supervisor, Leo Wolman, who was working as the labor advisor to the NRA. Wolman gave him a job with the NRA. When the NRA disbanded in 1936, Barkin bumped into Sidney Hillman, whom he had met while working with the NRA. Hillman offered Barkin a job with the Textile Workers Organizing Committee headed by Emil Rieve (see Chapter 4). Barkin worked for the TWUA for over two decades as director of research. During that time, he published numerous articles in academic journals and public interest magazines. Thus, he was a New Dealer who strongly supported unions, as well as an academically oriented economist and a labor pundit.[69]

While at Columbia, Barkin had studied with Clark and was captivated by his theory of social overhead costs. Barkin called his version of the theory the social costs of labor and made it a central part of his economic thinking. The concept paralleled the ideal of the New Deal that workers had to earn a living wage. From Barkin's perspective, unions were the best way for workers to attain this living wage and when they were unable to do so, the government had to step in.

To bolster his case for union and government intervention, Barkin started with a hypothetical view of the market economy. In a typical manufacturing industry with many firms using similar methods of production, those firms will have similar cost structures. Competition among the firms would make price increases difficult. Instead, when recessions hit, firms would try to reduce costs and cutting wages was the fastest way to achieve cost reductions.[70] The problem with this approach was that it did not reduce the social costs of labor. They were transferred to the worker or to society in the form of charity, welfare payments, or the reduced capability of the workforce. The gist of this idea was that there was no social gain from having business compete on the basis of sweatshop wages. The NRA Codes were supposed to take care of the problem by letting businesses in an industry collaborate to maintain or increase prices and avoid wage reductions to attain fair profits and living wages. But the NRA had not been able to achieve this goal.

The NRA had also strengthened the bargaining power of unions and the NLRA added to that bargaining power. Unions used that bargaining power to attain two goals, wage stability and security. To pursue those goals, they tried to bargain for uniform wages for workers in all firms in an industry, taking wages out of the competitive struggles of business. They also negotiated multiyear contracts that established a fixed wage pattern to attain stability and give workers the security of knowing their wages would not be reduced.[71] To the extent that unions attained stable wages for all workers in an industry, they would establish labor cost parity where no firm in the industry could gain a competitive edge by cutting wages.

In the textile industry, however, the TWUA had not been able to negotiate a wage scale for the entire textile industry. Instead, unionized firms had to compete with non-union firms, especially in the South. As a result, the unionized firms in the industry found it difficult to remain profitable and still pay union wages. National collective bargaining was needed to attain a social cost wage for workers, but national collective bargaining was proving difficult to attain.[72] In that case, the remedy was to have government impose a minimum wage on all firms.

During his years with the TWUA, Barkin served as chair of the CIO Committee on Fair Labor Standards and responded to critics of the minimum wage before numerous Congressional hearings. He based the CIO support for the FLSA on the social costs of labor. From this perspective, employers who did not pay a living wage were being subsidized by society, which had to make up the difference between the wages being paid by those firms and the full costs of living faced by workers. President Roosevelt had stated that "no industry which depends for existence on less than living wages has a right to continue to exist" and Barkin agreed.[73] For fair-minded employers who wanted to pay a living wage, the FLSA was a way to moderate the type of competition that led to low wages by providing "a realistic wage floor to which no employer can truly object if he wants to pay his workers a wage which represents some modicum of decency."[74]

In terms of the textile industry, Barkin found that the FLSA had helped to eliminate the ruinous competition that had kept wages low. During the Depression, for example, the crepe silk section of the industry had paid workers 10–15 cents an hour in the mid-1930s. After the FLSA was passed, wages were raised to the first minimum of 25 cents an hour and then to 30 cents with no negative impact on employers or employment levels.[75] While these increased wages were important, Barkin never accepted that they represented a living wage.

Throughout his career, Barkin tried to answer two questions about the living wage. How do we define the living wage and how do we ensure that workers earn it? In answering those questions, he refined the concept of a living wage.

For example, during World War II, the federal government in the USA controlled wages and prices in an effort to avoid the building up of inflationary pressures. Wage increases had to be approved by the War Labor Board. During the war, Barkin appeared before the Board to argue in favor of wage increases for textile workers on the grounds that their existing wages were substandard. To make his case, he started with a basic minimum standard of living as had been defined by the 1935 Emergency Subsistence Budget produced by the Works Progress Administration. He then re-priced that basic standard of living using prices derived from three New England and two Southern textile communities. He also surveyed textile workers to see if their household incomes were high enough to pay for the basic standard of living, that is, whether they had a living wage for the household. From this approach, he argued that textile workers did not earn a living wage. By adding in data on textile company profits to show that the companies could pay higher wages, Barkin convinced the Board to grant textile workers a wage increase.[76] In doing so, Barkin brought the definition of a living wage back to a base in terms of need.

Barkin would continue to make a living wage part of his union economics. In 1948, for example, he contributed an article, "Labor's Attitude toward Wage Incentive Plans," to the *Industrial and Labor Relations Review* for July. In it, he noted a trend where employers and workers were considering the place wage incentive programs had in a system of collective bargaining. Union leaders were skeptical of such plans but many workers in companies that used them were satisfied with them. Barkin observed this contradiction and found its basis in a living wage. He wrote,

> Employers who offer wage incentive programs to workers as a means of helping them attain a basic living wage usually arouse antipathy and opposition. The worker expects a living wage not as a reward for additional effort but as a normal by-product of employment.[77]

Workers did not readily see a connection between their wages and their productivity because they recognized that what they produced was greatly affected by how well management ran the factory.

Workers who made substandard wages were especially opposed to wage incentive systems. Workers who earned above a living wage, however, were more willing to accept "the belief current in our society that an individual's reward should be measured by his individual contribution."[78] Those systems gave them a way to increase their incomes and they were especially popular among unionized craft workers. The upshot of it to Barkin was that workers needed to earn a living wage before they would respond positively to incentives. Since many workers did not earn a living wage, wage incentive plans would be counterproductive.

Barkin's interest in a living wage reflected not only his intellectual attachment to Clark's theory of social overhead costs, it also was in tune with his commitment to his work with a member union of the CIO. Unions had long argued that a living wage would make workers more efficient. Barkin refined this idea by arguing that a living wage would also make business' use of incentive wage plans more efficient.

Conclusion

Following up on one of the goals of the NIRA, the FLSA as proposed by Roosevelt was meant to establish a living wage by requiring all firms to pay a minimum wage. The Secretary of Labor, Perkins, saw the minimum wage as a necessary step to establishing economic security as it countered the harshness of the market economy as seen in sweatshop wages. From her perspective, the minimum wage was a way to stop the race to the bottom of wage reductions. Roosevelt further emphasized its importance in his New Deal program by saying of the FLSA, "Except perhaps for the Social Security Act, it is the most far-reaching, far-sighted program for the benefit of workers ever adopted here or in any other country. Without question it starts us toward a better standard of living."[79] Unionists, such as those belonging to the CIO, insisted that a better standard of living would create a consumer society that kept the economy growing.

Writing in the early1950s, Milton Friedman found that the goal of a living wage had always been an underlying agenda in debates over minimum wage legislation that had previously taken place, and he objected to the approach.[80] While it is arguable whether the living wage had an impact on the debates in the Congress over the FLSA, the idea that the FLSA set the USA on the road to a living wage was widely accepted. That idea, however, has proven to be overly optimistic.

The FLSA set a minimum flat rate of 25 cents an hour in the first year and 30 cents in the second with flexibility for mandated wages to be higher, as long as that minimum did not exceed 40 cents per hour. In that way, it allowed for regional differences. As required by the Act, the regional differences were eliminated soon after the end of World War II and a national minimum wage of 40 cents an hour was put in place, with the recovery by the economy during the war making that step redundant. Since then, the exemptions to coverage by the law have been reduced and the minimum wage has been increased multiple times by the Congress starting in 1949. In 2009, the most recent increase brought it to $7.25 per hour and efforts are underway to increase it again. It is a legacy of the New Deal that the controversy surrounding the minimum wage revolves around whether or not to increase it, and never to eliminate it. Although the debate over the economic impact of the minimum wage continues, the minimum wage is another example of a New Deal regulation that has been broadly accepted. But it has not achieved a living wage for workers covered by the FLSA.

There are two reasons for this. First, the minimum wage did not start out as a living wage, as many proponents thought it should. Second, the FLSA did not take inflation into account. Rather it left it to the Congress to raise the minimum wage when and how it saw fit. As a result, even though the minimum wage has been increased numerous times over the last 75 years, the real minimum wage has fluctuated. Through the end of the 1960s, the minimum wage was increased faster than inflation; since then it has not kept up with inflation. No one would argue that the gains in the real minimum wage have reached a point where it is a living wage.

Notes

1. Roosevelt, 1933f.
2. Roosevelt, 1937a.
3. Roosevelt, 1933f.
4. Pigou, 1932.
5. Pigou, 1932, pp. 599–600.
6. Hovenkamp, 1991, pp. 72, 77 and 171.
7. Mitchell, 1947, p. 235.
8. Weber, 1930.
9. Weber, 1930, p. 1.
10. Weber, 1930, p. 2.
11. Weber, 1930, pp. 4–5.
12. Weber, 1930, p. 5.
13. Weber, 1930, p. 5.
14. Weber, 1930, pp. 5–6.
15. Weber, 1930, p. 8.
16. Armstrong, 1932, p. 17.
17. Armstrong, 1932, p. 93–105.
18. Armstrong, 1932, pp. 158–9.
19. Armstrong, 1932, pp. 162–5.
20. Armstrong, 1932, p. 167.
21. Perkins, 1933b. p. 24.
22. Perkins, 1933b. pp. 24 and 56.
23. Carlson, 1988, p. 26.
24. Downey, 2009, p. 260.
25. Perkins, 1945.
26. Supreme Court, 1937a. p. 23.

27. Supreme Court, 1937a. p. 24.
28. Supreme Court, 1937a. p. 26.
29. Sunstein, 2004, p. 523–529, brackets from Sunstein.
30. US Supreme Court, 1923.
31. Sunstein, 2004, pp. 535–42, the ellipses are Sunstein's.
32. Douglas, 1938, p. 184. Douglas' attribution of influence to the Webbs is consistent with the arguement of Bruce Kaufman (Kaufman 2009) that the Webbs were pioneers along with Clark in the development of the social cost theory of wages.
33. Douglas, 1938, pp. 195–6.
34. Douglas, 1938, p. 200.
35. Douglas, 1938, p. 202.
36. Douglas, 1938, p. 214.
37. Douglas, 1938, p. 216.
38. Douglas and Hackman, 1938. p. 491.
39. Douglas and Hackman, 1938. p. 514.
40. Douglas and Hackman, 1939. pp. 29–34.
41. Douglas and Hackman, 1939. p. 38.
42. Douglas and Hackman, 1939. p. 39–43.
43. Forsythe, 1939, pp. 465–470.
44. Forsythe, 1939, p. 466.
45. Prasch, 2000, p. 258.
46. Nordlund, 1997, p. 35.
47. Figart, Mutari and Power, 2002, p. 117.
48. Figart, Mutari and Power, 2002, p. 117.
49. Forsythe, 1939, pp. 467–69.
50. Forsythe, 1939, p. 469.
51. Forsythe, 1939, p. 470.
52. Forsythe, 1939, p. 478.
53. Forsythe, 1939, p. 478.
54. Boles, 1940, p. 498.
55. Boles, 1940, p. 499.
56. Leuchtenburg, 1963, pp. 261–63.
57. US Department of Labor, 2011, p. 1.
58. *American Federationist*, 1937, p. 709.
59. *American Federationist*, 1937, pp. 725–6.
60. Green, 1938a, pp. 689–90.
61. Green, 1938b, pp. 806–7.
62. *American Federationist*, 1938, pp. 1102–3, 1197–1202 and 1327–30.
63. *CIO News*, 1937a, p. 3.
64. *CIO News*, 1937a, p. 1.
65. *CIO News*, 1938a, p. 3.

66. *CIO News*, 1938b, p. 4.
67. *CIO News*, 1938c, p. 3.
68. *CIO News*, 1938d, p. 8.
69. Stabile, 1993b, pp. 10–14.
70. Barkin, 1946, p. 8.
71. Barkin, 1940, p. 3.
72. Barkin, 1946, p. 8.
73. Roosevelt, 1933f; Stabile, 1993b, p. 13.
74. Barkin, 1949, p. 6.
75. Barkin, 1949, p. 1.
76. Barkin, 1944.
77. Barkin, 1948, p. 554.
78. Barkin, 1948, p. 555.
79. Roosevelt, 1938b.
80. Friedman, 1966, p. 5.

CHAPTER 7

Collective Bargaining, Social Insurance, and the Minimum Wage: A Program for a Living Wage

Throughout this book, I have described arguments made by Roosevelt, living wage advocates, and supporters of the New Deal for how their policies—collective bargaining, social insurance, and the minimum wage—were a program to promote a living wage. Using a model established by the WIB and its NWLB, the New Deal first tried a system of cooperative planning under the NIRA as the best way to implement these three policies. To be sure, the NIRA had many goals, including the increase of purchasing power, but Roosevelt and his followers also indicated that it had a goal of instituting a living wage program. When that approach did not work, they turned to the NLRA, the SSA, and the FLSA to reach the same goal. To what extent, I will ask in this chapter, did they feel that they had succeeded in establishing a living wage?

A starting point in answering this question can be found in the words of President Roosevelt. On September 11, 1940, he gave a speech to the Teamsters Union Convention in Philadelphia. In that speech, he presented a picture of what his New Deal had accomplished for workers and especially for union members. He spoke of his accomplishments as follows:

> The last seven years have seen a series of laws enacted to give to labor a fairer share of the good life to which free men and women in a free nation are entitled as a matter of right. Fair minimum wages are being established for workers in industry; decent maximum hours and days of labor have been set, to bring about the objective of an American standard of living and

D. Stabile, *The Political Economy of a Living Wage*,
DOI 10.1007/978-3-319-32473-9_7

> recreation; child labor has been outlawed in practically all factories; a system of employment exchanges has been created; machinery has been set up and strengthened and successfully used in almost every case for the mediation of labor disputes. Over them all has been created a shelter of social security, a foundation upon which we are trying to build protection from the hazards of old age and unemployment.[1]

The New Deal had brought about collective bargaining, social insurance, and a minimum wage and accomplished its goal of helping labor. Although Roosevelt indicated there was more to be done, he did feel a sense of accomplishment in what had been done. Even if he did not use the term, a living wage, "a fairer share of the good life" was his definition of social justice.

Regardless of how he phrased it, this accomplishment was also consistent with ideals of the living wage movement and the programs for government to bring about a living wage as set forth by John Ryan and the Progressives. In 1909, Ryan presented a comprehensive list of labor legislation that included a minimum wage, the eight-hour day, protection for peaceful picketing, unemployment insurance and government employment offices, and funds to help workers when they became ill, injured, or elderly.[2] The Progressives had followed up with a set of policies for attaining Ryan's list, although they never rivaled the scope of his writing. Perhaps the closest work to Ryan's was Barbara Armstrong's book with its prescient title: *Insuring the Essentials. Minimum Wage Plus Social Insurance—A Living Wage Program.*[3]

In researching and writing this book, I have focused on contemporaneous assessments of Roosevelt's policies with regard to their ability to counter the hardships for labor of the market economy and to replace them with a living wage. In this chapter, I will look at how the supporters of a living wage interpreted the overall accomplishments of the New Deal. Then, I will address the legacy of the New Deal to consider why the components of its program for a living wage did not result in all workers attaining that standard. The finding of this chapter is that the rise of Keynesian economics and consumerism shifted the focus of the Progressives away from the achievement of a living wage.

George Soule and the New Deal Legacy

George Soule (1888–1970) was an economist and editor for *The New Republic*, with a long and consistent commitment to the idea of economic security.[4] In January 1939, he was invited to give the Storrs Lectures on Jurisprudence at the Yale School of Law. In the first lecture, "The Peril to Democracy," Soule began with the idea that the New Deal was over and that it had changed the structure of the US economy in ways that were irreversible. By saying the New Deal was over, Soule did not mean that its impact was at an end. Rather, the New Deal would vanish from the minds of the people of the USA because its changes had been so complete. He wrote,

> It is not probable that many of the New Deal measures will be repealed or even substantially amended. Nor can it be said that they will pass into forgetfulness without continuing to exert an important influence on our society. What will appear, however, is that they have been assimilated into the background; they are beginning to be taken for granted even by many of their traditional opponents.[5]

Once a program was taken for granted, it became part of the political and economic environment.

The programs I have outlined in the book, collective bargaining, social insurance, and the minimum wage, all had a goal of helping workers attain a living wage. Soule was on the mark in saying that they would never be repealed or substantially amended. To be sure, they have been altered. The NLRA was changed by the Taft-Hartley Act of 1948, and the SSA was expanded to cover more members of the workforce, include disability income, and bring about medical coverage through Medicare and Medicaid. The FLSA remains intact and debates over it center on whether or not to raise the minimum wage and not over abolishing the law. Not surprisingly, contemporaneous accounts of what the New Deal accomplished with respect to economic security centered on collective bargaining, social insurance, and the minimum wage, that is, a living wage as defined by the Progressives.

The New Republic Reviews the New Deal

Throughout the first two Roosevelt Administrations, *The New Republic* had been a thoughtful supporter of New Deal programs. On May 20, 1940, it took a broad look at those programs in a 21-page article, "The New Deal in Review: 1936–1940." The article analyzed nine elements of the New Deal. Here, we will be concerned with one of those elements, regulation.

A key theme in this book has been the use of regulation of business by the New Deal as part of its program of a living wage. Those regulations had been part of a larger reform program that aimed at a fairer distribution of income by keeping prices from being too high and setting the incomes of farmers and, more important to our theme, the wages of workers at higher levels. *The New Republic* gave the New Deal mixed ratings on this effort in its third topic, economic regulation. The prices of manufactured goods were still too high and the federal government was not certain what to do about it. There had been no direct regulation of prices charged by business, although tariff reductions and competition from government agencies such as the Tennessee Valley Authority might have exerted some downward pressure on prices.

A more direct regulation of the price of labor (wages) had taken place due to the FLSA, which resulted in pay increases for about three million workers. Some industries had their advisory committees that existed under the FLSA (see Chapter 6) recommend minimum wages above the level mandated by the law. Conservatives criticized the FLSA for holding production down. That might be true, the article noted, but production had been low before the FLSA was enacted. That production had remained low despite labor costs being reduced due to higher labor productivity. Regardless of the gains to labor from the FLSA, the article insisted that the New Deal had not gone far enough "to solve the problems of our economy by planned intervention to reduce unduly high prices and to expand production and employment."[6] Its efforts had been too piecemeal and reliant on business to solve the problem of low national output.

The article covered another important topic in regulation in a section on collective bargaining. Section 7A of the NIRA had tried to attain collective bargaining rights for workers. It was replaced by the NLRA and the formation of the NLRB. During its initial period, however, the NLRB had been hindered by attack from business on its constitutional status. At the same time, the Congress had been distracted by the fight over the

FLSA, which the article interpreted as an effort "to carry out another purpose of the NRA."[7] Once the US Supreme Court upheld the NLRA, the NLRB went into action and union membership greatly increased. *The New Republic* considered this growth of union membership to be an important accomplishment of the New Deal and believed it was "likely to be of overwhelming importance in the future."[8]

The next several sections of the article touched on topics that are not germane to the theme of this book, such as agriculture and international trade. It then offered a section with a title, "Looking Backward." In this case, the article looked backward to the days before the New Deal. In 1932, the economy was in deep trouble and President Herbert Hoover was too wedded to the market economy to do much about it. He was turned out of office and a different approach was tried. *The New Republic* put it this way: "We have reaffirmed in these past eight years an early American doctrine that had been all but forgotten in preceding decades: that the country exists for the welfare and happiness of all its inhabitants."[9]

From this perspective, the article concluded that the New Deal had accomplished more in improving the well-being of US citizens "than any administration in the previous history of the nation." The most important of its accomplishments had been the strengthening of labor through the NLRA and the FLSA. These gains for labor had to be kept in mind in light of the New Deal's failure to find "a genuine remedy for the stagnation of our economy."[10] Recovery had not come about, but the reforms of the New Deal had gone a long way toward attaining economic security.

Ryan and a Better Economic Order

As pointed out in Chapter 1, Ryan was the author of a pivotal book, *A Living Wage*,[11] in the movement to provide workers with a living wage. He became well-known in the Progressive circles, especially because he continued to write books and articles on the overarching concept of social justice. By the 1930s, he became linked with the New Deal, as can be seen in several of his works during this period.

The first work I will consider is his book, *A Better Economic Order*, published in 1935. As indicated in Chapter 3, Ryan used the book to continue his support of the NIRA. But he wanted to see it strengthened and approved of the Wagner Bill that had recently been proposed with a goal of adding some clout to the NIRA. He indicated that to strengthen the NIRA, a new labor law needed to outlaw company unions, and provide for collective bargaining agents to be determined by a majority vote of workers in a company and for the use of a national labor board.[12] Since these ideas became the key components of the NLRA and the NLRB, we can infer that Ryan approved the New Deal's change in the US labor law. Ryan's autobiography, *Social Doctrine in Action*, supports this inference. There, he referred to the NLRA as "probably the most just, beneficent and far-reaching piece of labor legislation ever enacted in the United States."[13] Such praise from Ryan would indicate that he believed that the NLRA had a goal of a living wage for workers.

Ryan also approved of the New Deal tax policy advocating higher income taxes, increased inheritance taxes, and the excess profits tax on business. He wrote of them, "The taxation proposals here advocated constitute one important means of bringing about the better distribution" of income consistent with social justice.[14] He also approved of the use of tax policy for other social programs as presented in the SSA. The Act had not been passed when he wrote, but he indicated that Roosevelt's recommendation of the Act in early 1935 reflected "an almost complete program of social insurance." To be sure, the income to be provided workers under the Act was not adequate, but "when the depression has ended the benefits can be readily increased."[15]

As indicated above, in his autobiography Ryan supported the NLRA as a component of a living wage. He was even more emphatic regarding his support for the minimum wage law enacted under the FLSA. He indicated that he had been a long-time supporter of minimum wage legislation[16] and had drafted a minimum wage law for the state of Minnesota that was enacted in 1913.[17] He also referred to the FLSA as "the latest important social reform enacted under the Roosevelt administration." To be sure, the minimum wage mandated by the FLSA was not a living wage, but Ryan was hopeful that it would become a living wage as soon as was politically practicable. He added, "When I began to advocate the establishment by law of a family living wage, I did not dare hope that so near an approach to it would be made by the federal government less than three and one half decades later."[18] Here is another indication that Ryan believed that the New Deal was bringing about a living wage.

Ryan had an opportunity to repeat his views in fall 1935 when Roosevelt sent him a letter asking for his view on the SSA, which had recently been put in place.[19] Ryan answered that he did not feel qualified to comment on the Act, "although I had the honor of serving as a member of the President's Advisory Council to the Committee on Economic Security."[20]

As noted in Chapter 5, the CES had been put in place to develop a proposal for the SSA and Ryan's membership on it is another indicator of his ties to the New Deal. Although he did not comment on social security, Ryan did return to the problem of low wages. He believed that for wages to be increased, "it will be necessary to re-establish the essential features of the NRA, particularly those related to minimum wages and maximum hours."[21] He believed, that it would take a constitutional amendment to bring back the NIRA, however. Regardless of whether that happened, Ryan told Roosevelt, "I have rejoiced over practically all the legislation that has been enacted since you assumed the high office of the President of the United States," adding, "But I do not believe that the legislative program of the New Deal is yet substantially complete."[22]

Ryan's ties with Roosevelt became stronger through a radio speech he gave on October 8, 1936, "Roosevelt Safeguards America." The speech was intended to defend the president from criticisms that he was a communist, especially as made by Father Charles C. Coughlin, the radio priest (See Chapter 3). These charges were misplaced according to Ryan. It was foolish to accuse the president and his advisors of communism when all that they were saying was "that the poor must obtain higher standards of living" and "that we must have a better distribution of wealth."[23] These views were consistent with the teaching of the Catholic Church and merely reflected a need for reform in the USA. The NLRA, for example, strengthened the right of labor to form unions, a right that was "strongly proclaimed by both Pope Leo XIII and Pope Pius XI." The NLRA and similar reforms of the New Deal such as the SSA were "mild installments of too long delayed social justice."[24]

If the citizens of the USA believed that communism was an evil, as Ryan surely did, the task was to provide an antidote to the primary reasons people believed in communism, that is, "poverty, insecurity and inequitable distributions of wealth and income." Roosevelt and his New Deal policies, by addressing these social problems, were effectively countering the spread of "destructive radicalism."[25] Ryan then indicated that he was especially interested in addressing wage workers, reminding them that he had been on their side for nearly half a century. He had been branded a radical for espousing the cause of labor and this branding of his espousal had been just as erroneous as was the charge of communism against the New Deal. His book, *A Living Wage*, "was the first publication in this country which placed the laborer's moral right to a living wage upon a solid basis of principle, fact and argument."[26] As a result, he had the proper credentials to tell workers that Roosevelt was on their side. He then asked them to vote for "the man who has shown a deeper and more sympathetic understanding of your needs and who has brought about more fundamental legislation for labor and for social justice than any other President in American history."[27]

In speaking of Roosevelt in such powerful terms, Ryan was strongly implying that the president and his policies were engaged on the side of labor in the movement for a living wage and he anticipated that the New Deal would continue its beneficial legislation until labor gained the social justice it had lacked. The NLRA and the SSA had been key laws in this movement. Not surprisingly, Roosevelt sent a telegram to Ryan, thanking him by telling him, "Your speech was magnificent."[28] The president followed up on his thanks by giving Ryan the honor of providing the invocation at his inauguration in 1937. On the occasion of Ryan's 70th birthday on May 25, 1939, Roosevelt sent Ryan a congratulatory letter to tell him, "You have pleaded the cause of social justice and the right of the individual to happiness through economic security, a living wage, and an opportunity to share in things that enrich and ennoble human life."[29] By printing this letter in his autobiography, Ryan clearly believed that Roosevelt was his ally in the movement for a living wage and Roosevelt added to that belief through his New Deal programs and by his honoring Ryan.

The New Deal and a Living Wage

Did Roosevelt and the New Deal have a living wage as a conscious objective of those programs? I have described in this book 22 examples where Roosevelt used the concept of a living wage in speeches and other statements—seven where he used the term a living wage and 15 where he referred to it by implication; he also referred to social justice 24 times that I have found, many of them also related to the living wage as an idea. A living wage was a leitmotif of the New Deal and it recurred on all those occasions when Roosevelt brought it into his rhetoric. This statement does not imply that he was as dedicated an advocate for a living wage as Ryan. A search of his online presidential papers for the words purchasing power came up with 126 hits during his years in office, much more than the combined uses of a living wage and social justice. Still, Roosevelt was a supporter of the idea of a living wage to a greater extent than has previously been recognized.

Among members of his administration, two top leaders of the NRA, Hugh Johnson and Douglas Cates, directly supported the idea of a living wage (Chapter 3); in Chapter 6 the Secretary of Labor, Frances Perkins, was quoted as using the term. Among academics and intellectuals who supported the New Deal, Max Rheinstein (Chapter 4), Maxwell Stewart (Chapter 5), Paul Douglas (Chapters 2 and 6), and Solomon Barkin (Chapter 6) used the term or expressed an affinity with the concept of a living wage. In the *Parrish Case*, the US Supreme Court referred to "wages so low as to be insufficient to meet the bare cost of living" (See Chapter 6), which meant that they were not a living wage. Union leaders at the AFL and later at the CIO, who were also supporters of the New Deal, continually used a living wage in their publications and linked it to the consumerist view of the purchasing power argument before anyone else did. And although it was used sparsely, the concept of a living wage entered into Congressional debates over the NLRA, SSA, and FLSA.

In addition, John Maurice Clark's theory of social overhead costs as a justification for a living wage was employed by Roosevelt in support of the NIRA (Chapter 3), by William Green in support of unions and collective bargaining (Chapter 4), by H.W. Story, P.W. Litchfield, the CES, and Edwin Witte in support of social security (Chapter 5), by Abraham Epstein in criticizing social security (Chapter 5), and by Frances Perkins, the US Supreme Court, Paul Douglas, and Solomon Barkin in support of the minimum wage (Chapter 6). The idea of a living wage was present in New Deal circles.

Oddly enough, I have found little evidence that opponents of the New Deal were critical of a living wage as a goal of the New Deal. The best examples of such criticism are the Brookings study that was critical of the NIRA and its efforts toward establishing a living wage[30] and the work of Charles Roos in his 1937 study of the NRA.[31] In addition, as described in Chapter 5, Carl Shoup offered a critique of Clark's social overhead justification of a living wage.[32] The New Deal was criticized for many things by its opponents but they did not criticize its goal of a living wage. To be sure, however, the Congress gave an implicit criticism of the idea of a living wage when it voted to remove living wage language from the SSA and the FLSA, but this implicit criticism has not been noticed, because it has not been recognized that living wage language was there in the first place. Consequently, no one has investigated the possibility, arguable at best, that by adding a living wage justification for its programs for labor the New Deal may have gotten more for workers than they would have with just the purchasing power approach.

Whether or not New Deal policies were consciously derived from the ideal of a living wage, the programs reviewed in this book, collective bargaining, social insurance, and the minimum wage, are lasting reminders of the New Deal push for economic security. They all can be interpreted as forms whereby members of a community engage in "chipping in" to help each other. Under the SSA, for example, everyone chips in through the payroll tax to provide unemployment benefits to those out of work and pensions for those who have reached an age where work is not possible. Less obvious, policies of regulation such as the FLSA and the NLRA also follow the practice of chipping in. If the FLSA and NLRA raise wages for labor with a corresponding increase in prices for consumers, that is just a way for consumers to chip in for higher wages. Ryan believed that consumers were obligated to pass by low prices that were the result of low wages and patronize firms that paid a living wage; low prices should not be based on low wages.[33] The NLRA and the FLSA pushed in that direction. This chipping in approach was the underlying philosophy of the New Deal.

Among the supporters of the New Deal I have surveyed in this chapter, *The New Republic* and Ryan recognized that the New Deal had accomplished much in its push for economic security but there was still more to do. Low-wage workers had not attained a living wage by the end of the 1930s in part because the economy had not yet recovered and in part because additional legislation was needed. Still, they believed that collective bargaining under the NLRA had put labor on a more equal footing with business and that augured well for a future where the chipping in process would reach the goals of the living wage movement. In this way, Clark's social overhead costs of labor would be incorporated into the price structure.

Ryan insisted that ethics and a living wage took precedence over economics and business' need for profit as well as the business owner's desire for a wealthy lifestyle and Roosevelt apparently agreed. Taxes and regulations were simply a community obligation that everyone must meet. In this way, the mutual assistance of the pre-capitalist era could be replicated in a mixed economy of government and business, but only if government took the lead.

What Went Wrong?

Each of the preceding three chapters ended by briefly looking at what went wrong with the policy reviewed in the chapter, collective bargaining, social security, and the minimum wage, in securing a living wage. In this section, I will take a look at the reasonableness of calls for a living wage during the New Deal. The starting point will be on the writings of Eleanor Roosevelt.

As the wife of President Roosevelt, Eleanor Roosevelt (1884–1962) has often been portrayed as the conscience of the New Deal, due to her trips around the country to investigate the plight of the poor. She used her position as first lady as well as the results of her investigations to influence many New Deal policies. Pertinent to the theme of this book, among those policies she "championed the concept of a living wage."[34]

A search of her papers on the website of the Eleanor Roosevelt Papers Project confirms her interest in a living wage. For an extended period she wrote a syndicated newspaper column, "My Day," and the search of her papers found 12 places during 1936–1960 where she referred to a living wage in one of those columns. In the earliest reference, on December 29, 1936, she wrote of the need of "putting young people as they come to working age into jobs which will provide them with a living wage." She then added a comment with the intention of measuring what she meant by a living wage, "I saw an article in yesterday's paper stating that $3600 a year was really the minimum on which an average family could lead a satisfactory existence, and most of us know that a very great percentage of our people see only from $200 to $600 cash in hand during the course of a year, and many, many others have incomes under $1000 or ranging from $1000 to $2000 a year."[35] What makes this quotation especially interesting is the amount she stated as needed for a living wage for a family, $3600. It was so out of reach that one worries that there might be a typographical error in her writing. After all, Mordecai Ezekiel set a considerably lower level of $2500 a year as abundance for a family of four and acknowledged that national income in 1934 amounted to $1000 per worker.[36] G. William Domhoff and Michael Webber cite an estimate of $1600 a year as the minimum amount needed by a family of four in 1936.[37]

As described earlier in this book, Sam Lewisohn, Paul H. Douglas, and Herbert J. Weber had investigated the feasibility of a living wage by looking at it in terms of national income and found that a living wage for all workers was not feasible. To Lewisohn, this result meant that it was not a good idea to overpromise on how much of a living wage one could deliver. Douglas and Weber added that the economy would have to grow at a high rate to make a living wage feasible. An implication of their attitude was that the middle of a serious economic depression was not a good time to be promising a living wage, much less implementing one. In his book on social security, Douglas raised this problem and calculated the cost of a living wage for two popular proposals being considered at the time. In the first, Dr. Francis Townsend proposed a government-funded pension of $200 a month for the elderly (See Chapter 5); Douglas estimated that the Townsend Plan would have taken up half of national income. With the second proposal, Representative Ernest Lundeen (1878–1940) of the Minnesota Farmer-Labor Party proposed a bill in the Congress for a federally funded unemployment insurance program that would pay every unemployed person the going wage rate in their local area; Douglas noted that proponents of the Lundeen Bill wanted to use these high benefits "as a lever to compel industry to pay a living wage to those who were employed," but the cost of the program would also amount to almost half of national income.[38] The economy would have to expand substantially to make good on any promises about a living wage.

To be sure, union leaders and Jett Lauck (see Chapter 2) along with Herbert J. Weber (see Chapter 6) had argued that a living wage would bring about an economic expansion. Using a dynamic approach, they argued that a living wage would foster increased efficiency among workers, provide for increased consumption demand from workers, and produce an incentive for businesses to use innovative technology to reduce the labor component of their production—all of which would stimulate the economy. Economists such as Douglas and Rexford Tugwell, however, did not accept this argument. They took a more static approach that business might not be able to afford to pay a living wage until something happened to make the economy grow. To them, economic growth had to precede social justice.

Another economist who offered a similar version of the argument for a cautious approach to President Roosevelt was John Maynard Keynes. In "An Open Letter to President Roosevelt" published in *The New York Times* on December 31, 1933, Keynes complimented Roosevelt for giving hope to reformers who wanted to remedy the economic problems the world faced "by reasoned experiment within the framework of the existing social system." If Roosevelt failed in his experiments, the hope for reasoned change would ebb, but success would bring about a "new economic era."[39]

Keynes worried that Roosevelt was risking failure due to his efforts to bring about both an end to the Great Depression and the enactment of reforms in business and society that were greatly needed. It would be better if the New Deal were to focus on bringing about a recovery and using its success in the recovery program to solidify its standing with the public and thereby bolster its chances for true reform. If reform undermined business' trust, it would impede the recovery. The reform Keynes had in mind was the NIRA and he wrote of it, "I cannot detect any material aid to recovery in N.I.R.A., though its social gains have been large."[40]

In the recent times, the slogan has been to not let an economic crisis go to waste but to use the opportunity it offers to push through social reforms. Here, Keynes was advising against the policies behind this slogan even when he favored them. Regarding the NIRA, he wrote the president, "I do not mean to impugn the social justice and social expediency of the redistribution of incomes aimed at by N.I.R.A." But the NIRA aimed at artificially raising prices and Keynes believed that increased prices were not acceptable unless they came from increased demand and thereby brought about increased production and employment. That was a better approach than raising prices by putting limits on production as the NIRA attempted to do.[41] Ryan had insisted that it was the ability to pay living wages that measured success and not profits and Roosevelt apparently agreed. Keynes was reminding them that profits were important for a recovery. Apparently, he agreed with Tugwell (see Chapter 3) that Roosevelt had made pursuit of a living wage a priority when it should not have been.

The question was how to increase demand and here Keynes offered a clear statement. Given the problems of trying to get consumers to spend more or to get business to invest more, the government should run deficits to give money to consumers to spend. He elaborated on this policy and explained it based on the experience of war when the government borrowed money to spend and thereby caused economic growth. The conventional view in economics and politics was that war could be taken as a reasonable time for the government to borrow and spend. By disregarding this conventional view Roosevelt, Keynes argued, was "free to engage in the interests of peace and prosperity the technique which hitherto has only been allowed to serve the purposes of war and destruction."[42]

In arguing this way, Keynes was using the argument he later made popular. These ideas would dominate economic thinking for the rest of the twentieth century. Roosevelt and Keynes did not get on very well when they first met, however, and Roosevelt did not accept his early advice, at least not until the 1937–1938 recessions. It took World War II to make Keynes' ideas supplant the older view of fiscal policy.

The New Deal, Keynes, and a Living Wage

The idea that the government should use fiscal policy during an economic downturn, deliberately running a budget deficit to stimulate the economy existed in the USA before the Great Depression. To give one example, it was considered at the Presidential Conference on Unemployment called by Herbert Hoover as the Secretary of Commerce.[43] By the early 1930s, the theory behind government spending programs during a recession, to the extent that we can call it a theory, was "pump-priming." When a pump loses the pressure needed to draw water up from a well, it is necessary to pour water down the pump to get it started again. With foresight, a bucket of water will be left next to the pump to be used in cases when the pump has to be primed. In a similar way, government could keep a reserve of money to get the economy started again. But what happens if the initial priming does not do the job and the pump does not work effectively? In that case, the metaphor of pump priming breaks down, for it involves a constant flow of water from multiple buckets to keep priming the pump and no one would have the foresight (or the buckets) to keep that much water available.

To get the economy to grow, the New Deal muddled along with a mix of policies, ranging from the NIRA as a way to cooperate with business to the NLRA, the SSA, and the FLSA as ways to increase consumption. It also launched a series of spending programs that resulted in budget deficits, followed by an effort to balance the federal budget which many believed had caused the recession of 1937–1938. These spending programs had some intellectual support. In the December 18, 1935, issue of *The New Republic*, for example, Stuart Chase took a look at fiscal policy in an article titled "Recovery." Chase found that starting with Hoover and continuing with Roosevelt, government spending from borrowing had been used to bring about recovery. Both presidents had taken savings that were not being invested by businesses and put them in the hands of government agencies to spend. This fiscal policy had not brought about a full recovery, however. Still, Chase argued, as long as the private sector did not revive its spending, the federal government had to keep spending for "as long as the government's credit holds out."[44] The idea that the government should keep spending for as long as its credit held out, however, could not be satisfying to economists. By the middle of the decade of the 1930s, a more satisfying theory for using fiscal policy to end the Depression was presented in the writings of Keynes.

Keynes must be considered the outstanding economic influence of the twentieth century for the way in which he reoriented economics toward the aggregate approach of macroeconomics. Economic thinking would never be the same once his book, *The General Theory of Employment, Interest and Money*, was published in 1936. I cannot hope to do justice to a book as complicated and abstract as *The General Theory* in a brief review such as being offered here. Fortunately, Keynes offered his own summary of his ideas which I can state briefly. His starting point was with the basic idea that when the economy grew and employment went up, total real income in the economy also went up. "The psychology of the community," however, would result in consumption not rising by as much as the rise in income. Total demand in the economy consisted of consumption and investment and when consumption did not rise as fast as income, investment had to make up the difference. When all of income was not spent on consumption it was because a portion of it was saved. The amount of savings did not determine investment, however. Instead, investment was determined by "the inducement to invest," which depended on "the marginal efficiency of capital," that is, the schedule of what business expected to gain from its use of investment in capital, compared to the interest rate. From the interaction of "the propensity to consume" and "the rate of new investment," there would be "only one level of employment consistent with equilibrium" because any other amount of employment would mean that aggregate supply and aggregate demand would be out of balance. The level of employment determined by consumption and investment demand, however, could be in equilibrium at a level that did not give a job to every worker who wanted one.[45]

The ideas Keynes set forth regarding consumption and investment were not new. I have previously described how William Foster and Waddill Catchings had argued that increased savings led to underconsumption and problems for the economy and underconsumption was viewed by many politicians and pundits as a key explanation for the severity of the Great Depression. In addition, Clark through his accelerator process had argued that declines in consumption reduced investment and produced a recession. Keynes did not just take these ideas over, however, but greatly amplified on them in new and important ways.

A key element of Keynes' new economics was his popularization of the concept of the "multiplier,"[46] which has now for decades been a standard concept in every macroeconomics textbook. The point of the multiplier is to show how changes in spending can generate larger changes in income. Keynes focused on an investment multiplier to show how small changes in investment led to larger changes in spending, but since he considered government spending as an investment,[47] it applied to government spending programs as well. Let us suppose that government spending increases through the hiring of people to build roads. When the workers who get those jobs spend their earnings on consumption items, their spending generates jobs and income in consumer goods industries. Workers in those industries also spend their income and the process continues, leading to a recovery. The multiplier effect will not go on forever, however, because at each step in the process, due to Keynes' theory of consumption, individuals will save a portion of their income and each step in the process will generate a smaller increase in income. Equally important, a decline in spending can cause a larger decline in income and consumption and bring about a recession.

Here was Keynes' rhetorical genius. Government spending of any type would stimulate the economy by giving people money to spend. When they spent that money on consumption goods, they would, through the multiplier effect, create jobs in the private sector. In addition, because of the multiplier, the income generated by government spending would be a greater amount than what the government spent. Taxes on that income would offset some of the government spending, with the result that the budget deficit might not be as large as originally planned. The point Keynes was making here is that government expenditures, whether useful or wasteful, will generate income for the persons engaged in working on government projects and through the multiplier their increased consumption spending would create more jobs. A missing element to the argument, pertinent to the theme of this book, was that Keynes never considered whether or not those jobs would pay a living wage.

Regardless, Keynes presented an alluring prospect to the Progressives that they could use government spending to manage the direction of the economy and counteract the Great Depression. Still, they could be concerned that the deficit spending of the 1930s had not ended the Great Depression. After all, the federal government deficits ranged from $2.3

to $3.5 billion from 1933 to 1940. Given that total federal government spending ranged from $5.1 to $10.1 billion during this period, as compared to national income of $56.4 to $101.4 billion, government spending would have been in the range of 10 percent of the GDP. To be sure, this was an increase compared to the 4–7 percent of GDP under Hoover, but it would have taken a very large multiplier for the fiscal stimulus of the New Deal to have brought about full employment. Larger deficits were called for by Keynesian theory.

It is now a commonplace that World War II ended the Great Depression by producing those larger deficits. Certainly government spending rose dramatically during the war, with the federal budget during the war taking up about 40 percent of total national income for the period of the war. As part of this spending, the government "hired" over ten million men and women directly in the effort to win the war, with another 16 million individuals working in defense plants. Not surprisingly, the unemployment rate fell to a record low of 1.2 percent in 1944. But the war effort remained mixed in terms of a social experiment in economic policy. A large portion of government spending was done on a contract basis with business, which would make it comparable to a fiscal stimulus program. Still, there was also an effort at planning by a War Production Board and then by the Office of War Mobilization. Prices were controlled by the Office of Price Administration, while a second NWLB regulated wages. Consumer goods were rationed. This version of economic control did not attain the luster of the WIB of World War I. Barber finds that the government in World War II relied more heavily on Keynesian policies.[48] The war certified to the Progressives that Keynes had been correct and government spending could counteract a recession.

The result of this view becoming commonplace, however, was that the period after the war became an age of Keynes with an emphasis on increasing consumption and not an age of Ryan and Roosevelt that led to implementation of a living wage through enactment of the second Bill of Rights (see Chapter 1). Just before his death, Roosevelt added to this age of Keynes by calling for the government to use its spending programs to generate full employment and a growing economy. Perhaps he thought the combination of these two goals would lead to a living wage. In the debates over this plan, however, a more conservative approach prevailed and the Employment Act of 1946 only called for government plans for attaining maximum employment. There is no mention in the Act or anywhere else of attaining a living wage for workers. According to Samuel Rosenman, the Congress completely ignored Roosevelt's second Bill of Rights.[49]

In place of the formula that collective bargaining plus social insurance plus a minimum wage would yield a living wage, the next 70 years would use a Keynesian formula that expansionary fiscal policy plus social welfare programs would lead to maximum employment regardless of whether it lead to a living wage. The age of Keynes coincided with an era of rapidly increased prosperity making a living wage more feasible, but no one was there to push for it. In looking at the JSTOR database for 1940–1950, I found no significant articles or books on a living wage. Politicians focused on spending programs that aimed at large corporations and unionized workers, which economists justified on Keynesian terms, and the working poor would have to hope that the benefits of expansionary fiscal policy would trickle down to them.

The result was the development of a consumer society where large corporations could produce as much as they wanted, safe in the security that government would do what was necessary with fiscal policy to maintain aggregate consumption demand. They could invest in increased plant size and be confident those investments would pay off with higher profits. Even the Federal Reserve was brought in to maintain total consumption and investment at high levels by keeping interest rates low.

The New Deal outcome of Keynesian fiscal policy and the regulation of business also included social costs. It is now commonly accepted that organized interest groups often lobby the federal government for favorable treatment as part of the process of rent seeking. Joseph Stiglitz makes this rent-seeking behavior a recurrent theme in his writings on inequality by arguing that rent-seeking activities worsen inequality.[50] He, thus, finds inequality to be an outcome of government policy choices, because large corporations and the wealthy use their influence to have government enact policies that confer benefits on them to the detriment of the less affluent. Since there is no organized interest group lobbying for a living wage, it does not get a hearing.

Stiglitz leaves out, however, that the process he rightly condemns also involves rent seeking on the part of members of the federal government. Politicians may seek campaign contributions and other financial benefits from the corporations they befriend along with promised votes from unions and community organizations in return for favorable policies. Government regulators often take jobs with the businesses they have previously regulated. Perhaps Plato was wise in suggesting that political leaders be accorded a living wage as a maximum amount (see Chapter 1). Whether by design or inadvertence—let us simply call it a negative externality, the New Deal, by expanding the scope and scale of the federal government and its regulatory bodies, also created more opportunities for mutual rent seeking in a return to the mercantilism that Adam Smith warned against (See Chapter 1). The NRA might have served as a warning that government, business, and labor were not suited for the role of promoting the general welfare. The New Deal did not invent crony capitalism, but it did expand the opportunities for rent seeking.

An early warning about this problem was given by Hoover, who is still wrongly characterized as a knee-jerk proponent of free markets. For a clearer perspective on his approach to markets, we can refer again to Walter Lippmann. He believed that Hoover's "historic position as an innovator has been greatly underestimated and that Mr. Roosevelt's pioneering has been greatly exaggerated,"[51] and highlighted many of Hoover's policies indicating that Roosevelt had merely followed them. With regard to the NIRA, for example, Hoover had long been a supporter of using trade associations to help plan an industry's production and prices. The NIRA had simply made the trade associations stronger and organized them in industries where they were lacking; it also brought home to them the importance of lobbying the federal government. Lippmann later recognized that the NIRA had meant that the federal government was involved with "the conferring of privileges on special interests."[52]

Lippmann, in making the case for Hoover not being a free-market advocate, perhaps went too far in the other direction. While Hoover did promote voluntary trade associations, he did not want the government to mandate them, as the NIRA proposed, because he, too, shared Lippmann's dislike for "the conferring of privileges on special interests." His main concern in keeping government out of the economy as much as possible was with the risks that attached to the growth of government. In his memoirs he warned, "Even if governmental conduct of business could give us more efficiency instead of less efficiency, the fundamental objection to it would remain unaltered and unabated. It would destroy political equality. It would increase rather than decrease abuse and corruption."[53] Indeed, long before he wrote his memoirs he had insisted that with a strong government economic decisions would be made under the patronage system of Tammany Hall.[54] Few Progressives appreciated that negative potential of government growth, least of all John Ryan.

Ryan Has a Final Word on Roosevelt and Social Justice

Roosevelt and Ryan, as described in various places in this book, had a relationship built on mutual admiration. A poignant link in that relationship was that they died in the same year, 1945, the president on April 16 and the priest on September 16. Although his health was failing, Ryan summoned the energy to write a valedictory article about Roosevelt, "Roosevelt and Social Justice," published in *The Review of Politics* for July 1945.

In order to determine the degree of social justice Roosevelt had accomplished for the USA, Ryan first had to define it. He wrote,

> Social justice is that form of justice which impels men to promote the common good; that is, the welfare of the community as such, as a unified entity, and also the common good as comprising the welfare of all members of society.[55]

Quoting Pope Pius XI, Ryan added that social justice meant caring for the "social organism" so that every person was able to live in a way as to be able to meet his or her "social functions." He then relied on the words of Pope Leo XIII to make clear that social justice was mainly concerned with "the weaker economic and social classes." Pope Leo had written, "the nation, as it were, of the rich is guarded by its own defenses and is in less need of government protection, whereas the suffering multitude, without the means to protect itself, relies especially on the protection of the state."[56] Roosevelt had taken this message to heart and had done more to help the members of US society most in need of social justice than any other president.

Having set the stage, Ryan then detailed all that Roosevelt had done to accomplish social justice in the USA. He went over the major legislation of the New Deal, from the Federal Deposit Insurance Act to the formation of the Farm Security Administration and described how each and added to social justice. He gave special attention to the programs featured in this book—the NIRA, the NLRB, the SSA, and the FLSA. Regarding the NIRA, he remained a supporter of it as trying to establish a guild system in the USA that was consistent with what the Catholic Church taught. To be sure, it had its faults but these could have been corrected. Even with those faults, "it represented the most comprehensive and fundamental measure for social justice that has been set up in modern times."[57] Its goal was to establish an organic economy as a buttress against collectivization and Ryan still supported it ten years after its demise. He also supported the NLRA as making labor's right to organize unions for collective bargaining effective, the SSA for providing protection against unemployment and old age, and the FLSA for ending "starvation wages." He concluded, "These three laws have done more to promote social justice than all the other federal legislation enacted since the adoption of the Constitution."[58]

Not only had these major programs of the New Deal promoted social justice, taken as a whole, they had brought about the most important element of social justice, the redistribution of income. Under Roosevelt, interest rates had declined, making it easier for the working poor to manage their debt. As a share of national income, interest on bonds and dividends on stock had declined between 1929 and 1943, while wages had increased. "This result," he added, "is in conformity with social justice." But there was still more to be done. Corporations retained a large amount of their profits within the business so the share going to ownership remained too large and not in complete "accord with the requirements of social justice."[59] Roosevelt's proposal in 1944 to use fiscal stimulus to bring about full employment was the next step. This program was also "in accord with social justice."[60]

Ryan devoted the last half of his eight-page article defending Roosevelt from a few specific critics. In general, they disliked the government intervention the New Deal had brought to the USA. To anticipate their arguments, Ryan quoted Roosevelt on the function of the government in attaining social justice. According to Roosevelt, the government "is the duly constituted representative of an organized society of human beings—created by them for their mutual protection and well-being."[61] Here, we have the organic view of society with the government at the heart of social life once Roosevelt put the USA on the path to a living wage. Ryan believed its function as the promoter of social justice would never abate.

Conclusion

When the New Deal was initially vindicated in the 1934 Congressional elections, Harry Hopkins, Roosevelt's right-hand man with regard to social welfare programs, stated that there would only be a limited time available to get all the social programs that the Progressives wanted to see enacted. [62] The large majority that the Democratic Party had consolidated in the elections gave the Progressives what they thought would be a unique, but short-term, opportunity to achieve the social reforms they had long wanted. They turned out to be correct in this assessment, as the NLRA, SSA, and FLSA, were all enacted in a three-year window. To make effective use of that limited time span, they bundled their reforms into a simple formula: collective bargaining, social insurance, and a minimum wage equaled a living wage. They did not get everything they wanted, however.

To give one example of recognition of this limited scope of accomplishment, Senator Robert Wagner later regretted the exclusion of agricultural and domestic workers from the NLRA, but he believed that a law that only applied to workers in industry was an improvement over no law at all.[63] This same recognition can be found in the drafting of the SSA. When the CES did the background work for the legislation that became the SSA, it produced a ten-volume report that was not published. It did publish a summary of that report. In its opening paragraphs. the summary report highlighted the difficulties it had faced in terms of providing a living wage through the use of unemployment insurance and pensions:

> The one almost all-embracing measure of security is an assured income. A program of economic security, as we vision it, must have as its primary aim the assurance of an adequate income to each human being in childhood, youth, middle age, or old age–in sickness or in health. It must provide safeguards against all of the hazards leading to destitution and dependency.[64]

The best they could be do at the time, however, was a "piecemeal approach." Still, the broader objective of economic security through a living wage could be retained by designing what could be accomplished in a way that could be developed into a "complete program." To have delayed in hopes of getting a complete program would have meant losing the opportunity to make a "substantial beginning…in the development of the safeguards which are so manifestly needed for individual security."[65]

The members of the Committee believed that they were working with a limited time frame. They did the best they could to create a program with the potential to develop into an economy where a living wage took precedence over profits and the luxury spending of the wealthy. As indicated at the end of Chapter 5, however, the SSA has not resulted in a living wage for all of the recipients of unemployment insurance or retirement benefits. Nor did the NLRA and the FLSA produce a living wage for all workers. There are two broad reasons for this limited success.

First, the ethical and economic perspective that Ryan and Roosevelt relied on did not, to use a current term, become a social construct. Ryan insisted that wages, and not profits, should be the measure of how successful a business was and Roosevelt agreed. For that perspective to become a social construct, however, business leaders had to be willing to sacrifice excessive profits and the luxuries they brought to business owners, consumers had to be willing to forgo low prices brought about by low wages, and workers had to form unions and use them for the greater good. None of this changed behavior has taken place.

Second, I have also presented an economic perspective on the living wage, as set forth by Clark. In this perspective, there are social overhead costs associated with work and if the workers' wages do not cover those costs someone else—charities, the government, or the society at large—must take care of them. For the social cost perspective to be effective, however, economists needed to develop social cost accounting to allocate the overhead costs of work to the firms that created them. Economists such as Dorothea Kittredge and Solomon Barkin tried to measure the costs of work in terms of the needs of workers and their families, but that was only a beginning. And as noted above, Lewisohn and Douglas tried to measure the burden a living wage would put on society by comparing it to national income, but no one has developed an effective system of social cost accounting although some accountants have tried.[66] As described in Chapter 5, Shoup pointed out that business firms are not equal in their ability to increase prices to cover the costs of higher wages and payroll taxes.[67] A system of social cost accounting would need to build those differences into its methodology. The best economists have come up with is the measure of economic welfare that adjusts the gross domestic product to include the value of household work and increased leisure time and deduct environmental damage, but does not take the costs of low wages into account.

Despite these failures, the New Deal did put economic security in play by making the beginning of a living wage a part of government policy, and the number of workers not earning a living wage today, currently estimated at around 40 percent of the workforce,[68] is less than Ryan's estimate that "it is altogether probable that sixty per cent of the adult male wage earners" did not earn a living wage at the beginning of the twentieth century.[69] Moreover, since the New Deal the basic formula of collective bargaining plus social insurance plus a minimum wage equates to a living wage has been expanded by extending collective bargaining to government workers, by adding many workers to the coverage of the SSA, by adding benefits ranging from the earned income tax credit to Obamacare, and by at least keeping the minimum wage in line with inflation—only it still has not added up to a living wage for low-paid workers.

As a result, the last two decades have seen a revival of a living wage movement comprised of a few unions, religious groups, and community organizations that has focused on helping low-wage workers in local areas get higher wages through the use of political action and moral persuasion.[70] The movement has made small gains in attaining its goal of a living wage, with success in about 100 municipal governments by 2003 and victories at some major universities.[71] In 2007, for example, the state of Maryland implemented a living wage law that required contractors doing business with it to pay their workers a living wage of $11.30 an hour in high-cost areas and $8.50 an hour in rural areas, just as the NWLB did in World War I and the NIRA did in the New Deal; in 2014, the respective rates were raised to $13.39 an hour and $10.06 an hour. San Francisco and Oakland, California, have also passed laws in 2014 mandating a living wage in the $14–$15 dollar an hour range. For the last four years there has been a struggle to create a national livable minimum wage by raising the federal minimum wage to a range of $15–$22 an hour. [72] The federal minimum wage represents a level of income that at least provides workers with the bare essential items needed to sustain life, while a living wage enables them to maintain a decent life. As a result, in his recent effort to base economic justice on political philosophy, Mark R. Reiff argues for increasing the minimum wage to a living wage level. He observes, "The minimum wage must be sufficient not only to satisfy each worker's basic needs, but also to acknowledge the dignity of each worker's labor."[73] Anthony Atkinson also makes a minimum wage as a living wage a key element of his proposed policies for reducing inequality.[74] To help in the pursuit of a living wage, the Massachusetts Institute of Technology has furnished a calculator that will estimate the level of a living wage for any community in the USA.[75]

While these efforts are ongoing, it is questionable that they will add up to a national program for a living wage as existed during the New Deal. The NIRA was an attempt to create a cooperative approach to attaining a living wage. When that did not work, regulation under the NLRA, SSA, and FLSA mandated a new approach to wages, but still did not attain a living wage for all workers. Present-day advocates for a living wage have tried to build on these programs by working to expand collective bargaining through reforms such as "card check," pushing for a living minimum wage and expanding social security retirement benefits. These efforts are very much in line with what Roosevelt, Ryan, and the other advocates for a living wage covered in this book believed was the right program for a living wage. This book has focused on how members and supporters of the New Deal thought that they were starting a process that would evolve into a complete living wage program. The conviction of current advocates for a living wage that they can attain their goal by extending that process is an indication that this focus has merit.

Notes

1. Roosevelt, 1940.
2. Broderick, 1963, p. 57.
3. Armstrong, 1932.
4. Stabile and Kozak, 2012, pp. 117, 123, 146 and 203.
5. Soule, 1939, p. 2.
6. *The New Republic*, 1940, p. 691.
7. *The New Republic*, 1940, p. 693.
8. *The New Republic*, 1940, p. 694.
9. *The New Republic*, 1940, p. 707.
10. *The New Republic*, 1940, pp. 707–708.
11. Ryan, 1906.
12. Ryan, 1935a, pp. 91.
13. Ryan, 1941, p. 261.
14. Ryan, 1935a, p. 108.
15. Ryan, 1935a, p. 113.
16. Ryan, 1941, pp. 90, 108 and 218–232.
17. Ryan, 1941, pp. 120–121.
18. Ryan, 1941, p. 259–260.
19. Roosevelt, 1935f.
20. Ryan, 1935b, p. 1.
21. Ryan, 1935b, p. 2.
22. Ryan, 1935b, p. 2.
23. Ryan, 1936, p. 5.
24. Ryan, 1936, p. 7.
25. Ryan, 1936, p. 10.
26. Ryan, 1936, p. 11.
27. Ryan, 1936, p. 12.
28. Roosevelt, 1936e.
29. Ryan, 1941, p. 281.

30. Lyon et al., 1935, p. 303.
31. Roos, 1937, pp. 52–3.
32. Shoup, 1939, p. 165.
33. Ryan, 1906, p. 267.
34. Eleanor Roosevelt Papers Project, 2014.
35. Eleanor Roosevelt, 1936a.
36. Ezekiel, 1936, pp. 4 and 14.
37. Domhoff and Webber, 2011, p. 4350.
38. Douglas, 1939, pp. 70 and 80.
39. Keynes, 1933.
40. Keynes, 1933.
41. Keynes, 1933.
42. Keynes, 1933.
43. Rothbard, 2000, pp. 2881–2911.
44. Chase, 1935, pp. 164–5.
45. Keynes, 1965 [1936], pp. 27–28.
46. Keynes, 1965 [1936], pp. 113–122.
47. Keynes, 1965 [1936], pp. 125–128.
48. Barber, 1996, p. 133.
49. Rosenman, 1952, p. 427.
50. Stiglitz, 2015, p. 4240.
51. Lippmann, 1935, p. 13.
52. Lippmann, 1938, p. 123.
53. Hoover, 1951, p. 203.
54. Hoover, 1922, p. 17–18.
55. Ryan, 1945, p. 297.
56. Ryan, 1945, p. 297.
57. Ryan, 1945, p. 298.
58. Ryan, 1945, p. 300.
59. Ryan, 1945, p. 301.
60. Ryan, 1945, p. 302.
61. Ryan, 1945, p. 302.
62. Sunstein, 2004, pp. 735–6.
63. Domhoff and Webber, 2011, pp. 3047–50.
64. Committee on Economic Security, 2014.
65. Committee on Economic Security, 2014.
66. Stabile, 1993a, pp. 179–84.
67. Shoup, 1939, p. 185.
68. The Job Gap, 2015; Zillman, 2015.
69. Ryan, 1906, p. 176.
70. Pollin and Luce, 2000, p. 1; Freeman, 2005, pp. 14–15.
71. Luce, 2004, pp. 33–35.

72. Pollin and Wicks-Lim, 2015; Dube, 2013.
73. Reiff, 2013, p. 14.
74. Atkinson, 2015, pp. 2478–2530.
75. MIT, 2015.

Bibliography

AEA. 1931. The business depression of nineteen hundred and thirty—Discussion. *The American Economic Review* 21(March): 183–201.

American Federationist. 1918. Avoidance and adjustment of labor disputes: A war measure. *American Federationist* 25(May): 369–370.

American Federationist. 1919. American federation of labor reconstruction program. *American Federationist* 26(February): 130–141.

American Federationist. 1930a. High wages increase prosperity. *American Federationist* 37(March): 667.

American Federationist. 1930b. Steady work—Steady Business. *American Federationist* 37(March): 668.

American Federationist. 1930c. Economic statistics. *American Federationist* 37(May): 591–594.

American Federationist. 1930d. A market for our goods. *American Federationist* 37(May): 595–597.

American Federationist. 1930e. Review of *principles of consumption* by Paul H. Nystron. *American Federationist* 37(May): 604–605.

American Federationist. 1933a. Recovery program. *American Federationist* 40(June): 627–631.

American Federationist. 1933b. An industrial covenant. *American Federationist* 40(July): 681–683.

American Federationist. 1933c. Recovery—Facts for code making. *American Federationist* 40(July): 698–701.

American Federationist. 1934. Four labor problems. *American Federationist* 41(March): 268–278.

D. Stabile, *The Political Economy of a Living Wage*,
DOI 10.1007/978-3-319-32473-9

American Federationist. 1935a. Economic security for the worker. *American Federationist* 42(March): 254–260.

American Federationist. 1935b. The national labor relations bill. Wagner Bill. *American Federationist* 42(March): 263–266.

American Federationist. 1937. Fair Labor Standards Bill. *American Federationist* 44(July): 709–726.

American Federationist. 1938. Wages and hours law. *American Federationist* 45(October, November and December): 1102–1103, 1197–1202, 1327–1330.

Aquinas, Saint T. 1953. Whether it is lawful to sell a thing for more than it is worth. *Summa Theoligica*. In *The political ideas of St. Thomas Aquinas*, ed. D. Rappaport, 143–147. New York: Haffner Press.

Aquinas, Saint T. 1968. Does man's happiness consist in wealth? *Summa Theologica*. In *The wisdom of Saint Thomas Aquinas*, eds. E. Freeman and T. Owens, 123–127. Greenwich: Fawcett Books.

Aristotle. 1986. *The politics*. Trans. Hippocrates G. Apostle and Lloyd P. Gerson. Grinnell: The Peripatetic Press.

Armstrong, Barbara N. 1932. *Insuring the essentials. Minimum wage plus social insurance—A living wage program*. New York: Macmillan.

Atkinson, Anthony B. 2015. *Inequality: What can be done?* Amazon Kindle edition. Cambridge, MA: Harvard University Press.

Barber, William J. 1996. *Designs within disorder: Franklin D. Roosevelt, the economists, and the shaping of American economic policy*. Cambridge: Cambridge University Press.

Barkin, Solomon. 1940. Industrial union wage policies. *Plan Age* 6(January): 1–14.

Barkin, Solomon. 1944. *Substandard conditions of living: A study of the cost of the emergency sustenance budget in five textile manufacturing communities in January–February 1944*. Textile Workers Union of America Research Department Report.

Barkin, Solomon. 1946. The significant change in wage demands. *Labor and Nation* 2 (February–March): 8–10.

Barkin, Solomon. 1948. Labor's attitude toward wage incentive plans. *Industrial and Labor Relations Review* 1(July): 553–572.

Barkin, Solomon. 1949. Testimony, Senate Labor and Public Welfare Committee. Revision of Fair Labor Standards Act (April): 1–23.

Beckerman, Wilfred. 2011. *Economics as applied ethics: Value judgments in welfare economics*. London/New York: Palgrave Macmillan.

Blakey, Roy G., and Gladys C. Blakey. 1939. Federal tax legislation, 1939. *The American Economic Review* 29(December): 695–707.

Boles Jr., Walter E. 1940. Some aspects of the Fair Labor Standards Act. *Southern Economic Journal* 5(April): 498–511.

Bortz, Abe. 2015. A brief history of social insurance. A training lecture for employees of the Social Security Administration developed in the early 1970s. http://www.socialwelfarehistory.com/organizations/social-security-a-brief-history-of-social-insurance/. Accessed 18 Feb 2015.

Brinkley, Alan. 1983. *Voices of protest: Huey Long, Father Coughlin, and the great depression*, Amazon Kindle edition. New York: Vintage Books.

Brinkley, Alan. 1996. *The end of reform: New deal liberalism in reform and war*, Amazon Kindle edition. New York: Vintage Books.

Broderick, Francis L. 1963. *Right reverend new dealer: John A. Ryan*. New York: Macmillan.

Bruère, Robert W. 1919. Can we eliminate labor unrest? *The Annals of the American Academy of Political and Social Science* 81(January): 95–100.

Carlson, Allan. 1988. The family wage problem, 1750–1940. In *The family wage: Work, gender and children in the modern economy*, ed. Bryce Christensen, 9–32. Rockford: The Rockford Institute.

Cates, Douglas. 1934. A current appraisal of the national recovery administration. *The Annals of the American Academy of Political and Social Science* 172(March): 130–138.

Chase, Stuart. 1925. *The tragedy of waste*. New York: Macmillan.

Chase, Stuart. 1935. Recovery. *The New Republic* (December 18): 162–166.

CIO News. 1937a. Low job standards show wage-hour bill needed. *CIO News* (December 15): 3.

CIO News. 1937b. Wage-hour bill defeat—A warning signal. *CIO News* (December 22): 1.

CIO News. 1938a. CIO has plan to fight business depression. *CIO News* (January 19): 3.

CIO News. 1938b. Wage-hour bill delay deepens depression. *CIO News* (March 12): 4.

CIO News. 1938c. Predict wage-hour bill will curb sweat shops. *CIO News* (June 18): 3.

CIO News. 1938d. See Wage-Hour Act aiding south. *CIO News* (July 23): 8.

Clark, John B. 1886. *The philosophy of wealth*. Boston: Ginn & Co.

Clark, John Maurice. 1923a. *Studies in the economics of overhead costs*. Chicago: University of Chicago Press.

Clark, John Maurice. 1923b. Some social aspects: An application of overhead cost to social accounting, with special reference to the business cycle. *The American Economic Review* 13(March): 50–59.

Clark, John Maurice. 1926. *The social control of business*. Chicago: University of Chicago Press.

Clark, John Maurice. 1934a. *Strategic factors in business cycles*. New York: The National Bureau of Economic Research.

Clark, John Maurice. 1934b. Economics and the national recovery administration. *The American Economic Review* 24(March): 11–25.

Clark, John Maurice. 1939. *The social control of business*, 2nd ed. Chicago: University of Chicago Press.

Clark, John Maurice. 1957. *Economic institutions and human welfare*. New York: Alfred A. Knopf.

Clark, John Bates. 1965 [1889]. *The distribution of wealth*. New York: Augustus M. Kelley Publishers.

Clark, John Bates. 1968 [1907]. *Essentials of economics theory*. New York: Augustus M. Kelley Publishers.

Cohen, Adam. 2009. *Nothing to fear: FDR's inner circle and the hundred days that created modern America*. New York: The Penguin Press.

Committee on Economic Security. 1937. *Social security in America*. Washington, DC: US Government Printing Office.

Committee on Economic Security. 2014. Body of the report. http://www.ssa.gov/history/reports/ces5.html. Accessed 4 Sept 2014.

Committee on Economic Security Appendix. 2014. Members of the Committee, Advisory Boards and Committee Staff. http://www.ssa.gov/history/reports/ces6.html. Accessed 4 Sept 2014.

Coughlin, Charles E. 1934. The national union for social justice. Radio Address, Sunday, November 11. Social Security Online History Pages. https://www.ssa.gov/history/fcspeech.html. Accessed 17 Dec 2015.

Coughlin, Charles E. 1935. A reply to general Hugh Johnson. Radio Address, Monday, March 11. Social Security Online History Pages. https://www.ssa.gov/history/fcspeech.html. Accessed 17 Dec 2015.

Coughlin, Charles E. 1936. Roosevelt and Ruin. Radio Address, June 19. www.austincc.edu/lpatrick/his2341/rooseveltandruin.htm. Accessed 17 Dec 2015.

Dauber, Michele Landis. 2013. *The sympathetic state: Disaster relief and the origins of the American welfare state*. Chicago: University of Chicago Press.

Domhoff, William G., and Michael Webber. 2011. *Class and power in the new deal: Corporate moderates, Southern democrats and the liberal-labor coalition*, Amazon Kindle edition. Stanford: Stanford University Press.

Donohue, Kathleen. 2003. *Freedom from want: American liberalism and the idea of the consumer*. Baltimore: The Johns Hopkins University Press.

Dorfman, Joseph. 1949. *The economic mind in American civilization*, vol. 3. New York: Viking Press.

Douglas, Paul H. 1927. *Wages and the family*, 2nd ed. Chicago: The University of Chicago Press.

Douglas, Paul H. 1936. The United States Social Security Act. *The Economic Journal* 46(March): 1–20.

Douglas, Paul H. 1937. American Labor Relations Acts. *The American Economic Review* 27(December): 735–761.

Douglas, Paul H. 1938. The economic theory of wage regulation. *The University of Chicago Law Review* 5(February): 184–218.

Douglas, Paul H. 1939. *Social security in the United States: An analysis and appraisal of the Federal Social Security Act*, 2nd ed. New York: McGraw-Hill Book Co.

Douglas, Paul H., and Joseph Hackman. 1938. The Fair Labor Standards Act of 1938 I. *Political Science Quarterly* 53(December): 491–515.

Douglas, Paul H. 1957 [1934]. *The theory of wages.* New York: Kelley and Millman.

Douglas, Paul H., and Joseph Hackman. 1939. The Fair Labor Standards Act of 1938 II. *Political Science Quarterly* 54(March): 29–55.

Douglas, Paul H., and Sam A. Lewisohn. 1923. Factors in wage determination—Discussion. *The American Economic Review* 13(March): 141–146.

Downey, Kirstin. 2009. *The woman behind the new deal: The life of Frances Perkins, FDR's secretary of labor and his moral conscience.* New York: Nan A. Talese/Doubleday.

Dube, Arindrajit. 2013. Statement before the US Senate Committee on Health, Education, Labor & Pensions Hearing on "Keeping up with a changing economy: Indexing the minimum wage". March 14. http://www.help.senate.gov/imo/media/doc/Dube1.pdf. Accessed 12 Feb 2015.

Edwards, Morris. 1933. The truce on the Sherman Law. *Nation's Business* 21(July): 13–16.

Eichengreen, Barry. 2015. *Hall of mirrors: The great depression, the great recession and the uses—And misuses—Of history.* Oxford: Oxford University Press.

Eleanor Roosevelt Papers Project. 2014. Question: What new deal policies did Eleanor Roosevelt influence? http://www.gwu.edu/~erpapers/teachinger/q-and-a/q20.cfm. Accessed 1 Sept 2014.

Elliot, John. 1981. *Marx and Engels on economics, politics and society.* Santa Monica: Goodyear Publishing Co.

Ely, Richard T. 1893. *An introduction to political economy.* New York: Hunt & Eaton.

Ely, Richard T. 1935. Letter to John A. Ryan. November 26. Box 11, Folder 7. Richard T. Ely Folder. John A. Ryan Papers, Subseries 1.1, Correspondents by Name. The American Catholic History Research Center and University Archives. Washington, DC: The Catholic University of America.

Epstein, Abraham. 1936a. *Insecurity: A challenge to America*, 2nd rev. ed. New York: Random House.

Epstein, Abraham. 1936b. Letter to John A. Ryan. February 6, Box 11, Folder 15. Abraham Epstein Folder. John A. Ryan Papers, Subseries 1.1, Correspondents by Name. The American Catholic History Research Center and University Archives. Washington, DC: The Catholic University of America.

Epstein, Abraham. 1938. Why cheer for social security? *Nation's Business* 26(December): 15–16, 66–69.

Ezekiel, Mordecai. 1936. *$2500 a year: From scarcity to abundance.* New York: Harcourt, Brace and Company.

Figart, Deborah M., Ellen Mutari, and Marilyn Power. 2002. *Living wages, equal wages, gender and labor market policies in the United States.* London/New York: Routledge.

Filene, Edward A. 1923. The minimum wage and efficiency. *The American Economic Review* 13(September): 411–415.

Forsythe, John S. 1939. Legislative history of the Fair Labor Standards Act. *Law and Contemporary Problems* 6(Summer): 464–490. http://scholarship.law.duke.edu/lcp/vol6/iss3/14. Accessed 2 Dec 2014.

Foster, William Trufant, and Waddill Catchings. 1924. *Money*, 2nd ed. Boston/New York: Houghton Mifflin Co.

Foster, William Trufant, and Waddill Catchings. 1925. *Profits.* Boston/New York: Houghton Mifflin Co.

Foster, William Trufant, and Waddill Catchings. 1928. *Business without a buyer.* Boston/New York: Houghton Mifflin Co.

Foster, William Trufant, and Waddill Catchings. 1930a. Mr. Hoover's road to prosperity. *Review of Reviews* 81(January): 50–52.

Foster, William Trufant, and Waddill Catchings. 1930b. Riotous saving. *Atlantic Monthly* 146(November): 667–672.

Frayne, Hugh. 1918. Organized labor and the war. *Proceedings of the Academy of Political Science in the City of New York* 7(February): 136–139.

Freeman, Richard. 2005. Fighting for other folks' wages: The logic and illogic of living wage campaigns. *Industrial Relations* 44(January): 14–31.

Frey, John. 1933. Business depends on wages. *American Federationist* 40(June): 583–585.

Friedman, Milton. 1966. The methodology of positive economics. In *Essays in positive economics.* 3–16, 30–43. Chicago: University of Chicago Press.

Fusfeld, Daniel R. 1956. *The economic ideas of Franklin D. Roosevelt and the origins of the new deal.* New York: Columbia University Press.

Gilbert, Richard V., George M. Hildebrand Jr., Arthur W. Stuart, Maxine Yaple Sweezy, Paul M. Sweezy, Lorrie Tarshis, and John D. Wilson. 1938. *An economic program for American democracy.* New York: The Vanguard Press.

Glickman, Lawrence B. 1997. *A living wage: American workers and the making of consumer society.* Ithaca: Cornell University Press.

Golden, Clinton S., and Harold J. Ruttenberg. 1942. *The dynamics of industrial democracy.* New York: Harper & Brothers Publishers.

Gompers, Samuel. 2015. Samuel Gompers quotations. *The Samuel Gompers Papers.* http://www.gompers.umd.edu/quotes.htm. Accessed 9 Feb 2015.

Goodwin, Craufurd D. 2014. *Walter Lippmann: Public economist.* Cambridge, MA: Harvard University Press.

Green, William. 1933a. New economic planning. *American Federationist* 40(June): 565–568.

Green, William. 1933b. Control the disorganizer. *American Federationist* 40(June): 568–569.

Green, William. 1933c. Labor states its case at code hearing. *American Federationist* 40(August): 802–810.

Green, William. 1934a. Recovery situation. *American Federationist* 41(December): 1289–1291.

Green, William. 1934b. Unemployment insurance. *American Federationist* 41(December): 1292–1293.

Green, William. 1936. The goals of organized labor. *The Annals of the American Academy of Political and Social Science* 184(March): 147–153.

Green, William. 1938a. Wages and Hours Act. *American Federationist* 45(July): 689–690.

Green, William. 1938b. Wages and Hours Act. *American Federationist* 45(August): 806–807.

Gregg, Richard B. 1919. The National War Labor Board. *Harvard Law Review* 33(November): 39–63.

Holtzman, Abraham. 1963. *The Townsend movement: A political study.* New York: Bookman Associates.

Hoover, Herbert. 1922. *American individualism.* Garden City: Doubleday, Page & Co.

Hoover, Herbert. 1951. *The memoirs of Herbert Hoover, vol. 2. The cabinet and the presidency, 1920–1933.* New York: Macmillan.

Hovenkamp, Herbert. 1991. *Enterprise and American law, 1836–1937.* Cambridge, MA: Harvard University Press.

Johnson, Alvin. 1926. Real wages and the control of industry. *The American Economic Review* 16(March): 54–58.

Johnson, Hugh S. 1935. The blue eagle from egg to earth. *Saturday Evening Post* 207(January): 5–7. 68–76.

Johnson, Hugh S. 1937. A Hokus-Pocus. *Vital Speeches of the Day* 4(December 1): 116–117.

Kaku, Sachio. 2001. Lugo Bretano on the compulsory insurance system for workers in Germany. In *The German historical school: The historical and ethical approach to economics*, ed. Yuichi Shionoya, 72–86. London/New York: Routledge.

Katznelson, Ira. 2013. *Fear itself: The new deal and the origins of our times*, Amazon Kindle edition. New York: Livewright Publishers.

Kaufman, Bruce E. 2000. The early institutionalists on industrial democracy and union democracy. *Journal of Labor Research* 21(June): 189–209.

Kaufman, Bruce E. 2008. *Managing the human factor: The early years of human resource management in American industry.* Ithaca: ILR Press.

Kaufman, Bruce. 2009. Promoting labour market efficiency and fairness through a legal minimum wage: The Webbs and the social cost of labour. *British Journal of Industrial Relations* 47(June): 306–326.

Kaufman, Bruce E. 2012. Wage theory, new deal labor policy, and the great depression: Were government and unions to blame? *Industrial and Labor Relations Review* 65(July): 501–532.

Kaufman, Bruce, and Michael Barry. 2014. IR theory built on the founders' principles with empirical application to Australia. *Industrial and Labor Relations Review* 67(October): 1203–1234.

Kendall, Henry P. 1919. Post-war standards for industrial relations. *The Annals of the American Academy of Political and Social Science* 81(January): 163–166.

Keynes, John M. 1933. An open letter to President Roosevelt. *The New York Times*, December 31. http://newdeal.feri.org/misc/keynes2.htm. Accessed 16 Mar 2015.

Keynes, John M. 1965 [1936]. *The general theory of employment, interest and money*. New York: Harcourt, Brace & World.

Kittredge, Dorothea Davis. 1923. A suggestion for determining a living wage. *The American Economic Review* 13(January): 225–229.

Laidler, Harry. 1932. Review of *Insuring the essentials. Minimum wage plus social insurance—A living wage program* by Barbara N. Armstrong. *Columbia Law Review* 32(December): 1467–1468.

Landon, Alfred M. 1936. I will not promise the moon. *Vital Speeches of the Day* 3(October 15): 26–28.

Lauck, W. Jett. 1922. *The industrial code: A survey of the postwar industrial situation*. New York: Funk & Wagnall's Co.

Lauck, W. Jett. 1929. *The new industrial revolution and wages*. New York: Funk & Wagnall's Co.

Lauck, W. Jett. undated. The practicality of a living wage. Copy of a mimeograph report. Washington, DC: Willard Wirtz Library, US Department of Labor, 1–43.

Leonard, Thomas C. 2012. From the progressives to the institutionalists: What the First World War did and did not do to American economics. Review essay on Rutherford, Malcolm. 2011. *The institutionalist movement in American economics, 1918–1947: Science and social control*. Cambridge: Cambridge University Press. http://www.princeton.edu/~tleonard/papers/Rutherford.pdf. Accessed 4 Apr 2015.

Leuchtenburg, William E. 1963. *Franklin D. Roosevelt and the new deal, 1932–1940*. New York: Harper Torchbooks.

Lewis, John L. 1922. Statement to the House Committee on Labor. *United Mine Workers Journal* 32(May 15): 10–13.

Lewisohn, Sam A. 1923. The living wage and the national income. *Political Science Quarterly* 38(June): 219–226.

Lewisohn, Sam A. 1935a. New aspects of unemployment insurance. *Political Science Quarterly* 50(March): 1–14.

Lewisohn, Sam A. 1935b. Major issues in unemployment insurance. *Proceedings of the Academy of Political Science* 16(June): 67–73.

Liberatore, Matteo. 1891. *Principles of political economy*. Trans. Edward H. Dering. London/New York: Art and Book Co./Benziger and Co.

Lippmann, Walter. 1935. *The new imperative*. New York: Macmillan.

Lippmann, Walter. 1937. *The Supreme Court: Independent or controlled?* New York: Harper & Brothers Publishers.

Lippmann, Walter. 1938. *An inquiry into the principles of the good society*. Boston: Little, Brown and Co.

Litchfield, P.W. 1936. The trend in industry. *Vital Speeches of the Day* 3(December 15): 146–149.

Long Beach Press-Gazette. 1933. Old age revolving pensions: A proposed national plan 'Youth for work age for leisure'. September 30. http://www.larrydewitt.org/SSinGAPE/oldage/townsend1.htm. Accessed 14 Nov 2015.

Love, Thomas B. 1918. The social significance of war risk insurance. *The Annals of the American Academy of Political and Social Science* 79(September): 46–51.

Lowe, Charles. 1922. Kentucky coal prices. *United Mine Workers Journal* 32(September15): 15.

Luce, Stephanie. 2004. *Fighting for a living wage*. Ithaca: ILR Press.

Lyon, Leverett S., Paul T. Honan, Lewis L. Lorwin, George Terborgh, Charles L. Dearing, and Leon C. Marshall. 1935. *The national recovery administration: An analysis and appraisal*. Washington, DC: The Brookings Institution.

Manly, Basil M. 1922. Moral influences in the adjustment of industrial disputes. *The Annals of the American Academy of Political and Social Science* 103(September): 40–44.

Marshall, Alfred. 1895. *Principles of economics*, 3rd ed. London: Macmillan and Co.

Marx, Karl. 1967. *Capital*, vol. 2. New York: International Publishers.

Marx, Karl. 1973. *Grundrisse*. Trans. Martin Nicolaus. New York: Vintage Books.

Marx, Karl. 1977. *Capital*, vol. 1. Trans. Ben Fowkes. New York: Vintage Books.

Mill, John Stuart. 1960. *Autobiography of John Stuart Mill*. New York: Columbia University Press.

Mill, John Stuart. 1969 [1909]. *Principles of political economy*. New York: Augustus M. Kelley Publishers.

MIT. 2015. Living wage calculator. Massachusetts Institute of Technology. http://livingwage.mit.edu/. Accessed 12 Feb 2015.

Mitchell, Broadus. 1947. *Depression decade: From New Era through New Deal, 1929–1941*. New York: Harper Torchbooks.

Moss, David A. 1996. *Socializing security: Progressive-era economists and the origins of American social policy*. Cambridge, MA: Harvard University Press.

Nation's Business. 1932. A panorama of economic planning. *Nation's Business* 20(February): 29–32.

Nation's Business. 1933. Business agrees to regulate itself. *Nation's Business* 21(June): 13–14, 17–18.

Nation's Business. 1938. Needs in the field of labor. *Nation's Business* 26(June): 37–38.

National Consumer's League. 1919. *A living wage for working women of the post-war world: One essential factor in reconstruction*, 1–11. New York: National Consumer's League.

National Recovery Administration. 1933. *Bulletin 1*. Washington, DC: US Government Printing Office.

NLRB. 1949. *Legislative history of the National Labor Relations Act, 1935*. Washington, DC: US Government Printing Office.

Nock, Albert J. 1936. The social security fad. *The American Mercury* 38(August): 483–486.

Nordlund, Willis J. 1997. *The quest for a living wage: The history of the federal minimum wage program*. Westport: Greenwood Press.

Ohl, John Kennedy. 1985. *Hugh S. Johnson and the new deal*. DeKalb: Northern Illinois University Press.

Parker, Randall E. 2007. *The economics of the great depression: A twenty-first century look back at the economics of the interwar era*. Cheltenham/Northampton: Edward Elgar.

Perkins, Frances. 1933a. Letter to John A. Ryan. March 31. Box 29, Folder 14. Frances Perkins Folder. John A. Ryan Papers. Subseries 1.1, Correspondents by Name. The American Catholic History Research Center and University Archives. Washington, DC: The Catholic University of America.

Perkins, Frances. 1933b. Why we need a minimum wage law. *Nation's Business* 21(July): 23–25, 56.

Perkins, Frances. 1933c. Letter to John A. Ryan. August 5. Box 29, Folder 15. Frances Perkins Folder. John A. Ryan Papers. Subseries 1.1, Correspondents by Name. The American Catholic History Research Center and University Archives. Washington, DC: The Catholic University of America.

Perkins, Frances. 1934a. *People at work*. New York: The John Day Co.

Perkins, Frances. 1934b. Letter to John A. Ryan. October 29. Box 29. Folder 15. Frances Perkins Folder. John A. Ryan Papers. Subseries 1.1, Correspondents by Name. The American Catholic History Research Center and University Archives. Washington, DC: The Catholic University of America.

Perkins, Frances. 1935a. Letter to John A. Ryan. May 10. Box 29. Folder 18. Frances Perkins Folder. John A. Ryan Papers. Subseries 1.1, Correspondents by Name. The American Catholic History Research Center and University Archives. Washington, DC: The Catholic University of America.

Perkins, Frances. 1935b. The Social Security Act. *Vital Speeches of the Day* 1(September 9): 792–794.

Perkins, Frances. 1936. A national labor policy. *The Annals of the American Academy of Political and Social Science* 184(March): 1–3.

Perkins, Frances. 1945. Letter to John A. Ryan. June 6. Box 29. Folder 18. Frances Perkins Folder. John A. Ryan Papers. Subseries 1.1, Correspondents by Name. The American Catholic History Research Center and University Archives. Washington, DC: The Catholic University of America.

Perlman, Selig. 1936. The principle of collective bargaining. *The Annals of the American Academy of Political and Social Science* 184(March): 154–160.

Phelps, Orme W., and John E. Jeuck. 1939. Criticisms of the National Labor Relations Act. *The Journal of Business of the University of Chicago* 12(January): 30–50.

Pigou, A.C. 1978 [1932]. *The economics of welfare*, 4th ed. London: Macmillan. Reprinted, New York: AMS Press.

Plato. 1888. *The republic.* Trans. Benjamin Jowett. Oxford: Clarendon Press.

Pollin, Robert, and Stephanie Luce. 2000. *The living wage: Building a fair economy.* New York: The New Press.

Pollin, Robert, and Jeannette Wicks-Lim. 2015. *A $15 U.S. minimum wage: How the fast-food industry could adjust without shedding jobs.* Political Economy Research Institute. January 13. http://www.peri.umass.edu/236/hash/6e68011c89cf49f210e4183f49b8f735/publication/643/. Accessed 12 Feb 2015.

Pollock, Channing. 1936. The survival of the unfittest. *The American Mercury* 38(August): 385–387.

Poole, Mary. 2006. *The segregated origins of social security: African Americans and the welfare state.* Chapel Hill: University of North Carolina Press.

Prasch, Robert E. 2000. John Bates Clark's defense of mandatory arbitration and minimum wage legislation. *Journal of the History of Economic Thought* 22(2): 251–263.

Prasch, Robert E. 1999. American economists in the progressive era on the minimum wage. *The Journal of Economic Perspectives* 13(Spring): 221–230.

Prasch, Robert E. 2010. Monsignor John Ryan on the ethics and economics of minimum wage legislation. In *Research in the history of economic thought and methodology*, vol. 28, ed. Ross B. Emmett and Jeff E. Biddle, 39–70. Bingley: Emerald Group Publishing.

Radosh, Ronald. 1972. The myth of the new deal. In *A new history of Leviathan: Essays on the rise of the American corporate state*, ed. Ronald Radosh and Murray N. Rothbard, 146–187. New York: E.P. Dutton & Co.

Rawls, John. 1999. *A theory of justice*, Revised ed. Cambridge, MA: The Belknap Press of Harvard University Press.

Rayback, Joseph G. 1966. *A history of American labor.* New York: The Free Press.

Reiff, Mark R. 2013. *Exploitation and economic justice in the liberal capitalist state.* Oxford: Oxford University Press.

Rheinstein, Max. 1939. Methods of wage policy I. *The University of Chicago Law Review* 6(June): 552–576.

Richberg, Donald M. 1917. Democratization of industry. *The New Republic* (May 12): 49–51.

Rieve, Emil. 1935. What labor demands of government. *The Annals of the American Academy of Political and Social Science* 178(March): 123–128.

Roos, Charles. 1937. *NRA economic planning*. Bloomington: The Principia Press.

Roosevelt, Franklin D. 1928. Letter to John A. Ryan. December 3. Box 31. Folder 27. Franklin D. Roosevelt Folder. John A. Ryan Papers. Subseries 1.1, Correspondents by Name. The American Catholic History Research Center and University Archives. Washington, DC: The Catholic University of America.

Roosevelt, Franklin D. 1932a. Letter to John A. Ryan. September 1. Box 31. Folder 27. Franklin D. Roosevelt Folder. John A. Ryan Papers. Subseries 1.1, Correspondents by Name. The American Catholic History Research Center and University Archives. Washington, DC: The Catholic University of America.

Roosevelt, Franklin D. 1932b. Campaign address on progressive government at the Commonwealth Club in San Francisco, California. September 23. Online by Gerhard Peters and John T. Woolley. *The American Presidency Project*. http://www.presidency.ucsb.edu/ws/?pid=88391. Accessed 23 Mar 2014.

Roosevelt, Franklin D. 1932c. Campaign address at Detroit, Michigan. October 2. Online by Gerhard Peters and John T. Woolley. *The American Presidency Project*. http://www.presidency.ucsb.edu/ws/?pid=88393. Accessed 10 July 2015.

Roosevelt, Franklin D. 1933a. *First inaugural address*. March 4: 1–9. Available at http://www.archives.gov/education/lessons/fdr-inaugural/. Accessed 14 June 2012.

Roosevelt, Franklin D. 1933b. Address of the President before the annual dinner of the chamber of commerce of the United States. May 4. President's Master Speech File. Hyde Park: Franklin D. Roosevelt Library, 1–3.

Roosevelt, Franklin D. 1933c. Fireside chat of May 7. In *The fireside chats of Franklin Delano Roosevelt*, Amazon Kindle edition, 2004, 67–180.

Roosevelt, Franklin D. 1933d. Message to congress on reemployment. May 17. President's Master Speech File. Hyde Park: Franklin D. Roosevelt Library, 1–21.

Roosevelt, Franklin D. 1933e. Mimeographed copy of statement on the National Industrial Recovery Act. June 16. President's Official Files 466: National Industrial Recovery Act. Box 1. Hyde Park: Franklin D. Roosevelt Library.

Roosevelt, Franklin D. 1933f. Statement on the National Industrial Recovery Act. June 16. http://docs.fdrlibrary.marist.edu/odnirast.html. Accessed 14 Nov 2013.

Roosevelt, Franklin D. 1933g. Statement on signing the National Industrial Recovery Act. June 16. Online by Gerhard Peters and John T. Woolley. *The*

American Presidency Project. http://www.presidency.ucsb.edu/ws/?pid=14669. Accessed 23 Nov 2013.

Roosevelt, Franklin D. 1933h. Fireside chat of July 24. In *The fireside chats of Franklin Delano Roosevelt*, Amazon Kindle edition, 2004, 180–294.

Roosevelt, Franklin D. 1933i. The President's reemployment agreement. July 27. Online by Gerhard Peters and John T. Woolley. *The American Presidency Project.* http://www.presidency.ucsb.edu/ws/?pid=14492. Accessed 23 Nov 2013.

Roosevelt, Franklin D. 1933j. Executive Order 6252 on the public works administration. August 19. Online by Gerhard Peters and John T. Woolley. *The American Presidency Project.* http://www.presidency.ucsb.edu/ws/?pid=14505. Accessed 11 Feb 2014.

Roosevelt, Franklin D. 1933k. Press conference. November 3. Online by Gerhard Peters and John T. Woolley. *The American Presidency Project.* http://www.presidency.ucsb.edu/ws/?pid=14543. Accessed 23 Nov 2013.

Roosevelt, Franklin D. 1934a. Letter to Emily R. Kneubuhl of the National Federation of Business and Professional Women's Clubs. March 3. Online by Gerhard Peters and John T. Woolley. *The American Presidency Project.* http://www.presidency.ucsb.edu/ws/index.php?pid=14819. Accessed 29 Sept 2014.

Roosevelt, Franklin D. 1934b. Letter to Hugh Johnson. September 25. President's Official Files 466: National Industrial Recovery Act. Box 2. Hyde Park: Franklin D. Roosevelt Library.

Roosevelt, Franklin D. 1935a. Messages to the new Congress. *Vital Speeches of the Day* 1(January 14): 226–229.

Roosevelt, Franklin D. 1935b. Message to Congress on the extension of the National Industrial Recovery Act. February 20. President's Official Files 466: National Industrial Recovery Act, Box 3. Hyde Park: Franklin D. Roosevelt Library.

Roosevelt, Franklin D. 1935c. Letter to John A. Ryan. May 15. Box 31. Folder 28. Franklin D. Roosevelt Folder. John A. Ryan Papers. Subseries 1.1, Correspondents by Name. The American Catholic History Research Center and University Archives. Washington, DC: The Catholic University of America.

Roosevelt, Franklin D. 1935d. Excerpts from the press conference. June 7. Online by Gerhard Peters and John T. Woolley. *The American Presidency Project.* http://www.presidency.ucsb.edu/ws/?pid=15071. Accessed 1 Aug 2012.

Roosevelt, Franklin D. 1935e. Message to Congress on Tax Revision. June 19. Online by Gerhard Peters and John T. Woolley. *The American Presidency Project.* http://www.presidency.ucsb.edu/ws/?pid=15088. Accessed 1 Aug 2012.

Roosevelt, Franklin D. 1935f. Letter to John A. Ryan. September 24. *American Catholic History Classroom.* http://cuomeka.wrlc.org/items/show/358. Accessed 17 Feb 2014.

Roosevelt, Eleanor. 1936a. *My Day*. December 29. Eleanor Roosevelt Papers Project. http://www.gwu.edu/~erpapers/myday/displaydoc.cfm?_y=1936&_f=md054526. Accessed 1 Sept 2014.

Roosevelt, Franklin D. 1936b. Acceptance speech for the renomination for the Presidency, Philadelphia, PA. June 27. Online by Gerhard Peters and John T. Woolley. *The American Presidency Project*. http://www.presidency.ucsb.edu/ws/?pid=15314. Accessed 23 Nov 2013.

Roosevelt, Franklin D. 1936c. Labor Day message to the workers of America. September 6. Online by Gerhard Peters and John T. Woolley. *The American Presidency Project*. http://www.presidency.ucsb.edu/ws/?pid=15121. Accessed 23 Nov 2013.

Roosevelt, Franklin D. 1936d. Rear-platform remarks at Dubuque, Iowa. October 9. Online by Gerhard Peters and John T. Woolley. *The American Presidency Project*. http://www.presidency.ucsb.edu/ws/?pid=15153. Accessed 29 Sept 2014.

Roosevelt, Franklin D. 1936e. Telegram to John Ryan. November 1. *American Catholic History Classroom*. http://cuomeka.wrlc.org/items/show/358. Accessed 17 Feb 2014.

Roosevelt, Franklin D. 1936f. Letter to John A. Ryan. November 16. Box 31. Folder 28. Franklin D. Roosevelt Folder. John A. Ryan Papers. Subseries 1.1, Correspondents by Name. The American Catholic History Research Center and University Archives. Washington, DC: The Catholic University of America.

Roosevelt, Franklin D. 1937a. Message to Congress on establishing minimum wages and maximum hours. May 24. Online by Gerhard Peters and John T. Woolley. *The American Presidency Project*. http://www.presidency.ucsb.edu/ws/?pid=15405. Accessed 23 Nov 2013.

Roosevelt, Franklin D. 1937b. Labor Day statement by the President. September 5. Online by Gerhard Peters and John T. Woolley. *The American Presidency Project*. http://www.presidency.ucsb.edu/ws/index.php?pid=15453. Accessed 23 Nov 2013.

Roosevelt, Franklin D. 1938a. Remarks to visiting protestant ministers. Washington, DC. January 31. Online by Gerhard Peters and John T. Woolley. *The American Presidency Project*. http://www.presidency.ucsb.edu/ws/?pid=15591. Accessed 29 Sept 2014.

Roosevelt, Franklin D. 1938b. Fireside chat. June 24. Online by Gerhard Peters and John T. Woolley. *The American Presidency Project*. http://www.presidency.ucsb.edu/ws/?pid=15662. Accessed 23 Nov 2013.

Roosevelt, Franklin D. 1938c. Radio address on the Third Anniversary of the Social Security Act. August 15. Online by Gerhard Peters and John T. Woolley. *The American Presidency Project*. http://www.presidency.ucsb.edu/ws/?pid=15523. Accessed 23 Nov 2013.

Roosevelt, Franklin D. 1939. Address at the National Parole Conference, White House, Washington, DC. April 17. Online by Gerhard Peters and John T. Woolley. *The American Presidency Project.* http://www.presidency.ucsb.edu/ws/?pid=15744. Accessed 6 Jan 2016.

Roosevelt, Franklin D. 1940. Address at Teamsters Union Convention, Washington, DC. September 11. Online by Gerhard Peters and John T. Woolley. *The American Presidency Project.* http://www.presidency.ucsb.edu/ws/?pid=16005. Accessed 14 Nov 2013.

Roosevelt, Franklin D. 1944a. State of the Union Message to Congress. January 11, 1944. Online by Gerhard Peters and John T. Woolley. *The American Presidency Project.* http://www.presidency.ucsb.edu/ws/?pid=16018. Accessed 14 Nov 2013.

Roosevelt, Franklin D. 1944b. Letter to John A. Ryan. May 30. Box 31. Folder 29. Franklin D. Roosevelt Folder. John A. Ryan Papers. Subseries 1.1, Correspondents by Name. The American Catholic History Research Center and University Archives. Washington, DC: The Catholic University of America.

Roosevelt, Theodore. 1912. Address before the convention of the National Progressive Party in Chicago. August. http://www.ssa.gov/history/trspeech.html. Accessed 13 Nov 2013.

Rosen, Harvey S. 2005. *Public finance*, 7th ed. New York: McGraw-Hill.

Rosenman, Samuel I. 1952. *Working with Roosevelt.* New York: Harper and Brothers, Publishers.

Rothbard, Murray N. 2000. *America's great depression*, 5th ed., Amazon Kindle edition. Auburn: The Ludwig von Mises Institute.

Rothbard, Murray N. 2006. *An Austrian perspective on the history of economic thought*, 2 vol., Amazon Kindle edition. Auburn: The Mises Institute.

Rutherford, Malcolm. 2011. *The institutionalist movement in American economics, 1918–1947.* Cambridge: The Cambridge University Press.

Ryan, John Augustine. 1906. *A living wage: Its ethical and economic aspects.* New York: Macmillan.

Ryan, John Augustine. 1916. *Distributive justice: The right and wrong of our present distribution of wealth.* New York: Macmillan.

Ryan, John Augustine. 1920. *A living wage: Its ethical and economic aspects.* New York: Macmillan.

Ryan, John Augustine. 1927. Letter to Abraham Epstein. January 7. Box 11. Folder 14. Abraham Epstein Folder. John A. Ryan Papers. Subseries 1.1, Correspondents by Name. The American Catholic History Research Center and University Archives. Washington, DC: The Catholic University of America.

Ryan, John Augustine. 1929. Letter to Franklin D. Roosevelt. January 11. Box 31. Folder 27. Franklin D. Roosevelt Folder. John A. Ryan Papers. Subseries 1.1, Correspondents by Name. The American Catholic History Research

Center and University Archives. Washington, DC: The Catholic University of America.

Ryan, John Augustine. 1932. Letter to Raymond Moley. November 29. *American Catholic History Classroom.* http://cuomeka.wrlc.org/items/show/349. Accessed 9 July 2014.

Ryan, John Augustine. 1934. Shall the NRA be scrapped? Address Delivered at the National Conference of Catholic Charities. Cincinnati, October 9: 3–16.

Ryan, John Augustine. 1935a. *A better economic order.* New York: Harper & Brothers Publishers.

Ryan, John Augustine. 1935b. Letter to Franklin D. Roosevelt. September 24. *American Catholic History Classroom.* http://cuomeka.wrlc.org/items/show/358. Accessed 17 Feb 2014.

Ryan, John Augustine. 1936. Roosevelt safeguards America. October 8. *American Catholic History Classroom.* http://cuomeka.wrlc.org/items/show/358. Accessed 17 Feb 2014.

Ryan, John Augustine. 1939. Letter to Franklin D. Roosevelt. March 22. Box 31. Folder 29. Franklin D. Roosevelt Folder. John A. Ryan Papers. Subseries 1.1, Correspondents by Name. The American Catholic History Research Center and University Archives. Washington, DC: The Catholic University of America.

Ryan, John Augustine. 1941. *Social doctrine in action: A personal history.* New York: Harper & Brothers.

Ryan, John Augustine. 1945. Roosevelt and social justice. *The Review of Politics* 7(July): 297–305.

Schechter. 1935. *A.L.A. Schechter Poultry Corporation v. United States, 295 U.S. 495.* May 27. http://caselaw.lp.findlaw.com/cgi-bin/getcase.pl?court=us&vol=295&invol=495. Accessed 14 June 2012.

Schieber, Sylvester J., and John B. Shoven. 1999. *The real deal: The history and future of social security.* New Haven: Yale University Press.

Schumpeter, Joseph A. 1964. *Business cycles: A theoretical, historical and statistical analysis of the capitalist process*, abridged edition. New York: McGraw-Hill.

Seager, Henry R. 1919. Effect of present methods on future wage adjustments. *Proceedings of the Academy of Political Science in the City of New York* 8(February): 109–118.

Shoup, Carl. 1939. Taxing for social security. *The Annals of the American Academy of Political and Social Science* 202(March): 165–175.

Smiley, Gene. 2002. *Rethinking the great depression.* Chicago: I.R. Way, American Ways Series.

Smith, Adam. 1976 [1776]. *An inquiry into the nature and causes of the wealth of nations*, 2 vol. Chicago: University of Chicago Press.

Social Security Administration. 2014a. *The Administration's 1935 Economic Security Bill, HR 4120.* January 17, 1935. http://www.ssa.gov/history/pdf/fdrbill.pdf. Accessed 19 Nov 2014.

Social Security Administration. 2014b. Report of the Committee on Economic Security & Professor Edwin Witte's Testimony—PART 1. http://www.ssa.gov/history/pdf/hr35report1.pdf. Accessed 19 Nov 2014.

Social Security Administration. 2014c. Perkins, Hon. Frances, Secretary of Labor—Part 1. http://www.ssa.gov/history/pdf/hr35perkins1.pdf. Accessed 19 Nov 2014.

Social Security Administration. 2014d. Green, William, president American Federation of Labor. http://www.ssa.gov/history/pdf/hr35afl.pdf. Accessed 20 Nov 2014.

Social Security Administration. 2014e. House debates on social security. http://www.ssa.gov/history/senate35.html. Accessed 21 Nov 2014.

Social Security Administration. 2014f. House debate. April 16, 1935. http://www.ssa.gov/history/pdf/h416.pdf. Accessed 20 Nov 2014.

Social Security Administration. 2014g. William Green president of the American Federation of Labor. http://www.ssa.gov/history/reports/35senate.html. Accessed 20 Nov 2014.

Social Security Administration. 2014h. Browder, Earl, New York City, representing the Communist Party. http://www.ssa.gov/history/pdf/s35browder.pdf. Accessed 20 Nov 2014.

Social Security Administration. 2014i. Senate debate June 15, 1935. http://www.ssa.gov/history/pdf/senate3.pdf. Accessed 20 Nov 2014.

Social Security Administration. 2014j. 1935 congressional debates on social security. http://www.ssa.gov/history/tally.html. Accessed 21 Nov 2014.

Soule, George. 1939. *An economic constitution for democracy.* New Haven: Yale University Press.

Spencer, William H. 1935. *The National Labor Relations Act: Its scope, purposes and implications.* Chicago: The University of Chicago Press.

Stabile, Donald R. 1997a. The intellectual antecedents of Thorstein Veblen: A case for John Bates Clark. *Journal of Economic Issues* 31(September): 817–825.

Stabile, Donald R. 1997b. Adam Smith and the natural wage: Sympathy, subsistence and social distance. *Review of Social Economy* 55(Fall): 292–311.

Stabile, Donald R. 2000. Unions and the natural standard of wages: Another look at 'the J.B. Clark problem'. *History of Political Economy* 32(3): 585–606.

Stabile, Donald R. 2008. *The living wage: Lessons from the history of economic thought.* Cheltenham/Northampton: Edward Elgar.

Stabile, Donald R., and Andrew F. Kozak. 2012. *Markets, planning and the moral economy: Business cycles in the progressive era and new deal.* Cheltenham/Northampton: Edward Elgar.

Stabile, Donald R. 1993a. Accountants and the price system: The problem of social costs. *Journal of Economic Issues* 27(March): 171–188.

Stabile, Donald R. 1993b. *Activist unionism: The institutional economics of Solomon Barkin.* Armonk: M. E. Sharpe.

Stewart, Maxwell S. 1935a. Security versus mathematics. *The Nation* 140 (January 16): 67–69.

Stewart, Maxwell S. 1935b. Congress discovers the class struggle. *The Nation* 140(February 27): 247–249.

Stiglitz, Joseph E. 2015. *The great divide: Unequal societies and what we can do about them*, Amazon Kindle edition. New York/London: W.W. Norton & Co.

Story, H.W. 1934. Sound unemployment protection. *Nation's Business* 22(October): 15–20, 60–62.

Studenski, Paul. 1936. Modern fiscal systems: Their characteristics and trends of development. *The Annals of the American Academy of Political and Social Science* 183(January): 27–38.

Sunstein, Cass R. 2004. *The second bill of rights: FDR's unfinished revolution and why we need it*, Amazon Kindle edition. New York: Basic Books.

Supreme Court. 1937a. *West Coast Hotel Company v. Parrish*, March 29. Arthur Steiner, ed., *Significant Supreme Court decisions: 1934–1937*, 2nd ed., 21–26. New York: John Wiley & Sons.

Supreme Court. 1937b. *National Labor Relations Board v. Jones & Laughlin Steel Corporation*, April 12. H. Arthur Steiner, ed., *Significant Supreme Court decisions: 1934–1937*, 2nd ed., 49–57. New York: John Wiley & Sons.

Supreme Court. 1937c. *Charles C. Steward Machine Company v. Harwell G. Davis*, May 24. H. Arthur Steiner, ed., *Significant Supreme Court decisions: 1934–1937*, 2nd ed., 65–71. New York: John Wiley & Sons.

Supreme Court. 1937d. *Guy T. Haverling v. George P. Davis*, May 24. H. Arthur Steiner, ed., *Significant Supreme Court decisions: 1934–1937*, 2nd ed., 72–75. New York: John Wiley & Sons.

Swope, Gerard. 1931. The Swope plan. Appendix A in Antony C. Sutton, *Wall Street and FDR*. http://www.reformation.org/wall-st-fdr-app-a.html. Accessed 14 June 2012.

Swope, Gerard. 1934. Letter to John A. Ryan. December 14. Box 35. Folder 20. Gerard Swope Folder. John A. Ryan Papers. Subseries 1.1, Correspondents by Name. The American Catholic History Research Center and University Archives. Washington, DC: The Catholic University of America.

The Job Gap. 2015. National findings. http://thejobgap.org/2015-low-wage-nation-national-findings/. Accessed 12 Nov 2015.

The Nation. 1935. Where is Security, Mr. Roosevelt? *The Nation* 139(January 30): 116.

The Nation. 1936. Mr. Landon's ethics. *The Nation* 140(October 10): 404–409.

The New Republic. 1935a. Inching toward social security. *The New Republic* (May 1): 327–328.

The New Republic. 1935b. How much social security? *The New Republic* (July 3): 209–210.

The New Republic. 1935c. A Judas Kiss for social security. *The New Republic* (October 14): 268.

The New Republic. 1940. The new deal in review, 1936–1940. *The New Republic* (May 20): 687–708.

Townsend, Francis. 1933. Prosperity for all. *Long Beach Press-Gazette*, September 30. http://www.larrydewitt.org/SSinGAPE/oldage/townsend1.htm. Accessed 14 Nov 2015.

Tugwell, Rexford Guy. 1927. *Industry's coming of age*. New York: Columbia University Press.

Tugwell, Rexford Guy. 1933. *The industrial discipline*. New York: Columbia University Press.

Tugwell, Rexford Guy. 1977. *Roosevelt's revolution: The first year—A personal perspective*. New York: Macmillan Publishing Co.

Tugwell, Rexford Guy, and Howard C. Hill. 1934. *Our economic society and its problems*. New York: Harcourt, Brace and Company.

United Mine Workers Journal. 1918a. Terms agreed upon by War Labor Board. *United Mine Workers Journal* 28(April 4): 10.

United Mine Workers Journal. 1918b. Living wage upheld by Frank Walsh. *United Mine Workers Journal* 28(June 13): 10.

United Mine Workers Journal. 1918c. What about after the war? *United Mine Workers Journal* 29(July 15): 11.

United Mine Workers Journal. 1921. Editorial. *United Mine Workers Journal* 32(October 15): 14–15.

United Mine Workers Journal. 1922a. The living wage. *United Mine Workers Journal* 33(November 15): 6.

United Mine Workers Journal. 1922b. Official circular. *United Mine Workers Journal* 33(June 1): 8.

United Mine Workers Journal. 1933a. Industrial Recovery Bill, about to become law, means emancipation of the wage slave. *United Mine Workers Journal* 44(June 1): 3.

United Mine Workers Journal. 1933b. Greatest Labor Victory in history achieved as Industrial Recovery Bill Becomes Law. *United Mine Workers Journal* 44(June 15): 3.

United Mine Workers Journal. 1933c. Appraisal of Industrial Recovery Act. *United Mine Workers Journal* 44(July 1): 7.

United Mine Workers Journal. 1933d. Statement by president on the Policies of the Industrial Recovery Act. *United Mine Workers Journal* 44(July 1): 10.

United Mine Workers Journal. 1934a. President Lewis says labor is in full accord with principles of National Recovery Act. *United Mine Workers Journal* 45(January15): 10–11.

United Mine Workers Journal. 1934b. President Lewis speaks in support of Bill to strengthen National Recovery Law. *United Mine Workers Journal* 45(April 1): 3–4.

United Mine Workers Journal. 1934c. Supreme Court Declares National Recovery Act unconstitutional. *United Mine Workers Journal* 45(June 1): 4.

United Mine Workers Journal. 1935. Passage of Wagner Bill is great victory for workers. *United Mine Workers Journal* 44(July 1): 5.

US Department of Labor. 2011. Wage and Hour Division. The Fair Labor Standards Act of 1938. May: 1–59. http://www.dol.gov/whd/regs/statutes/FairLaborStandAct.pdf. Accessed 28 Nov 2014.

US Supreme Court. 1923. Adkins v. Children's Hospital. (April 9). https://www.law.cornell.edu/supremecourt/text/261/525. Accessed March 7, 2016.

von Mises, Ludwig. 1920. Economic calculation in the socialist commonwealth. Trans. G. Sandler, 1–47. Auburn: The Ludwig von Mises Institute, 1990.

Wagner, Robert F. 1935a. Speech on the National Labor Relations Act. February 21. *Congressional Record*, 74th Cong., 1st sess., vol. 79: 2371–2372.

Wagner, Robert F. 1935b. Toward security. *Forum and Century* 93(May): 294–296.

Wagner, Robert F. 1935c. Letter to John A. Ryan. May 10. Box 37. Folder 15. Robert F. Wagner Folder. John A. Ryan Papers. Subseries 1.1, Correspondents by Name. The American Catholic History Research Center and University Archives. Washington, DC: The Catholic University of America.

Walsh, Frank P. 1918. Labor day. *The American Federationist* 25(October): 894–897.

Waltman, Jerold L. 2004. *The case for a living wage*. New York: Algora Publishing.

Weber, Herbert J. 1930. *A living wage*. Intro. by Thomas N. Carver and Paul H. Douglas. Chicago: Webb-Linn Printing Co., 9 pp.

Wilson, Woodrow. 1916. Address at Sea Girt, New Jersey accepting the democratic nomination for president. September 2. Online by Gerhard Peters and John T. Woolley. *The American Presidency Project*. http://www.presidency.ucsb.edu/ws/?pid=65393. Accessed 13 Sept 2015.

Wilson, Woodrow. 1919. 7th annual message. December 2. Online by Gerhard Peters and John T. Woolley. *The American Presidency Project*. http://www.presidency.ucsb.edu/ws/?pid=29560. Accessed 13 Sept 2015.

Withers, William. 1939. *Financing economic security in the United States*. New York: Columbia University Press.

Witte, Edwin E. 1937. Old age security in the Social Security Act. *The Journal of Political Economy* 45(February): 1–44.

Witte, Edwin E. 1938. Letter to John A. Ryan. March 10. Box 38. Folder 20. Edwin Witte Folder. John A. Ryan Papers. Subseries 1.1, Correspondents by Name. The American Catholic History Research Center and University Archives. Washington, DC: The Catholic University of America.

Woll, Matthew. 1919. Editorial: Insist on the living wage. *The American Federationist* 25(February): 151–153.

Zillman, Claire. 2015. Who makes less than $15 an hour? http://fortune.com/2015/04/13/who-makes-15-per-hour/. Accessed 12 Nov 2015.

Index

D. Stabile, *The Political Economy of a Living Wage*,
DOI 10.1007/978-3-319-32473-9

Kolibri 360 GmbH
Ferdinand-Jühlke-Straße 7
99095 Erfurt, Deutschland
produktsicherheit@kolibri360.de